LEGAL WRITING: ETHICAL AND PROFESSIONAL CONSIDERATIONS
Second Edition

LEGAL WRITING: ETHICAL AND PROFESSIONAL CONSIDERATIONS

Second Edition

MELISSA H. WERESH
Professor of Law
Director of Legal Writing
Drake University Law School

ISBN: 978-1-4224-7305-4

Library of Congress Cataloging-in-Publication Data

Weresh, Melissa H.
Legal writing : ethical and professional considerations / Melissa H. Weresh. -- 2nd ed.
p. cm.
Includes index.
ISBN 978-1-4224-7305-4 (perfect bound) 1. Legal composition. 2. Legal ethics--United States.
I. Title.
KF250.W438 2009
808'.06634--dc22
2009015289

Editorial Offices
744 Broad Street, Newark, NJ 07102 (973) 820-2000
201 Mission St., San Francisco, CA 94105-1831 (415) 908-3200
www.lexisnexis.com

MATTHEW◆BENDER

(2009–Pub.3207)

ACKNOWLEDGMENTS

I would like to thank my research assistant, Brant Leonard, for his valuable contributions to the second edition. I would also like to thank members of the Drake Law Library faculty who provided valuable assistance with this and the first edition, including Karen Wallace and Karen Herman. Finally, I would like to acknowledge the encouragement of my family, who make all my accomplishments worthwhile.

The author acknowledges the permissions kindly granted to reproduce excerpts from the materials indicated below

American Bar Association, Model Code of Professional Responsibility. Copyright © 1980, American Bar Association. Reprinted by permission of the American Bar Association.

American Bar Association, Model Rules of Professional Conduct. Copyright © 2008, American Bar Association. Reprinted by permission of the American Bar Association. Copies of ABA Model Rules of Professional Conduct, 2008, are available from: Service Center, American Bar Association, 321 North Clark Street, Chicago, IL 60610, 1-800-285-2221.

American Bar Association, Formal Ethics Opinions 92-363, 94-383, 99-413, 06-442. Copyright © 1992, 1994, 1999, and 2006, American Bar Association. Reprinted by permission of the American Bar Association. Copies of ABA Ethics Opinions are available from: Service Center, American Bar Association, 321 North Clark Street, Chicago, IL 60610, 1-800-285-2221.

Harris, Allen K., *The Professionalism Crisis — The 'Z' Word and Other Rambo Tactics: The Conference of Chief Justices' Solution*, 53 S.C. L. Rev. 549, 558–9 (2002). Copyright © 2002. South Carolina Law Review. Reprinted by permission of Allen K. Harris and the South Carolina Law Review.

Lorence, Jordan W.; Sears, Alan E.; & Bull, Benjamin W., *No Official High or Petty: The Unnecessary, Unwise, and Unconstitutional Trend of Prescribing Viewpoint Orthodoxy in Mandatory Continuing Legal Education*, 44 S. Tex. L. Rev. 263, 274 (2002). Copyright © South Texas Law Review. Reprinted by permission of the South Texas Law Review.

Pennsylvania Bar Association Committee on Legal Ethics and Professional Responsibility, Formal Ethics Opinion Number 2007-500, Copyright © 2007, Pennsylvania Bar Association. Reprinted by permission of the Pennsylvania Bar Association.

San Diego County Bar Association Formal Opinion 2006-1. Copyright © 2006, San Diego County Bar Association. Reprinted by permission of the San Diego County Bar Association.

Schiltz, Patrick J. *On Being a Happy, Healthy, and Ethical Member of an Unhappy, Unhealthy, and Unethical Profession*, 52 Vand. L. Rev. 871 (1999). Copyright © 1999, Vanderbuilt Law Review. Reprinted by Permission of the Vanderbuilt Law Review.

Smith, Michael R., *Advanced Legal Writing*, 123-4 (2d ed., Aspen 2008). Copyright © 2008, Aspen Publishers. Reprinted by permission of Aspen Publishers.

Veasey, E. Norman. *Making it Right — Veasey Plans Action to Reform Lawyer Conduct*, Business Law Today 7(4): 42 (March/April 1998). Copyright © 1998. Reprinted by permission of the American Bar Association.

A NOTE ON EDITORIAL PRACTICES

All of the principal cases in this text have been edited. Omissions from principal cases or quoted material are indicated in most instances, with the exceptions noted below. Most footnotes and authorities within the principal cases have been omitted for ease of reading. Footnotes and citations that remain have been retained for substance. Those footnotes that have been included retain their original number. Ellipses (. . .) signal the omission of words, sentences, or citations from within a paragraph, although in many instances citations are omitted without indication. Centered asterisks (* * *) signal the omission of a paragraph or more.

In the text, I have endeavored to use gender-neutral language. For ease of reading, I have used either "he" or "she," rather than "he or she."

Table of Contents

Table of Contents

Table of Contents

Chapter 1

ATTORNEY REGULATION: SOURCES OF ETHICAL AND PROFESSIONAL CONSIDERATIONS

The most important determinant of an attorney's success may well be other people's perception of the attorney's integrity and trustworthiness. It is difficult to earn the high regard of others for one's integrity, and that regard can be lost in an instant by one unprofessional action; worse, once it is lost, that high regard is rarely ever recovered.

> — Jan M. Levine, Associate Professor and
> Director, Duquesne University School of Law

Ethical rules are meaningful only when compliance comes at a price. Anyone can be ethical in the abstract or when nothing significant is on the line. The true measure of character is following the rules of ethics when doing so disadvantages one's position or short-term interests. And it is in these situations that one must appreciate that the short-term loss is well worth the long term gains of respect and honor.

> — Michael R. Smith, Winston S. Howard
> Distinguished Professor of Law and Director
> of Legal Writing, University of Wyoming College of Law

I. REGULATION OF LAWYERS

This book is titled ethical *considerations* associated with legal writing. The term *considerations* was chosen to reflect the fact that there are a variety of sources for these considerations, some of which are codified in the form of laws or rules, and others that are more informal. The most evident influence in this regard is the adoption of rules that govern the legal profession. However, it is important to recognize how the conduct of lawyers is governed and enforced in order to understand the ethical rules themselves. In terms of ethical and professional standards, lawyers as a profession are self-regulating. That means that, generally, lawyers are subject to rules of ethics by virtue of their admission to the bar in a particular state and regulation of lawyers takes place within the judiciary. The American Law Institute's Restatement of the Law Governing Lawyers notes that "Upon admission to the bar of any jurisdiction, a person becomes a lawyer and is subject to applicable law governing such matters as professional discipline, procedure and evidence, civil remedies, and criminal sanctions." Restatement (Third) of the Law Governing Lawyers § 1 (1998). As explained in the Preamble to the American Bar Association Model Rules of Professional Conduct ("Model Rules"):

> The legal profession is largely self-governing. Although other profes-
> sions also have been granted powers of self-government, the legal profes-

sion is unique in this respect because of the close relationship between the profession and the processes of government and law enforcement. This connection is manifested in the fact that ultimate authority over the legal profession is vested largely in the courts.

Model Rules of Prof'l Conduct, Preamble 9 (2008).

In the context of ethical rules, most states have adopted some form of the various ethical rules promulgated by the American Bar Association ("ABA"). The two main sources, the Model Rules and the ABA Model Code of Professional Responsibility ("Model Code"), are described below. However, it is worth noting that both incarnations of the ethical rules produced by the ABA are titled "Model" for good reason — the ABA is a private organization with no inherent authority to impose rules upon lawyers. Therefore, it is the adoption of the rules by state bar associations or state court systems that gives effect to the rules themselves. It is also worth noting that not all jurisdictions treat the ethical rules with the same degree of authority. In some jurisdictions the rules are treated as having the force of law. In other jurisdictions the courts have treated the rules as mere guidelines. Consequently, the primary source for ethical and professional regulation comes in the form of ethical and professional codes adopted at the state and local level, which are then applicable to lawyers who are admitted to practice within those jurisdictions. Many states have also adopted professionalism codes, which reinforce ethical rules and often contain components that require civility among members of the bar. Finally, rules of civil procedure, rules of appellate procedure, federal and state constitutional provisions, and local rules of court may impose ethical and professional obligations upon lawyers.

A.   ABA Ethics Rules

The ABA has been the primary source for producing rules that are designed to regulate the conduct of lawyers. Its first publication of a set of ethical rules in 1908 was the Canons of Professional Ethics. The Canons remained in effect until the production of the Model Code. First published in 1969, the Model Code was designed to be a national model for states to follow in adopting legal ethics rules. The Model Code is comprised of nine Canons, which are described in the Preamble to the ABA Code as "axiomatic norms, expressing in general terms the standards of professional conduct expected of lawyers in their relationships with the public, with the legal system, and with the legal profession." For example, Canon 1 of the Model Code states "A lawyer should assist in maintaining the integrity and competence of the legal profession." Model Code of Prof'l Responsibility Canon 1 (1981). Ethical Considerations (ECs) correspond to the Canons. The ECs are aspirational and "represent the objectives toward which every member of the profession should strive." Model Code of Prof'l Responsibility Preamble (1981). An EC that corresponds to Canon 1 provides:

> A lawyer should maintain high standards of professional conduct and should encourage fellow lawyers to do likewise. He should be temperate and dignified, and should refrain from all illegal and morally reprehensible conduct. Because of his position in society, even minor violations of law by a lawyer may tend to lessen public confidence in the legal profession. Obedience to law exemplifies respect for law. To lawyers especially, respect for law should be more than a platitude.

Model Code of Prof'l Responsibility EC 1-5 (1981). Finally, the ABA Code contains Disciplinary Rules (DRs), which, unlike the ECs, are mandatory and "state the minimum level of conduct below which no lawyer can fall without being subject to disciplinary action." Model Code of Prof'l Responsibility Preamble (1981). Consequently, DR1-101(A) provides: "A lawyer is subject to discipline if he has made a materially false statement in, or if he has deliberately failed to disclose a material fact requested in connection with, his application for admission to the bar." Model Code of Prof'l Responsibility DR 1-101(A) (1981). Designed as a system under which lawyer conduct could be evaluated, the ABA intended the enforcing agency at the state level to apply the DRs by using "the interpretive guidance in the basic principles embodied in the Canons and in the objectives reflected in the [ECs]". Model Code of Prof'l Responsibility Preamble (1981). The Model Code was widely accepted at its inception and within a few years after its initial publication most states had adopted ethical rules modeled after the Model Code.

The Model Code, while widely adopted, was also criticized, largely for its aspirational and therefore arguably vague quality. In 1977 the ABA formed a commission to prepare a new set of rules. That commission, commonly identified by its first chairperson, Robert J. Kutak, endeavored to come up with a Restatement-style set of black-letter rules followed by explicative comments. The Model Rules of Professional Conduct, adopted by the ABA House of Delegates in 1983, were designed to supplant the Model Code. In an introductory "Scope" section of the Model Rules, the Rules are described as "rules of reason . . . partly obligatory and disciplinary and partly constitutive and descriptive in that they define a lawyer's role." Model Rules of Prof'l Conduct Preamble 14 (2008). The Comments to the Rules are designed to "explain[] and illustrate[] the meaning and purpose of the Rules" and "are intended as guides to interpretation." Model Rules of Prof'l Conduct Preamble 21 (2008). Intended to be set forth as black letter rules, Rule 1.1 provides: "A lawyer shall provide competent representation to a client. Competent representation requires the legal knowledge, skill, thoroughness and preparation reasonably necessary for the representation." Model Rules of Prof'l Conduct R. 1.1 (2008).

Following the adoption of the Model Rules, many states modified their rules of ethics to reflect material in the Model Rules. According to the Center for Professional Responsibility, 47 jurisdictions have adopted some form of the Model Rules. However, many states modify the rules within their jurisdictions. Consequently, it is important to be familiar with not only the Model Code and Model Rules, but also with state rules and statutes regarding legal ethics. In addition, many local rules of court include rules governing lawyer conduct that impose ethical and professional obligations.

B.   Professionalism Standards

In addition to rules relating to legal ethics, there are a variety of rules that relate specifically to professionalism in the legal profession. Professionalism codes are common at the state and local levels. For example, many state bar associations have codes, creeds, or pledges of professionalism that apply to all lawyers who are admitted to practice within the state. In addition, some local bar associations, such as the Dallas, Houston, and San Antonio bar associations, maintain codes of professionalism. Further, some groups within the ABA, such as the Young Lawyers Division and the Section on Litigation, have adopted professionalism codes specific to the division. Many of the professionalism codes reiterate the aspirations of the ethical rules, including loyalty to the client. Others adopt a more directed approach at courtesy and civility within the practice of law. The West Virginia State Bar Association's Standards of Professional Conduct provide that

> A lawyer should treat all counsel, parties, and witnesses in a civil and courteous manner, not only in court, but also in all other written and oral communications. A lawyer should not, even when called upon by a client to do so, abuse or indulge in offensive conduct, disparaging personal remarks or acrimony toward other counsel, parties, or witnesses.

> A lawyer should not, absent good cause, attribute bad motives or improper conduct to other counsel or bring the profession into disrepute by unfounded accusations of impropriety.

> A lawyer will speak and write civilly and respectfully in all communications with the court.

Similarly, the Alameda County Bar Association Statement of Professionalism and Civility provides:

> As attorneys, we engage in a profession devoted to serving the interests of clients and the public. As officers of the court, counselors, and advocates, we aspire to professional standards of behavior. In addition to adhering to the letter and spirit of rules of professional conduct, we believe the following principles foster success in — and contribute to the enjoyment of — the practice of law:

> Treating other participants in the justice system with courtesy and respect;

> Upholding the integrity of the justice system; and

> Striving to eliminate prejudice and ensure fairness in the justice system.

While these admonitions may seem self-evident, much has been written about the lack of professionalism and courtesy in the practice of law and, particularly how lapses in civility undermine the integrity of the profession. As the President of the Oregon State Bar noted in her 2005 speech to graduating law students, "Clients come and go. Cases are won and lost. Fees are awarded or denied. You will spend your entire career building a reputation and it can come crashing down with either a momentary lapse in judgment or through a pattern and practice of abusive behavior. Do not let [this] happen to you." Nena Cook, *Professionalism*, 65-APR Or. St. B. Bull. 49 (2005). Likewise, in discussing the reasons for a loss of lawyer professionalism, Cornell law professor Roger C. Cramton writes:

> Some years ago the fidelity and loyalty owed to clients was balanced by a generally accepted understanding that the lawyer's primary obligation was to the procedures and institutions of the law. When tension arose between client interests and those of the legal system, the lawyer's respect for the rule of law — the maintenance and improvement of just and efficient legal institutions — almost always prevailed. Our greatest need today is to regenerate this common faith.

Allen K. Harris, *The Professionalism Crisis — The 'Z' Word and Other Rambo Tactics: The Conference of Chief Justices' Solution*, 53 S.C. L. Rev. 549, 558–559

(2002) (citing Roger C. Cramton, *On Giving Meaning to "Professionalism,"* in Teaching and Learning Professionalism).

Scholars have struggled to characterize the difference between ethics and professionalism, although most agree that there is a distinction. As one ABA report noted,

> Professionalism is a much broader concept than legal ethics. For the purposes of this report, professionalism includes not only civility among members of the bench and bar, but also competence, integrity, respect for the rule of law, [participation in pro bono and community service,] and conduct by members of the legal profession that exceeds the minimum ethical requirements. Ethics rules are what a lawyer must obey. Principles of professionalism are what a lawyer should live by in conducting his or her affairs. Unlike disciplinary rules that can be implemented and enforced, professionalism is a personal characteristic.

Jordan W. Lorence, Alan E. Sears, & Benjamin W. Bull, *No Official High or Petty: The Unnecessary, Unwise, and Unconstitutional Trend of Prescribing Viewpoint Orthodoxy in Mandatory Continuing Legal Education*, 44 S. Tex. L. Rev. 263, 274 (2002) (citing A National Action Plan on Lawyer Conduct and Professionalism: A Report of the Working Group on Lawyer Conduct and Professionalism, National Action Plan on Lawyer Conduct and Professionalism 62 (submitted to the CCJ Committee on Professionalism and Lawyer Competence July 17, 1998)). Similarly, on the relationship between ethics and professionalism, one state supreme court justice commented:

> What is the difference between ethics and professionalism? Ethics is a set of rules that lawyers must obey. Violations of these rules can result in disciplinary action or disbarment. Professionalism, however, is not what a lawyer must do or must not do. It is a higher calling of what a lawyer should do to serve a client and the public.

Gus Chin, *Standard 2 — Civility, Courtesy and Fairness*, 18-APR Utah B.J. 35, 36 (2005) (citing Chief Justice E. Norman Veasey, "Making it Right-Veasey Plans Action to Reform Lawyer Conduct," Bus. L. Today, Mar.–Apr. 1998, 42, 44). So, ethics and professionalism are related concepts. In order to become a competent and respected lawyer, students should be familiar with ethical and professional rules that regulate the conduct of lawyers.

C.   Personal Integrity

Finally, students arrive at law school with a sense of personal integrity — knowing right from wrong. They also come to the practice of law with an innate sense of responsibility to the public associated with personal and professional behavior. The considerations set forth in the text should reinforce those principles, particularly insofar as they impact the representation of clients and the meaningful participation in the practice of law. I hope that, to the extent that the ethical and professional rules in fact reinforce those closely held notions of integrity, this text will encourage students to take pride in their professional and ethical discourse.

II. RELATIONSHIP BETWEEN THESE SOURCES AND THE PRACTICE OF LEGAL WRITING

This textbook is not designed to teach students how to prepare the documents that are the subject of later chapters. This textbook also does not endeavor to set forth all of the nuances related to the ethical rules addressed within the text. Indeed, that is the subject of a separate course in professional responsibility, which is required at all ABA-accredited law schools. Rather, the purpose of this textbook is to identify the types of ethical and professional considerations that are associated with particular types of documents. It is my hope that this textbook will educate lawyers on the types of ethical and professional considerations that are related to legal writing.

I also hope to encourage lawyers generally to engage in an ethical, professional, and courteous discourse practice. Much has been written about the state of law practice and the moral and ethical compass of the profession. This body of scholarship often paints a dim picture of the legal profession. My hope is to illustrate the incentives for ethical, professional, and moral behavior. Clearly, one incentive is to comport your behavior with the ethical rules so as to maintain your license to practice law. Additionally, engaging in a moral, ethical, professional, and courteous law practice will make you a more effective lawyer.

With respect to how ethical and professional behavior contributes to the efficacy of a lawyer's practice, consider the three rhetorical components of persuasion: ethos, pathos, and logos. Logos pertains to the logic or rationale of an argument. Pathos refers to persuasion by appealing to the emotion of the audience. Ethos is often conceptually related to the concept of ethics and refers to persuading by establishing credibility vis-à-vis the audience. As Michael Smith notes in his textbook, Advanced Legal Writing: Theories and Strategies in Persuasive Writing,

> A strong argument could be made that ethos is more important to persuasive legal writing than either logical argument (logos) or appeals to emotions (pathos). In fact, the effectiveness of both emotional and logical arguments depends in large part on perceptions of the advocate's credibility. Consider, for example, the role of credibility in an emotional appeal. A highly emotional argument, if presented by someone with little credibility, will likely be met with skepticism rather than acceptance. When an emotional argument is made by someone who possesses little credibility, it often comes across as an effort to manipulate or distract the decision-maker. Conversely, when an advocate who possesses credibility makes an emotional argument, the audience is more likely to receive it as it was intended, as a supplement to the arguments based on logic and reason.

> Likewise, credibility is important in arguments based on logic and reason. The law relevant to any particular legal issue is often susceptible to multiple interpretations, many of which could be reasonable. Arguments based on the logical application of legal authorities rarely point to a single clear conclusion. Not surprisingly, then, when a decision-maker is forced to choose between alternative logical conclusions, an advocate's credibility can play a significant role in the decision-maker's deliberations.[1]

---

[1] Michael R. Smith, Advanced Legal Writing: Theories and Strategies in Persuasive Writing, 123–4 (2d ed., Aspen Publishers 2008).

Smith's text notes that lawyers can establish credibility in writing by evincing good will, intelligence, and good moral character, characteristics which are reflected in the three sources of influence discussed in this chapter.

Smith explains how lawyers can evince good moral character traits such as truthfulness, candor, respect, and professionalism in writing by explaining the law and facts accurately and honestly and by crafting a neat, professional-looking document that complies with local rules. Similarly, a lawyer can evince intelligence in writing by following format and citation rules, organizing complex material clearly, and including proper authority to support legal arguments. Many of these characteristics of effective, professional legal writing are mandated or informed by ethical and professional considerations. Thus, they are not only a required or expected component of good legal writing, but they have a significant impact on the efficacy of the document and, in turn, the advocate.

Similarly, adherence to ethical and professional considerations has an impact on the level of satisfaction of a life in the law. Meeting the expectations of peers with respect to ethical and professional considerations has its own rewards, not the least of which is the likelihood that ethical, professional, and civil behavior will be returned by peers. As Justice Levinson of the Supreme Court of Hawaii notes:

> I feel impelled to get off my chest some additional and personal observations that are born of almost twenty-two years in the legal profession, almost seventeen of them as a private practitioner. If I have learned anything in that time, it is that what "goes around" truly does "come around" and that lawyers represent their clients' interests best when they discharge their responsibilities in accordance with the preamble to the Hawai'i Rules of Professional Conduct . . .

*   *   *   *   *

*   *   *

Former Chief Justice Burger, who unquestionably had the credentials to assume his self-appointed role as the nation's "commentator general" on legal etiquette, was right on the mark when he observed that:

> lawyers who know how to think but have not learned how to behave are a menace and a liability . . . to the administration of justice. . . . [T]he necessity for civility is relevant to lawyers because they are . . . living exemplars-and thus teachers-every day in every case and in every court; and their worst conduct will be emulated . . . more readily than their best.

*   *   *   *   *

*   *   *

My comments regarding the importance of "civility" in the conduct of the legal profession apply equally to all of its members, including myself. Collectively, every one of us must be better monitors of our daily professional behavior.

Matter of Hawaiian Flour Mills, Inc., 868 P.2d 419, 435–37 (Haw. 1994) (Levinson, J. concurring) (citations omitted).

Behaving ethically, professionally and civilly toward peers in the law should reinforce positive relationships which make a law practice gratifying. And the process of conducting a law practice ethically and professionally begins in law school — indeed, in the earliest phases of instruction. Consider the following remarks by Professor Patrick J. Schiltz:

Patrick J. Schiltz, On Being a Happy, Healthy, and Ethical Member of an Unhappy, Unhealthy, and Unethical Profession
52 Vand. L. Rev. 871 (1999)

* * *

A. Practicing Law Ethically

Let's first be clear on what I mean by practicing law ethically. I mean three things.

First, you generally have to comply with the formal disciplinary rules — either the Model Rules of Professional Conduct, the Model Code of Professional Responsibility, or some state variant of one or the other. As a law student, and then as a young lawyer, you will often be encouraged to distinguish ethical from unethical conduct solely by reference to the formal rules. Most likely, you will devote the majority of the time in your professional responsibility class to studying the rules, and you will, of course, learn the rules cold so that you can pass the Multi-State Professional Responsibility Exam ("MPRE"). In many other ways, subtle and blatant, you will be encouraged to think that conduct that does not violate the rules is "ethical," while conduct that does violate the rules is "unethical."

It is in the interests of your professors, the organized bar, and other lawyers to get you to think about ethics in this way. It is a lot easier for a professor to teach students what rules say than it is to explore with students what it means to behave ethically. (Fortunately, many professors resist the temptation to teach only the rules, but many others do not.) Defining ethics with reference to rules puts tremendous power in the hands of the organized bar that writes those rules. And many lawyers want "the absence of disciplinary measures and adherence to the profession's own Model Rules of Professional Conduct" to be sufficient to qualify a lawyer as "ethical," simply because it is easy to avoid disciplinary measures and to adhere to at least the letter of the formal rules.

I don't have anything against the formal rules. Often, they are all that stands between an unethical lawyer and a vulnerable client. You should learn them and follow them. But you should also understand that the formal rules represent nothing more than "the lowest common denominator of conduct that a highly self-interested group will tolerate." For many lawyers, "(e)thics is a matter of steering, if necessary, just clear of the few unambiguous prohibitions found in rules governing lawyers." But complying with the formal rules will not make you an ethical lawyer, any more than complying with the criminal law will make you an ethical person. Many of the sleaziest lawyers you will encounter will be absolutely scrupulous in their compliance with the formal rules. In fact, they will be only too happy to tell you just that. Complying with the rules is usually a necessary, but never a sufficient, part of being an ethical lawyer.

The second thing you must do to be an ethical lawyer is to act ethically in your work, even when you aren't required to do so by any rule. To a substantial extent, "bar ethical rules have lost touch with ordinary moral intuitions." To practice law ethically you must practice law consistently with those intuitions. For the most part, this is not complicated. Being an ethical lawyer is not much different from being an ethical doctor or mail carrier or gas station attendant. Indeed, long before you applied to law school, your parents had probably taught you all that you need to know to practice law ethically. You should treat others as you want them to treat you. Be honest and fair. Show respect and compassion. Keep your promises. Here is a good rule of thumb: If you would be ashamed if your parents or spouse or children knew what you were doing, then you should not do it.

The third thing you must do to be an ethical lawyer is to live an ethical life. Many big firm lawyers — who can be remarkably "smug[ ]about the superiority of the ethical standards of large firms" — ignore this point. So do many law professors who, when writing about legal ethics, tend to focus solely on the lawyer at work. But being admitted to the bar does not absolve you of your responsibilities outside of work — to your family, to your friends, to your community, and, if you're a person of faith, to your God. To practice law ethically, you must meet those responsibilities, which means that you must live a balanced life. If you become a workaholic lawyer, you will be unhealthy, probably unhappy, and, I would argue, unethical.

*   *   *

Because practicing law ethically will depend primarily upon the hundreds of little things that you will do almost unthinkingly every day, it will not depend much upon your thinking. You are going to be busy. The days will fly by. When you are on the phone negotiating a deal or when you are at your computer drafting a brief or when you are filling out your time sheet at the end of the day, you are not going to have time to reflect on each of your actions. You are going to have to act almost instinctively.

What this means, then, is that you will not practice law ethically — you cannot practice law ethically — unless acting ethically is habitual for you. You have to be in the habit of being honest. You have to be in the habit of being fair. You have to be in the habit of being compassionate. These qualities have to be deeply ingrained in you, so that you can't turn them on and off — so that acting honorably is not something you have to decide to do — so that when you are at work, making the thousands of phone calls you will make and writing the thousands of letters you will write and dealing with the thousands of people with whom you will deal, you will automatically apply the same values in the workplace that you apply outside of work, when you are with family and friends.

*   *   *

On Being a Happy, Healthy, and Ethical Lawyer

*   *   *

This is the best advice I can give you: Right now, while you are still in law school, make the commitment — not just in your head, but in your heart — that, although you are willing to work hard and you would like to make a comfortable living, you are not going to let money dominate your life to the exclusion of all else. And don't just structure your life around this negative; embrace a positive. Believe in something — care about something — so that when the culture of greed presses in on you from all sides, there will be something inside of you pushing back. Make the decision now that you will be the one who defines success for you — not your classmates, not big law firms, not clients of big law firms, not the National Law Journal. You will be a happier, healthier, and more ethical attorney as a result.

* * *

Develop the Habit of Acting Ethically

As I have explained, whether you practice law ethically will depend primarily upon the hundreds of mundane things that you will do almost unthinkingly every day. To behave ethically, day in and day out, you need to be in the habit of doing so. Developing the habit of acting ethically is no different from developing the habit of putting on your seatbelt or cracking your knuckles: You have to do it a lot. If you are going to practice law ethically, you need to decide now, while you are still in law school, what kind of lawyer you want to be, and then act as that kind of lawyer would act. Always. Everywhere. In big things and small. Do not take that first step toward being an unethical lawyer.

So, in your first year of law school, as you begin your legal education and learn how to research and write the documents that lawyers use to communicate in law practice, decide what kind of lawyer you want to be. I hope that this text will help you learn those habits which make your legal discourse instinctively ethical, professional, civil and courteous. Welcome to law school and to your life in the law.

Chapter 2

ENGAGING THE CLIENT — CONFLICTS

You will not always win. Sometimes damage control is all you can do for your client, and that damage control will be a worthy service in and of itself. Sometimes just having your competent representation is the best your client can hope for, and being able to exercise that fundamental right to representation may mean the world to your client. At the end of the day, if you have done your very best work for your client, and you have remained within the ethical boundaries of the profession and your own conscience, you will sleep well at night. You will have made your contribution to justice.

> — Professor Sue Liemer, Director of Lawyering Skills,
> Southern Illinois University School of Law

Lawyers owe a duty of undivided loyalty to clients. To that end, they must avoid any conflict of interest that would undermine that duty. Conflicts can arise between current clients, between current and former clients, and between the lawyer and client. All must be either avoided or, where permissible under the ethical rules, the conflict must be explained to the client and the client must consent to the representation notwithstanding the conflict. While this text cannot possibly address all the nuances associated with conflicts of interest, suffice it to say that lawyers must understand the rules relating to conflicts before embarking on representation of a client.

I. CONFLICTS OF INTEREST BETWEEN CURRENT CLIENTS

The rules in most jurisdictions tend to reinforce the general principle that a lawyer owes an undivided loyalty to a client. Consequently, under Model Rule 1.7, a lawyer may not represent a client if her representation of the client will be directly adverse to another client or if there is a "significant risk that the representation of one or more clients will be materially limited by the lawyer's responsibilities to another client, a former client or a third person or by a personal interest of the lawyer." Similarly, Canon 5 of the Model Code requires that a lawyer exercise independent professional judgment on behalf of a client.

Some conflicts may be resolved by obtaining written consent from all affected clients. In order to obtain proper consent, the lawyer must ensure that the affected clients are "aware of the relevant circumstances and of the material and reasonably foreseeable ways that the conflict could have adverse effects on the interests of that client." Model Rules of Prof'l Conduct R. 1.7 cmt. 18 (2008). Similarly, the EC 5-16 requires that, "before a lawyer may represent multiple clients, he should explain fully to each client the implications of the common representation and should accept or continue employment only if the clients consent."

Under the Model Rules there are certain types of representations that cannot be undertaken in the face of a conflict notwithstanding the client's consent — they are nonconsentable. "Consentability is typically determined by considering whether the interests of the clients will be adequately protected if the clients are permitted to give their informed consent. . . . ." Model Rules of Prof'l Conduct R. 1.7 cmt. 15 (2008). Therefore, in a situation in which a lawyer could not properly provide competent and diligent representation, the conflict cannot be waived by the client (indeed, the lawyer should not request it). In addition, if representation is prohibited by law, the conflict cannot be waived. For example, some jurisdictions prohibit a lawyer from representing more than one defendant in a capital trial. In addition, a lawyer cannot obtain consent to represent opposing parties in the same litigation. Finally, under some circumstances it may be impossible for the lawyer to make the necessary disclosure to obtain consent.

The lawyer's primary responsibility with regard to current clients requires that he be able to: (1) clearly identify clients; (2) determine whether there are potential conflicts; and (3) decide whether it is possible to resolve the conflict with the clients' consent. If the lawyer determines that he can resolve the conflict by obtaining the clients' consent, he must obtain confirmation of the consent in writing. Note that the rule does not require that the consent be in writing — written confirmation may include a letter in which the lawyer confirms in writing the client's oral consent. Model Rules of Prof'l Conduct R. 1.0(b) (2008).

II.   CONFLICTS OF INTEREST BETWEEN CURRENT AND FORMER CLIENTS

Model Rule 1.9 sets forth the lawyer's obligation to former clients, noting that "[a]fter termination of a client-lawyer relationship, a lawyer has certain continuing duties with respect to confidentiality and conflicts of interest.. . . ." Model Rules of Prof'l Conduct R. 1.9 cmt. 1 (2008). Generally, a lawyer is prohibited from representing a new client whose interests are materially adverse to those of the former client (who the lawyer either personally represented or who was represented by a firm with which the lawyer was associated), unless the former client consents to the conflict. In addition, under Model Rule 1.9, a lawyer who has formerly represented a client, or who was associated with a firm that represented the client, is generally prohibited from using or revealing information related to the representation.

In terms of determining whether there is a conflict, the comments to the rule provide some insight on when a lawyer's involvement in a previous client matter precludes her from representing a new client absent consent. With regard to evaluating the lawyer's involvement with the prior matter, Comment 2 explains that

> When a lawyer has been directly involved in a specific transaction, subsequent representation of other clients with materially adverse interests in that transaction clearly is prohibited. On the other hand, a lawyer who recurrently handled a type of problem for a former client is not precluded from later representing another client in a factually distinct problem of that type even though the subsequent representation involves a position adverse to the prior client . . . .

Model Rules of Prof'l Conduct R. 1.9 cmt. 2 (2008). Further, in evaluating whether the matter of the former client is "substantially related" to the new client's matter,

Comment 3 notes that, where matters "involve the same transaction or legal dispute or if there otherwise is a substantial risk that confidential factual information as would normally have been obtained in the prior representation would materially advance the client's position in the subsequent matter." Model Rules of Prof'l Conduct R. 1.9 cmt. 3 (2008).

The comments to the rule acknowledge that issues of conflict become more complicated when lawyers move between firms. The comments explain that, under those circumstances, there are competing considerations. First, the former client is entitled to a remaining assurance of loyalty. In addition, the rule should not be so broadly construed so as to undermine the ability of clients to select a lawyer. Finally, the rule should not hinder a lawyer who leaves a practice from representing new clients. Indeed, the comments point out that "If the concept of imputation were applied with unqualified rigor, the result would be radical curtailment of the opportunity of lawyers to move from one practice setting to another and of the opportunity of clients to change counsel." Model Rules of Prof'l Conduct R. 1.9 cmt. 4 (2003). The underlying principle is one of actual knowledge of information that would give rise to a conflict. Absent such knowledge, the lawyer's representation of a subsequent client, even in a matter that conflicts with the former client's matter, is not compromised. "Thus, if a lawyer while with one firm acquired no knowledge or information relating to a particular client of the firm, and that lawyer later joined another firm, neither the lawyer individually nor the second firm is disqualified from representing another client in the same or a related matter even though the interests of the two clients conflict." Model Rules of Prof'l Conduct R. 1.9 cmt. 5 (2008).

Consequently, a lawyer who begins representation of a new client should evaluate whether his representation of a former client will be compromised by the new representation. He must also evaluate whether his association with a prior law firm and his involvement with client matters in that setting compromise the new representation.

III.   CONFLICTS OF INTEREST BETWEEN LAWYER AND CLIENT

Rule 1.8 identifies a variety of prohibited relationships between a lawyer and his client. For example, absent certain exceptions, a lawyer should not acquire ownership or pecuniary interests adverse to a client. Lawyers should generally not solicit gifts from clients or prepare documents that have the legal effect of giving the lawyer such gifts. Further, lawyers should not generally make or negotiate agreements in which the lawyer acquires media or literary interests based on information relating to the representation. Finally, lawyers generally should not provide financial assistance to clients in connection with pending or contemplated representation. In the Model Code, prohibited conflicts between lawyer and client are similar to those set forth in the Model Rules and are addressed under Canon 5, which requires a lawyer to exercise independent professional judgment on behalf of a client.

Chapter 3

E-MAIL COMMUNICATION

Your professional reputation and your client's case are just as much at play in e-mail as it is in any memo, brief or client letter. One of the best lessons that I have learned about reviewing e-mails for proper tone and polish is that the recipient's e-mail address should be the very *last* thing to add, not the first.

— Ruth Anne Robbins, Clinical Professor of Law,
Rutgers School of Law—Camden

Lawyers communicate with a variety of constituencies via e-mail. They may send advice or information to clients by e-mail, or they may communicate with opposing counsel. They may communicate with third parties, including witnesses, insurance agents, accountants, and court staff. E-mails do constitute "writings" under Model Rule 1.0, such that any ethical rule that addresses a writing implicates e-mail communication. The ethical obligations associated with e-mail communications will vary according to the objective and content of the communication. Where the objective of the e-mail communication is, for example, client advice, you should consult the chapters on interoffice memoranda and client letters for additional considerations. If the objective of the e-mail is to explore settlement prior to the initiation of a lawsuit, consult the chapter on demand letters. However, there are some ethical issues which specifically relate to electronic communication by e-mail. These focus primarily on inadvertent disclosure or receipt of confidential information, and the prohibition on live solicitation of clients. This chapter will deal briefly with certain content-based ethical considerations, and will also address considerations of professionalism — particularly those involving format — applicable to e-mail communication.

I. CONTENT-BASED CONSIDERATIONS

A. Overview

i. Disclosure of Confidential Information

Under Model Rule 1.6, lawyers are expressly prohibited from revealing information relating to a client unless the client gives informed consent. Information under the rule is construed broadly to include not only information received from a client, but also from other sources, including public sources. In this respect the prohibition against disclosure contained in Model Rule 1.6 should be distinguished from the attorney-client privilege. The latter is a rule pertaining to the admissibility of evidence at trial. "Confidential" information subject to the restriction under Model Rule 1.6 includes, but is not limited to privileged information.

In the context of communicating information by means of e-mail, the comments to Rule 1.6 caution that "When transmitting a communication that includes information relating to the representation of a client, the lawyer must take reasonable precautions to prevent the information from coming into the hands of unintended recipients." Model Rules of Prof'l Conduct 1.6 cmt. 17 (2008). The comments note that lawyers do not need to employ special security measures to transmit information if the method of transmittal affords a reasonable expectation of privacy. Because electronic documents do contain embedded information known as "metadata," including information regarding authorship and prior versions and modifications to the document, lawyers should be cognizant of the ability of the recipient to obtain this form of information from an electronically transmitted document. It is becoming increasingly common practice to remove such data by "scrubbing" the document prior to transmittal. Lawyers may also use encrypted e-mail. For particularly sensitive information, lawyers should evaluate whether an alternative transmission method is warranted. Comment 17 to the rule further provides that "A client may require the lawyer to implement special security measures not required by this Rule or may give informed consent to the use of a means of communication that would otherwise be prohibited by this Rule." Model Rules of Prof'l Conduct 1.6, cmt. 17 (2008).

The duty of confidentiality under Model Rule 1.6 survives the termination of the lawyer-client relationship and extends to information which is disclosed by a lawyer's employees. To the extent that the electronic transmission of documents may include embedded data, lawyers must be particularly careful when sending information electronically.

ii.   Inadvertent Receipt of Confidential Information

Model Rule of Prof'l Conduct 4.4(b) states that a "lawyer who receives a document relating to the representation of the lawyer's client and knows or reasonably should know that the document was inadvertently sent shall promptly notify the sender." The comments specifically include electronic transmission such as e-mail and provide that "[i]f a lawyer knows or reasonably should know that a document was sent inadvertently, then this Rule requires the lawyer to promptly notify the sender in order to permit that person to take protective measures." Model Rule of Prof'l Conduct 4.4 cmt. 2 (2008). It is unclear whether a lawyer can use information which was inadvertently disclosed. This issue is addressed later in this chapter.

iii.   Advertising/ Communication with Someone Represented by Counsel

Model Rule 4.2 prohibits a lawyer from communicating directly with a person the lawyer knows to be represented by counsel. This rule "contributes to the proper functioning of the legal system by protecting a person who has chosen to be represented by a lawyer in a matter against overreaching by other lawyers who are participating in the matter. . . ." Model Rules of Prof'l Conduct R. 4.2 cmt. 1 (2008).

Chapter 7 of the Model Rules addresses information about legal services, and places certain advertising restrictions on lawyers. Model Rule 7.3 restricts lawyers from advertising for services in real time communications, including electronic communications. This prohibition is based on the potential for abuse, including the possibility of unduly influencing clients who are not in a position to fully evaluate all of their available alternatives. Comment 1 notes that "[t]here is a potential for abuse inherent in direct in-person, live telephone or real-time electronic contact by a lawyer with a prospective client. . . ." Model Rule of Prof'l Conduct R. 7.3 cmt. 1 (2008). Generally, e-mail communications are treated as written solicitations rather than real time communications, largely because they do not present the potential for overreaching associated with a real time communication.

B.   Disclosure of Confidential Information

Lawyers routinely correspond with clients, opposing counsel, and third parties by e-mail. Electronic transmission of legal documents gives rise to concerns about electronic interception of materials, as well as inadvertent transmission of client information which is embedded in an electronic version of a document. Most jurisdictions agree that e-mail is an acceptable method of transmitting information, and affords the sender a reasonable expectation of privacy. In 1999, the American Bar Association concluded that e-mail was an acceptable method of transmitting client information. ABA Comm. on Ethics and Prof'l Responsibility, Formal Op. 99-413 (1999). The opinion, reproduced below, provides a detailed discussion of a lawyer's responsibility when communicating via e-mail.

American Bar Association
ABA Formal Op. 99-413

PROTECTING THE CONFIDENTIALITY OF UNENCRYPTED E-MAIL

March 10, 1999

A lawyer may transmit information relating to the representation of a client by unencrypted e-mail sent over the Internet without violating the Model Rules of Professional Conduct (1998) because the mode of transmission affords a reasonable expectation of privacy from a technological and legal standpoint. The same privacy accorded U.S. and commercial mail, land-line telephonic transmissions, and facsimiles applies to Internet e-mail. A lawyer should consult with the client and follow her instructions, however, as to the mode of transmitting highly sensitive information relating to the client's representation.

The Committee addresses in this opinion the obligations of lawyers under the Model Rules of Professional Conduct (1998) when using unencrypted electronic mail to communicate with clients or others about client matters. The Committee (1) analyzes the general standards that lawyers must follow under the Model Rules in protecting "confidential client information"[1] from inadvertent disclosure; (2) compares the risk of interception of unencrypted e-mail with the risk of interception of other forms of communication; and (3) reviews the various forms of

---

[1] As used in this opinion, "confidential client information" denotes "information relating to the representation of a client" under Model Rule 1.6(a), which states:

(a) a lawyer shall not reveal information relating to representation of a client unless a client consents after consultation, except for disclosures that are impliedly authorized in order to carry out the representation

e-mail transmission, the associated risks of unauthorized disclosure, and the laws affecting unauthorized interception and disclosure of electronic communications.

The Committee believes that e-mail communications, including those sent unencrypted over the Internet, pose no greater risk of interception or disclosure than other modes of communication commonly relied upon as having a reasonable expectation of privacy. The level of legal protection accorded e-mail transmissions, like that accorded other modes of electronic communication, also supports the reasonableness of an expectation of privacy for unencrypted e-mail transmissions. The risk of unauthorized interception and disclosure exists in every medium of communication, including e-mail. It is not, however, reasonable to require that a mode of communicating information must be avoided simply because interception is technologically possible, especially when unauthorized interception or dissemination of the information is a violation of law.[2]

The Committee concludes, based upon current technology and law as we are informed of it, that a lawyer sending confidential client information by unencrypted e-mail does not violate Model Rule 1.6(a) in choosing that mode to communicate. This is principally because there is a reasonable expectation of privacy in its use.

The conclusions reached in this opinion do not, however, diminish a lawyer's obligation to consider with her client the sensitivity of the communication, the costs of its disclosure, and the relative security of the contemplated medium of communication. Particularly strong protective measures are warranted to guard against the disclosure of highly sensitive matters. Those measures might include the avoidance of e-mail,[3] just as they would warrant the avoidance of the telephone, fax, and mail. See Model Rule 1.1 and 1.4(b). The lawyer must, of course, abide by the client's wishes regarding the means of transmitting client information. See Model Rule 1.2(a).

A. Lawyers' Duties Under Model Rule 1.6

The prohibition in Model Rule 1.6(a) against revealing confidential client information absent client consent after consultation imposes a duty on a lawyer to take reasonable steps in the circumstances to protect such information against unauthorized use or disclosure. Reasonable steps include choosing a means of communication in which the lawyer has a reasonable expectation of privacy.[4] In order to comply with the duty of confidentiality under Model Rule 1.6, a lawyer's

---

[2] The Electronic Communications Privacy Act amended the Federal Wiretap Statute by extending its scope to include "electronic communications." The ECPA now commonly refers to the amended statute in its entirety. The ECPA provides criminal and civil penalties for the unauthorized interception or disclosure of any wire, oral, or electronic communication.

[3] Options other than abandoning e-mail include using encryption or seeking client consent after apprising the client of the risks and consequences of disclosure.

[4] Whether a lawyer or a client has a reasonable expectation of privacy also governs whether a communication is "in confidence" for purposes of the attorney-client privilege. As a result, analysis under the attorney-client privilege is often relevant to this opinion's discussion of e-mail and the duty of confidentiality. The relevance of privilege is not exhaustive, however, because of its more restrictive application in prohibiting the introduction of privileged communications between a lawyer and client in any official proceeding. In contrast to the requirement imposed by the duty of confidentiality to avoid disclosing any information "relating to the representation" of the client, see Model Rule 1.6(a), supra n. 1, the attorney-client privilege applies only to actual "communications" made "in confidence" by the client to the lawyer. See JOHN H. WIGMORE, 8 EVIDENCE § 2295 (McNaughton rev. 1961).

expectation of privacy in a communication medium need not be absolute; it must merely be reasonable.

It uniformly is accepted that a lawyer's reliance on land-line telephone, fax machine, and mail to communicate with clients does not violate the duty of confidentiality because in the use of each medium, the lawyer is presumed to have a reasonable expectation of privacy.[5] The Committee now considers whether a lawyer's expectation of privacy is any less reasonable when she communicates by e-mail.

B. Communications Alternatives To E-Mail

In order to understand what level of risk may exist without destroying the reasonable expectation of privacy, this Section evaluates the risks inherent in the use of alternative means of communication in which lawyers nonetheless are presumed to have such an expectation. These include ordinary U.S. mail; land-line, cordless, and cellular telephones; and facsimile transmissions.

1. U.S. and Commercial Mail

It uniformly is agreed that lawyers have a reasonable expectation of privacy in communications made by mail (both U.S. Postal Service and commercial). This is despite risks that letters may be lost, stolen or misplaced at several points between sender and recipient. Further, like telephone companies, Internet service providers (ISPs), and on-line service providers (OSPs), mail services often reserve the right to inspect the contents of any letters or packages handled by the service. Like e-mail, U.S. and commercial mail can be intercepted and disseminated illegally. But, unlike unencrypted e-mail, letters are sealed and therefore arguably more secure than e-mail.

2. Land-Line Telephones

It is undisputed that a lawyer has a reasonable expectation of privacy in the use of a telephone. For this reason, the protection against unreasonable search and seizure guaranteed by the Fourth Amendment applies to telephone conversations.[6] It also is recognized widely that the attorney-client privilege applies to conversations over the telephone as long as the other elements of the privilege are present. However, this expectation of privacy in communications by telephone must be considered in light of the substantial risk of interception and disclosure inherent in its use. Tapping a telephone line does not require great technical

---

[5] See infra Section B. It should be noted that a lawyer's negligent use of any medium — including the telephone, mail and fax — may breach the duty of confidentiality. The relevant issue here, however, is whether, despite otherwise reasonable efforts to ensure confidentiality, breach occurs solely by virtue of the lawyer's use of e-mail.

[6] It should be noted that the ECPA preserves the privileged character of any unlawfully intercepted "wire, oral, or electronic communication." The inclusion of e-mail in this provision is important for two reasons. First, implicit in this provision is the assumption that electronic communications are capable of transmitting privileged material. To argue that the use of e-mail never is "in confidence" or constitutes an automatic waiver of otherwise privileged communications therefore appears to be inconsistent with an assumption of this provision of federal law. Second, the identical federal treatment of e-mail with other means of communication long assumed consistent with the maintenance of privilege likewise is inconsistent with the assertion that the use of e-mail poses unique threats to privileged communications.

sophistication or equipment, nor is the know-how difficult to obtain. Multiple extensions provide opportunities for eavesdropping without the knowledge of the speakers. Technical errors by the phone company may result in third parties listening to private conversations. Lastly, phone companies are permitted by law to monitor phone calls under limited conditions.

Despite this lack of absolute security in the medium, using a telephone is considered to be consistent with the duty to take reasonable precautions to maintain confidentiality.

3. Cordless and Cellular Phones

Authority is divided as to whether users have a reasonable expectation of privacy in conversations made over cordless and cellular phones. Some court decisions reached the conclusion that there is no reasonable expectation of privacy in cordless phones in part because of the absence, at the time, of federal law equivalent to that which protects traditional telephone communications. After the 1994 amendment to the Wiretap Statute, which extended the same legal protections afforded regular telephone communications to cordless phone conversations, at least one ethics opinion addressed the advisability of using cordless phones to communicate with clients and concluded that their use does not violate the duty of confidentiality.

The nature of cordless and cellular phone technology exposes it to certain risks that are absent from e-mail communication. E-mail messages are not "broadcast" over public airwaves. Cordless phones, by contrast, rely on FM and AM radio waves to broadcast signals to the phone's base unit, which feeds the signals into land-based phone lines. Therefore, in addition to the risks inherent in the use of a regular telephone, cordless phones also are subject to risks of interception due to their broadcast on radio signals that may be picked up by mass-marketed devices such as radios, baby monitors, and other cordless phones within range. Further, the intercepted signals of cordless and analog cellular telephones are in an instantly comprehensible form (oral speech), unlike the digital format of e-mail communications.

Similarly, cellular phones transmit radio signals to a local base station that feeds the signals into land-based phone lines. The broadcast area from the phone to the station is larger than that of a cordless phone, and receivers and scanners within range may intercept and overhear the conversation. Although the Committee does not here express an opinion regarding the use of cellular or cordless telephone, it notes that the concerns about the expectation of privacy in the use of cordless and cellular telephones do not apply to e-mail transmitted over land-based phone lines.[7]

---

[7] The risks of interception and disclosure may be lessened by the recent introduction of digital cellular phones, whose transmissions are considered more difficult to intercept than their analog counterparts. New communications technology, however, does not always advance privacy concerns. The use of airplane telephones, for example, exposes users to the interception risks of cellular telephones as well as a heightened risk of disclosure due to eavesdropping on the airplane itself. Most recently, a world-wide, satellite-based cellular telephone system called Iridium has been introduced by Motorola. The principles articulated in this opinion should be considered by a lawyer when using such systems.

4. Facsimile

Authority specifically stating that the use of fax machines is consistent with the duty of confidentiality is absent, perhaps because, according to some commentators, courts assume the conclusion to be self-evident. Nonetheless, there are significant risks of interception and disclosure in the use of fax machines. Misdirection may result merely by entering one of ten digits incorrectly. Further, unlike e-mail, faxes often are in the hands of one or more intermediaries before reaching their intended recipient, including, for example, secretaries, runners, and mailroom employees. In light of these risks, prudent lawyers faxing highly sensitive information should take heightened measures to preserve the communication's confidentiality.

C. Characteristics of E-Mail Systems

The reasonableness of a lawyer's use of any medium to communicate with or about clients depends both on the objective level of security it affords and the existence of laws intended to protect the privacy of the information communicated. We here examine the four most common types of e-mail and compare the risks inherent in their use with those of alternative means of communication, including the telephone (regular, cordless and cellular), fax, and mail.

Like many earlier technologies, "e-mail" has become a generic term that presently encompasses a variety of systems allowing communication among computer users. Because the security of these e-mail systems is not uniform, the Committee here evaluates separately the degree of privacy afforded by each. As set forth below, we conclude that a lawyer has a reasonable expectation of privacy in such use.

1. "Direct" E-Mail

Lawyers may e-mail their clients directly (and vice versa) by programming their computer's modem to dial their client's. The modem simply converts the content of the e-mail into digital information that is carried on land-based phone lines to the recipient's modem, where it is reassembled back into the message. This is virtually indistinguishable from the process of sending a fax: a fax machine dials the number of the recipient fax machine and digitally transmits information to it through land-based phone lines. Because the information travels in digital form, tapping a telephone line to intercept an e-mail message would require more effort and technical sophistication than would eavesdropping on a telephone conversation by telephone tap.

Based on the difficulty of intercepting direct e-mail, several state bar ethics opinions and many commentators recognize a reasonable expectation of privacy in this form of e-mail. Further, in two recent federal court decisions, the attorney-client and work-product privileges were considered applicable to e-mail communications. The Committee agrees that there is a reasonable expectation of privacy in this mode of communication.

2. "Private System" E-Mail

A "private system" includes typical internal corporate e-mail systems and so-called "extranet" networks in which one internal system directly dials another private system. The only relevant distinction between "private system" and "direct" e-mail is the greater risk of misdirected e-mails in a private system. Messages mistakenly may be sent throughout a law firm or to unintended recipients within the client's organization. However, all members of a firm owe a duty of confidentiality to each of the firm's clients. Further, unintended disclosures to individuals within a client's private e-mail network are unlikely to be harmful to the client.

The reliance of "private system" e-mail on land-based phone lines and its non-use of any publicly accessible network renders this system as secure as direct e-mail, regular phone calls, and faxes. As a result, there is a widespread consensus that confidentiality is not threatened by its use, and the Committee concurs.

3. On-line Service Providers

E-mail also may be provided by third-party on-line service providers or "OSPs." Users typically are provided a password-protected mailbox from which they may send and retrieve e-mail.

There are two features of this system that distinguish it from direct and private-system e-mail. First, user mailboxes, although private, exist in a public forum consisting of other fee-paying users. The added risk caused by the existence of other public users on the same network is that misdirected e-mails may be sent to unknown users. Unlike users of private system e-mail networks who, as agents of their employers, owe a duty of confidentiality to them and, in the case of a law firm, to all firm clients, the inadvertent user owes no similar duties. The risk of misdirection is, however, no different from that which exists when sending a fax. Further, the misdirection of an e-mail to another OSP can be avoided with reasonable care.[8]

The second distinctive feature of e-mail administered by an OSP is that the relative security and confidentiality of user e-mail largely depends on the adequacy of the particular OSP's security measures meant to limit external access and its formal policy regarding the confidentiality of user e-mail. Together, they will determine whether a user has a reasonable expectation of privacy in this type of e-mail.

The denial of external access ordinarily is ensured by the use of password-protected mailboxes or encryption. The threat to confidentiality caused by the potential inspection of users' e-mail by OSP system administrators who must access the e-mail for administrative and compliance purposes is overcome by the adoption of a formal policy that narrowly restricts the bases on which system administrators and OSP agent are permitted to examine user e-mail.

---

[8] If the inadvertent recipient is a lawyer, then the lawyer must refrain from examining the information any more than necessary to ascertain that it was not intended for her and must notify the sender, ABA Comm. on Ethics and Professional Responsibility, Formal Op. 92-368 (1992), an obligation that extends to information received by e-mail or fax, ABA Comm. on Ethics and Professional Responsibility, Formal Op. 94-382 (1994).

Moreover, federal law imposes limits on the ability of OSP administrators to inspect user e-mail, irrespective of the OSP's formal policy. Inspection is limited by the ECPA to purposes "necessary to the rendition of services" or to the protection of "rights or property." Further, even if an OSP administrator lawfully inspects user e-mail within the narrow limits defined by the ECPA, the disclosure of those communications for purposes other than those provided by the statute is prohibited.

Accordingly, the Committee concludes that lawyers have a reasonable expectation of privacy when communicating by e-mail maintained by an OSP, a conclusion that also has been reached by at least one case as well as state bar ethics committees and commentators.

4. Internet E-Mail

E-mail may be sent over the Internet between service users without interposition of OSPs. Internet e-mail typically uses land-based phone lines and a number of intermediate computers randomly selected to travel from sender to recipient. The intermediate computers consist of various Internet service providers or "routers" that maintain software designed to help the message reach its final destination.

Because Internet e-mail typically travels through land-based phone lines, the only points of unique vulnerability consist of the third party-owned Internet services providers or "ISPs," each capable of copying messages passing through its network. Confidentiality may be compromised by (1) the ISP's legal, though qualified, right to monitor e-mail passing through or temporarily stored in its network, and (2) the illegal interception of e-mail by ISPs or "hackers."

The ISPs' qualified inspection rights are identical to those of OSPs. The same limits described above therefore apply to ISPs. In addition, the provider of an electronic communications service may by law conduct random monitoring only for mechanical or service quality control checks.

The second threat to confidentiality is the illegal interception of e-mail, either by ISPs exceeding their qualified monitoring rights or making unauthorized disclosures, or by third party hackers who use ISPs as a means of intercepting e-mail. Although it is difficult to quantify precisely the frequency of either practice, the interception or disclosure of e-mail in transit or in storage (whether passing through an ISP or in any other medium) is a crime and also may result in civil liability.

In addition to criminalization, practical constraints on the ability of third parties and ISPs to capture and read Internet e-mail lead to the conclusion that the user of Internet e-mail has a reasonable expectation of privacy. An enormous volume of data travelling at an extremely high rate passes through ISPs every hour. Further, during the passage of Internet e-mail between sender and recipient, the message ordinarily is split into fragments or "packets" of information. Therefore, only parts of individual messages customarily pass through ISPs, limiting the extent of any potential disclosure. Because the specific route taken by each e-mail message through the labyrinth of phone lines and ISPs is random, it would be very difficult consistently to intercept more than a segment of a message by the same author.

Together, these characteristics of Internet e-mail further support the Committee's conclusion that an expectation of privacy in this medium of communication is reasonable. The fact that ISP administrators or hackers are capable of intercepting Internet e-mail — albeit with great difficulty and in violation of federal law — should not render the expectation of privacy in this medium any the less reasonable, just as the risk of illegal telephone taps does not erode the reasonable expectation of privacy in a telephone call.

Conclusion

Lawyers have a reasonable expectation of privacy in communications made by all forms of e-mail, including unencrypted e-mail sent on the Internet, despite some risk of interception and disclosure. It therefore follows that its use is consistent with the duty under Rule 1.6 to use reasonable means to maintain the confidentiality of information relating to a client's representation.

Although earlier state bar ethics opinions on the use of Internet e-mail tended to find a violation of the state analogues of Rule 1.6 because of the susceptibility to interception by unauthorized persons and, therefore, required express client consent to the use of e-mail, more recent opinions reflecting lawyers' greater understanding of the technology involved approve the use of unencrypted Internet e-mail without express client consent.

Even so, when the lawyer reasonably believes that confidential client information being transmitted is so highly sensitive that extraordinary measures to protect the transmission are warranted, the lawyer should consult the client as to whether another mode of transmission, such as special messenger delivery, is warranted. The lawyer then must follow the client's instructions as to the mode of transmission. See Model Rule 1.2(a).

NOTES

1. Some jurisdictions have suggested that lawyers have a heightened obligation to protect client confidences transmitted electronically. For example, in Opinion 782, the New York State Bar Association Committee on Professional Ethics concluded that a lawyer should "exercise reasonable care" to protect client's confidential information. The opinion notes "[w]hat constitutes reasonable care will vary with the circumstances, including the subject matter of the document, whether the document was based on a 'template' used in another matter for another client, whether there have been multiple drafts of the document with comments from multiple sources, whether the client has commented on the document, and the identity of the intended recipients of the document." With respect to the mode of transmission, the court concluded that reasonable care might "call for the lawyer to stay abreast of technological advances and the potential risks in transmission in order to make an appropriate decision with respect to the mode of transmission."

The Opinion further examined the responsibility of the recipient with respect to the use of the information. The Committee concluded that "Lawyer-recipients also have an obligation not to exploit an inadvertent or unauthorized transmission of client confidences or secrets . . . [W]e conclude[] that the use of computer technology to access client confidences and secrets revealed in metadata constitutes 'an impermissible intrusion on the attorney-client relationship in violation of the

Code.' " This issue is further explored in the following section.

C.   Inadvertent Receipt of Confidential Information

Model Rule 4.4(b) states that a "lawyer who receives a document relating to the representation of the lawyer's client and knows or reasonably should know that the document was inadvertently sent shall promptly notify the sender." The comments specifically include electronic transmission such as e-mail and provide that "[i]f a lawyer knows or reasonably should know that a document was sent inadvertently, then this Rule requires the lawyer to promptly notify the sender in order to permit that person to take protective measures." Model Rule of Prof'l Conduct 4.4 cmt. 2 (2008). The lawyer's responsibility with respect to reviewing and/or using inadvertently transmitted material is not entirely clear. The comments merely note that "[s]ome lawyers may choose to return a document unread, for example, when the lawyer learns before receiving the document that it was inadvertently sent to the wrong address. Where a lawyer is not required by applicable law to do so, the decision to voluntarily return such a document is a matter of professional judgment ordinarily reserved to the lawyer." Model Rule of Prof'l Conduct 4.4 cmt. 3 (2008). The following case illustrates the difference of opinion among state bar associations with respect to ethical or professional restrictions on lawyers' use of inadvertently transmitted client information.

Pennsylvania Bar Association Committee on Legal Ethics and Professional Responsibility
MINING METADATA
Formal Opinion Number 2007-500
2007

I. Introduction

This Formal Opinion provides ethical guidance to lawyers on the subject of metadata received from opposing counsel in electronic materials, including documents, spreadsheets and PowerPoint presentations under circumstances in which it is clear that the materials were not intended for the receiving lawyer. As more fully set forth below, it is the opinion of this Committee that each attorney must, as the Preamble to the Rules of Professional Conduct states, "resolve [the issue] through the exercise of sensitive and moral judgment guided by the basic principles of the Rules" and determine for himself or herself whether to utilize the metadata contained in documents and other electronic files based upon the lawyer's judgment and the particular factual situation.

In reaching this conclusion, the Committee notes that there is no specific Pennsylvania Rule of Professional Conduct determining the ethical obligations of a lawyer receiving inadvertently transmitted metadata from another lawyer, his client or other third person; and, there is no specific Pennsylvania Rule of Professional Conduct requiring the receiving lawyer to assess whether the opposing lawyer has violated any ethical obligation to the lawyer's client. Thus, the decision of how or whether a lawyer may use the information contained in the metadata will depend upon many factors, including:

- The judgment of the lawyer;
- The particular facts applicable to the situation;

- The lawyer's view of his or her obligations to the client under Rule of Professional Conduct 1.3, and the relevant Comments to this Rule;[9]
- The nature of the information received;
- How and from whom the information was received;
- Attorney-client privilege and work product rules; and,
- Common sense, reciprocity and professional courtesy.

Although the waiver of the attorney-client privilege with respect to privileged and confidential materials is a matter for judicial determination, the Committee believes that the inadvertent transmissions of such materials should not constitute a waiver of the privilege, except in the case of extreme carelessness or indifference.

II. Background

Metadata, which means "information about data," is data contained within electronic materials that is not ordinarily visible to those viewing the information. Although most commonly found in documents created in Microsoft Word, metadata is also present in a variety of other formats, including spreadsheets, PowerPoint presentations and Corel WordPerfect documents. Metadata generally contains seemingly harmless information. However, metadata may also contain privileged and/or confidential information, such as previously deleted text, notes and tracked changes, which may provide information about, *e.g.*, legal issues, legal theories and other information that was not intended to be disclosed to opposing counsel.

Attorneys who receive electronic documents from other attorneys can easily use a variety of software to discover and utilize this metadata, with potentially disastrous consequences to the other side. For example, in a products liability lawsuit involving the prescription drug Vioxx, the metadata contained within documents produced by Merck, the manufacturer of the drug, revealed that Merck had edited out negative information from a drug study. Because the problems with metadata have become increasingly common, and because the software that permits review of the data is inexpensive and easy to use, the ability to discover and utilize metadata presents serious challenges to the protection of the confidentiality of information provided by counsel.

III. Discussion

Pa.R.P.C. 1.6 ("Confidentiality of Information") governs an attorney's disclosure of information relating to the representation of a client. The Rule states:

> (a) A lawyer shall not reveal information relating to representation of a client unless the client gives informed consent, except for disclosures that are impliedly authorized in order to carry out the representation, and

---

[9] Comment 1 to R.P.C. 1.3 states:

[1] A lawyer should pursue a matter on behalf of a client despite opposition, obstruction or personal inconvenience to the lawyer, and take whatever lawful and ethical measures are required to vindicate a client's cause or endeavor. A lawyer must also act with commitment and dedication to the interests of the client and with zeal in advocacy upon the client's behalf. A lawyer is not bound, however, to press for every advantage that might be realized for a client. For example, a lawyer may have authority to exercise professional discretion in determining the means by which a matter should be pursued. See Rule 1.2. The lawyer's duty to act with reasonable diligence does not require the use of offensive tactics or preclude the treating of all persons involved in the legal process with courtesy and respect.

except as stated in paragraphs (b) and (c).

The Comment to Rule 1.6 states in relevant part:

[2] A fundamental principle in the client-lawyer relationship is that, in the absence of the client's informed consent, the lawyer must not reveal information relating to the representation. See Rule 1.0(e) for the definition of informed consent. This contributes to the trust that is the hallmark of the client-lawyer relationship. The client is thereby encouraged to seek legal assistance and to communicate fully and frankly with the lawyer even as to embarrassing or legally damaging subject matter. The lawyer needs this information to represent the client effectively and, if necessary, to advise the client to refrain from wrongful conduct. Almost without exception, clients come to lawyers in order to determine their rights and what is, in the complex of laws and regulations, deemed to be legal and correct. Based upon experience, lawyers know that almost all clients follow the advice given, and the law is upheld.

[3] The principle of client-lawyer confidentiality is given effect by related bodies of law: the attorney-client privilege, the work product doctrine and the rule of confidentiality established in professional ethics. The attorney-client privilege and work-product doctrine apply in judicial and other proceedings in which a lawyer may be called as a witness or otherwise required to produce evidence concerning a client. The rule of client-lawyer confidentiality applies in situations other than those where evidence is sought from the lawyer through compulsion of law. The confidentiality rule, for example, applies not only to matters communicated in confidence by the client but also to all information relating to the representation, whatever its source. A lawyer may not disclose such information except as authorized or required by the Rules of Professional Conduct or other law.

[4] Paragraph (a) prohibits a lawyer from revealing information relating to the representation of a client. This prohibition also applies to disclosures by a lawyer that do not in themselves reveal protected information but could reasonably lead to the discovery of such information by a third person. A lawyer's use of a hypothetical to discuss issues relating to the representation is permissible so long as there is no reasonable likelihood that the listener will be able to ascertain the identity of the client or the situation involved.

The Comment, "Acting Competently to Preserve Confidentiality," further states:

[23] A lawyer must act competently to safeguard information relating to the representation of a client against inadvertent or unauthorized disclosure by the lawyer or other persons who are participating in the representation of the client or who are subject to the lawyer's supervision. See Rule 1.1, 5.1 and 5.3.

[24] When transmitting a communication that includes information relating to the representation of a client, the lawyer must take reasonable precautions to prevent the information from coming into the hands of unintended recipients. This duty, however, does not require that the lawyer use special security measures if the method of communication affords a reasonable expectation of privacy. Special circumstances, however, may

warrant special precautions. Factors to be considered in determining the reasonableness of the lawyer's expectation of confidentiality include the sensitivity of the information and the extent to which the privacy of the communication is protected by law or by a confidentiality agreement. A client may require the lawyer to implement special security measures not required by this Rule or may give informed consent to the use of a means of communication that would otherwise be prohibited by this Rule.

In addition, Rule 4.4(b) ("Respect for Rights of Third Persons") states:

> (b) A lawyer who receives a document relating to the representation of the lawyer's client and knows or reasonably should know that the document was inadvertently sent shall promptly notify the sender.

The Comment to Rule 4.4 states:

> [2] Paragraph (b) recognizes that lawyers sometimes receive documents that were mistakenly sent or produced by opposing parties or their lawyers. If a lawyer knows or reasonably should know that a document was sent inadvertently, then this Rule requires the lawyer to promptly notify the sender in order to permit that person to take protective measures. Whether the lawyer is required to take additional steps, such as returning the original document, is a matter of law beyond the scope of these Rules, as is the question of whether the privileged status of a document has been waived. Similarly, this Rule does not address the legal duties of a lawyer who receives a document that the lawyer knows or reasonably should know may have been wrongfully obtained by the sending person. For purposes of this Rule, "document" includes e-mail or other electronic modes of transmission subject to being read or put into readable form.

> [3] Some lawyers may choose to return a document unread, for example, when the lawyer learns before receiving the document that it was inadvertently sent to the wrong address. Where a lawyer is not required by applicable law to do so, the decision to voluntarily return such a document is a matter of professional judgment ordinarily reserved to the lawyer. See Rules 1.2 and 1.4.

When Rule 4.4(b) and the Comments to the Rule are read in conjunction with Rule 1.6, it is possible to conclude that the Pennsylvania Supreme Court has determined that attorneys in Pennsylvania who receive inadvertently disclosed documents have an ethical obligation to promptly notify the sender in order to permit that person to take protective measures. The absence of a specific Rule addressing the inadvertent disclosure of metadata may also be viewed as analogous to the inadvertent disclosure of a document and not an act consciously undertaken by counsel.

Various Ethics Committees have considered whether it is ethically permissible to review the metadata contained within documents produced by opposing counsel.

The American Bar Association Standing Committee on Ethics and Professional Responsibility considered the review and use of metadata in *Formal Opinion 06-442* (August 5, 2006), concluding that the ABA Model Rules of Professional Conduct "generally permit" a lawyer to review and use metadata contained in e-mail and other electronic documents, "whether [they are] received from opposing counsel, an adverse party or an agent of an adverse party." *Id.* Finding Model Rule 4.4(b) most closely applicable, the Committee stated that, although Rule 4.4(b) provides that "[a] lawyer who receives a document relating to the representation of the lawyer's client and knows or reasonably should know that the document was inadvertently sent shall promptly notify the sender," the rule is silent on the issue of whether or not an attorney can review or use such information. *Id.* The Committee therefore concluded that the Rule's sole requirement of promptly notifying the sender of inadvertently sent documents was "evidence of the intention to set no other specific restrictions on the receiving lawyer's conduct . . ." *Id.* The Committee suggested several methods by which counsel could protect himself or herself from inadvertently disclosing metadata, including negotiation of a confidentiality agreement or protective order that allows the transmitting attorney to "pull back" transmitted documents. *Id.* These methods of protection, however, will not always adequately protect an attorney, such as when the transferred metadata contains information about a client's willingness to settle and/or the terms by which the client may be willing to do so.

Consistent with the ABA Opinion, the District of Columbia Bar Association issued *Ethics Opinion 341* in September 2007, in which it concluded:

> A receiving lawyer is prohibited from reviewing metadata sent by an adversary only where he has actual knowledge that the metadata was inadvertently sent. In such instances, the receiving lawyer should not review the metadata before consulting with the sending lawyer to determine whether the metadata includes work product of the sending lawyer or confidences or secrets of the sending lawyer's client.

The D.C. Bar further opined that, "In all other circumstances, a receiving lawyer is free to review the metadata contained within the electronic files provided by an adversary."

Several Ethics Opinions issued by various states have concluded, contrary to the ABA and D.C. Committees, that a party may not use inadvertently disclosed metadata. *See, e.g.*, New York Committee on Professional Ethics, *Opinion 749* (December 14, 2001) and *Opinion 782* (December 8, 2004). In *Opinion 749*, the Committee addressed the use of computer software to surreptitiously examine metadata contained in e-mails and other electronic documents. The New York Committee concluded that such a use of metadata "constitutes an impermissible intrusion on the attorney-client relationship in violation of the [Code of Professional Responsibility]." Noting that the Code "prohibits a lawyer from engaging in conduct 'involving dishonesty, fraud, deceit or misrepresentation . . .' and 'conduct that is prejudicial to the administration of justice . . .' " the Committee opined that "in light of the strong public policy in favor of preserving confidentiality as the foundation of the lawyer-client relationship," such a use of metadata would go against the spirit of the Code. The Committee paralleled the use of inadvertently transmitted metadata to the use of inadvertently transmitted communications in general, which the Committee had previously found impermissible under the Code because the conduct involved "dishonesty, fraud, deceit or misrepresentation, [was] prejudicial to the administration of justice' " and would "undermine confidentiality and the attorney-client relationship." The Committee concluded that the use of software to examine metadata was more impermissible than the use of inadvertently transmitted communication in general noting that, whereas in the latter scenario the transmitting attorney's carelessness caused the inadvertent transmission, in the former scenario, the transmitting attorney unwillingly and unknowingly transmitted the metadata, which the receiving attorney then secretly and deceitfully accessed.

In *Opinion 782*, the New York Committee addressed the e-mailing of documents that may contain metadata "reflecting client confidences and secrets." The Committee concluded that "Lawyers must exercise reasonable care to prevent the disclosure of confidences and secrets contained in 'metadata' in documents they transmit electronically to opposing counsel or other third parties." Identifying the various rules under the Lawyer's Code of Professional Responsibility that provide guidance in these situations, the Committee stated:

> The Lawyer's Code of Professional Responsibility (the "Code") prohibits lawyers from "knowingly" revealing a client confidence or secret, DR 4-101(B)(1), except when permitted under one of five exceptions enumerated in DR 4-101(C). DR 4-101(D) states that a lawyer "shall exercise reasonable care to prevent his or her employees, associates, and others whose services are utilized by the lawyer from disclosing or using confidences or secrets of a client." See also EC 4-5 ("Care should be exercised by a lawyer to prevent the disclosure of the confidences and secrets of one client to another"). Similarly, a lawyer who uses technology to communicate with clients must use reasonable care with respect to such communication, and therefore must assess the risks attendant to the use of that technology and determine if the mode of transmission is appropriate under the circumstances. See N.Y. State 709 (1998) ("an attorney must use reasonable care to protect confidences and secrets"); N.Y. City 94-11 (lawyer must take reasonable steps to secure client confidences or secrets).

The Committee opined that "Reasonable care may, in some circumstances, call for the lawyer to stay abreast of technological advances and the potential risks in transmission in order to make an appropriate decision with respect to the mode of transmission," implying that attorneys have the responsibility to take steps to prevent the transmission of metadata when e-mailing documents. The Committee noted, however, that "Lawyer-recipients also have an obligation not to exploit an inadvertent or unauthorized transmission of client confidences or secrets." Therefore, while finding that attorneys may have to take steps to prevent the transmission of metadata, the Committee continued to hold that it is unethical for receiving attorneys to use technology to secretly view and use metadata.

The Professional Ethics Committee of The Florida Bar and Alabama State Bar Office of General Counsel have reached similar conclusions. In *Professional Ethics of the Florida Bar Opinion 06-2* (September 15, 2006), the Florida Committee addressed the duties of both transmitting and receiving attorneys with respect to metadata contained in electronic documents. With respect to transmitting attorneys, the Committee examined Fl.R.P.C. 4-1.6(a), which is virtually identical to Pa.R.P.C. 1.6, for guidance. The Committee concluded that "Florida lawyers must take reasonable steps to protect confidential information in all types of documents and information . . . including electronic documents and electronic communications with other lawyers and third parties" in order to maintain confidentiality as required by Rule 4-1.6(a). With respect to receiving attorneys, the Committee relied on Fl.R.P.C. 4-4.4(b), which is substantially similar to Pa.R.P.C. 4.4(b), for guidance, concluding:

It is the recipient lawyer's concomitant obligation, upon receiving an electronic communication or document from another lawyer, not to try to obtain from metadata information relating to the representation of the sender's client that the recipient knows or should know is not intended for the recipient. Any such metadata is to be considered by the receiving lawyer as confidential information which the sending lawyer did not intend to transmit.

. . . If the recipient lawyer inadvertently obtains information from metadata that the recipient knows or should know was not intended for the recipient, the lawyer must "promptly notify the sender." *Id.*

Id. (footnote omitted) The Committee concluded that the duties of transmitting and receiving attorneys mentioned above "may necessitate a lawyer's continuing training and education in the use of technology in transmitting and receiving electronic documents in order to protect client information under Rule 4-1.6(a)," noting that Rule 4-1.6's Comment addressing competency states that a lawyer "should engage in continuing study and education" to maintain the skills and knowledge necessary for competent representation.

In *Alabama Bar Formal Ethics Opinion 2007-02* (March 14, 2007), the Alabama State Bar Office of General Counsel, concluded that "an attorney has an ethical duty to exercise reasonable care when transmitting electronic documents to ensure that he or she does not disclose his or her client's secrets and confidences," noting that what constitutes reasonable care will vary based on the circumstances of each case. Relying upon Ala. R. Prof. C. 1.6 and 8.4, which are substantially similar to Pa.R.P.C. 1.6 and 4.4, the Opinion also concluded that "Just as a sending lawyer has an ethical obligation to reasonably protect the confidences of a client, the receiving lawyer also has an ethical obligation to refrain from mining an electronic document." The Alabama Bar specifically agreed with New York *Opinion 749* that the use of computer technology to view and utilize metadata "constitutes an impermissible intrusion on the attorney-client relationship in violation of the Alabama Rules of Professional Conduct," noting that the protection of the confidence of the client is "a fundamental tenet of the legal profession."

In a similar vein, the Maryland State Bar Association Committee on Ethics issues Opinion 2007-09, in which it concluded that lawyers who produce electronic materials in discovery have a duty to take reasonable measures to avoid the disclosure of confidential information embedded in the metadata within the documents. Citing the recent amendments to the Federal Rules of Civil Procedure, the Committee further concluded that lawyers who receive electronic discovery materials have no ethical duty to refrain from viewing or using metadata.

These various opinions reach different conclusions, although each offers a persuasive rationale. This Committee believes, however, that it would be difficult to establish a rule applicable in all circumstances and that, consequently, the final determination of how to address the inadvertent disclosure of metadata should be left to the individual attorney and his or her analysis of the applicable facts.

IV. Conclusion

The utilization of metadata by attorneys receiving electronic documents from an adverse party is an emerging problem. Although a transmitting attorney has tools at his disposal that can minimize the amount of metadata contained in a document he or she is transmitting, those tools still may not remove all metadata.

Therefore, this Committee concludes that, under the Pennsylvania Rules of Professional Conduct, each attorney must determine for himself or herself whether to utilize the metadata contained in documents and other electronic files based upon the lawyer's judgment and the particular factual situation. This determination should be based upon the nature of the information received, how and from whom the information was received, attorney-client privilege and work product rules, and common sense, reciprocity and professional courtesy. Although the waiver of the attorney-client privilege with respect to privileged and confidential materials is a matter for judicial determination, the Committee believes that the inadvertent transmissions of such materials should not constitute a waiver of the privilege, except in the case of extreme carelessness or indifference.

NOTES

1. What is a lawyer's obligation with respect to information included in an unsolicited e-mail? For example, does a lawyer have the obligation to safeguard confidential information sent by a prospective client seeking representation? In Formal Opinion 2006-1, the San Diego County Bar Association examined whether a lawyer has a duty to preserve the confidentiality of information sent via e-mail from a prospective client. Recognizing that the duty of confidentiality may attach even though no attorney-client relationship has formed, the Association nonetheless concluded that the "listing [of] a public e-mail address on the State Bar of California's website, along with other public information, such as address and telephone number, without more, [does not] constitute prior words or conduct which create a reasonable expectation that the lawyer has agreed to a consultation." Because the mere listing of the attorney's address on the State Bar of California's website did "not constitute an invitation to the public at large to communicate confidential information," the lawyer did not have an obligation to safeguard information communicated by a prospective client.

The Committee did distinguish a situation in which the prospective client utilized an attorney e-mail address provided in an advertisement. In that situation "the only inference to be drawn from listing the e-mail address is to invite prospective clients to contact the attorney for legal advice or representation, giving rise to a further inference that private information divulged to the attorney would be confidential."

2. In *Chemcraft Holdings Corp. v. Shayban*, an unpublished decision of the North Carolina Superior Court, a lawyer, Rossabi, was disqualified from representing a client on the basis of an e-mail attachment he received — but never opened — from a prospective client. *Chemcraft Holdings Corp. v. Shayban*, 2006 NCBC LEXIS 15 (N.C. Sup. Ct. Oct. 6, 2006). The court noted that "Mr. Rossabi had a duty to thoroughly review the contents of Mr. Gottlieb's e-mail and its attachments just as if he had received a letter in the mail from him. By receiving the e-mail, he was on constructive notice of his possession of sensitive documents and should have taken steps to avoid a conflict of interest related to those documents." *Id.* at **15. Finding that there was no violation of the Rules of Professional Conduct, the court

nonetheless disqualified Rossabi from representing a client with an adverse interest. The court explained that

> [T]he Rules of Professional Conduct need not be violated in order to create an appearance of impropriety with the potential to undermine the credibility of the courts in the eyes of litigants. In this regard, the Court finds that the perception of a problem on [the prospective client's] part is real and justifiable and that he did not create the problem . . . Were this Court to allow Mr. Rossabi to continue participating in this case, both Defendant and the public at large could justifiably question the integrity of the legal system.

Id. at **16–17.

The court also noted that Rossabi had the e-mail attachment in his possession for a number of months. *Id.* at **18. His disqualification was further warranted by the "significant harm" standard of the Rules of Professional Conduct. Rejecting Rossabi's argument that mere access to, rather than review of the documents, was insuffient to justify disqualification, the court noted:

> The record shows that Mr. Rossabi received confidential information regarding [the prospective client's] dispute with Chemcraft and that he retained possession of them for months. This gives rise to the presumption . . . that Mr. Rossabi learned of the contents of [the prospective client's] writings. Mr. Rossabi's assertions that he did not open or read the confidential attachments cannot overcome . . . . this Court's duty to uphold the public reputation of the legal system by guarding against the appearance of impropriety on the part of counsel.

Id. at **22.

II.   FORMAT AND PRACTICE CONSIDERATIONS

While the format of e-mail communications is not specifically addressed in the rules regulating the professional conduct of lawyers, there are some format considerations which should influence the lawyer to communicate more effectively in an electronic format.

A.   Overview

i.   Diligence

A lawyer charged with the responsibility of representing a client has an obligation to provide that representation diligently. Model Rules of Prof'l Conduct R. 1.3 (2008). This obligation is apparent in the context of e-mail communications, as clients will expect that a lawyer routinely communicate the status of the case via e-mail.

ii.   Civility and Professionalism

While neither the Model Rules nor the Model Code expressly require that lawyers play nicely with one another, a lack of civility may give rise to sanctions for a failure in professionalism. Many states have adopted codes of professionalism that have specific civility obligations. For example, the Idaho State Bar

Association's Standards for Civility in Professional Conduct provide, in part,

> We will treat all other counsel, parties and witnesses in a civil and courteous manner, not only in court, but also in all other written and oral communications;

> We will not, even when called upon by a client to do so, abuse, or indulge in offensive conduct directed to other counsel, parties or witnesses. We will abstain from disparaging personal remarks or acrimony toward other counsel, parties, or witnesses.

To the extent that a lawyer uses abusive or disrespectful language in an e-mail, she may be subject to disapproval or sanctions under applicable professionalism codes.

B. General Format Considerations: Competence and Professionalism in Electronic Communication

i. Preferred manner of communication

As an initial matter, consider whether e-mail is the most efficient, effective, and appropriate method for communicating. For example, given the content of the exchange, consider whether it would be preferable to make a phone call, or go to the office of the recipient for a face to face exchange. This would be preferred if you have a number of questions on a client matter, and anticipate that a conversation would be helpful. Also, consider whether there are confidentiality issues, such that a phone call or direct exchange would be preferable to avoid communicating confidential content. Finally, consider your relationship and prior exchanges with the recipient. Because electronic exchanges lack the visual cues of a face-to-face conversation, they can lead to misunderstandings. Attempts at humor or sarcasm may fail in an electronic dialogue, and emoticons are rarely appropriate in a law office setting. Therefore, if there seems to be this type of misunderstanding developing in an e-mail exchange, consider transitioning to a face-to-face or phone conversation.

One caveat: Lawyers are exceptionally busy people. This makes electronic exchanges particularly useful because they enable people to compose and respond at times and places that are convenient. So, wherever possible and given considerations of content and tone, consider whether an e-mail exchange would be the most efficient manner given the circumstances.

ii. Formatting considerations

E-mail in a law office setting differs from e-mail in an informal setting, or in a formal, school setting. E-mails in law practice are lawyering communications, and should be treated with a degree of formality associated with the business of a law practice. So, there are several formatting issues to consider when sending e-mail in practice.

a. Recipient: An initial consideration is to whom the e-mail will be addressed.

1. *Use of "To," "CC, and "BCC":* There are three choices for addressing the e-mail, and you should carefully consider the appropriate recipient, if any, for each category. The "To" option should be fairly apparent — the addresses here are for people to whom the e-mail content is directly addressed. The "CC" option, also

known as courtesy or carbon copy, is for people who need to know the information contained in the e-mail for tangential reasons. They may be actively monitoring, but not working on the file. Copying these individuals serves a "For your information" function, and distinguishes these individuals from the primary contacts in the "To" option. Avoid including too many recipients in this category — limit the use of the "CC" function to those people who have a legitimate interest in the material. Again, lawyers are exceptionally busy and not terribly interested in being copied on e-mails that are not relevant to their practice. The "BCC" option, also known as blind courtesy or carbon copy, is used to communicate the content of the e-mail privately. Recipients in the "To" and "CC" categories will not be aware of the recipients in the "BCC" category. Carefully consider whether there are any appropriate recipients for this category. However, because other recipients do not see recipients in the "BCC" category, this is a useful function when sending an e-mail to multiple recipients who do not need to know each other's e-mail addresses.

2. *Use of "Reply All":* In an informal e-mail exchange between friends, people often use the "reply all" function to keep all recipients, including those in the "to," "cc," and "bcc" categories, in the exchange. In a law office practice, recognize that the "reply all" function generates multiple e-mails to multiple recipients. Carefully consider whether all of the recipients are keenly interested in your reply.

3. *Forwarding function:* If you need to forward a message to someone, read carefully through the prior exchange to strip any extraneous information. This will shorten the message for the recipient and make it easier to read. It will also force you to read back through the exchange to ensure that you do not inadvertently forward information not appropriate for the recipient. Also, be sure to include proper material in the subject matter clause to ensure that the recipient has some context for your forwarded message. As with all forms of e-mail in an office setting, use the forward function judiciously, and only for matters and to people who would consider the material relevant to law office practice.

4. *Use of Delivery Confirmation and Read Receipts:* As a general matter, it is not necessary to use delivery confirmation or read receipts for interoffice or general law practice e-mail correspondence. If you want to confirm that your message has been received, it is preferable to simply ask the recipient to confirm receipt.

5. *Use of High Priority Designation:* Do not overuse the high priority function. Most e-mails sent in law practice do not warrant this function.

b. Subject Clause

1. In an *original e-mail,* use the subject matter field routinely to concisely communicate the content and purpose of the e-mail — give the recipient some context for what they are receiving. If you have to send a lengthy e-mail, it is also appropriate to include the word "Long" in the subject matter field to indicate to the recipient that the e-mail will take some time to read.

2. In a *reply e-mail,* be sure that the subject matter material remains on the response. Also, for e-mail responses make sure to include information from the original message that is pertinent to the response. Be sure that the responsive material in the message is distinguishable from the original message.

c. Content

1. *Brevity:* E-mail messages should be concise and to the point. Messages that are longer than necessary are frustrating to the recipient and undermine the efficiency of an e-mail exchange.

2. *Formatting*

a. <u>Salutation:</u> For most e-mail messages, a standard salutation such as "Dear Mr. Smith" is appropriate. If you normally address the recipient by her first name, that would also be appropriate. If you are responding to an e-mail, or have a close relationship with the recipient and are sending somewhat informal information, you may omit the salutation.

b. <u>Responses:</u> When you are responding to an e-mail that asks several questions, be sure that the responses are clear. It is acceptable to embed the responses in the sender's message, but be sure that the response is set apart with extra space between the original text and the response. You might also use a distinct font type or color for the response. As with other methods of responding to questions in practice, be sure to respond as quickly as possible. If a response will take a few days to complete, it is appropriate to respond, letting the sender know you have received the e-mail and are working on a response.

c. <u>Abbreviations:</u> Consider the audience and content. For example, in an environmental law practice, commonly understood environmental acronyms are typically appropriate. However, note that you will likely be communicating with people of all ages. Therefore avoid electronic shorthand like "LOL," which could be misinterpreted by the recipient as "lots of love" rather than "laugh out loud." Informal electronic communication acronyms such as BTW (by the way) and IMO (in my opinion) are only appropriate when you absolutely know that the recipient will understand this form of shorthand.

d. <u>Emoticons and Smilies:</u> Emoticons and smilies are textual visual cues to communicate the writer's emotions. For example, the use of a colon, followed by a dash, followed by an end parenthesis (ex. :-)) signifies a smiley face. These are very rarely appropriate in a law practice setting and should be generally avoided.

e. <u>Grammar, Punctuation, and Spelling:</u> While e-mail communication outside of practice can be very informal, in a law office setting your e-mail communication will reflect on you and your law firm. Therefore, traditional rules of grammar, punctuation, and spelling should be observed.

f. <u>Allcaps:</u> Allcaps in written communication is the electronic equivalent of shouting at your recipient. With the exception of acronyms that are relevant to the content of the exchange and well known by the recipient, avoid the use of allcaps in all forms of written communication.

g. <u>Signatures:</u> To ensure that the recipient knows who you are and how to contact you, be sure your signature line includes your name, firm affiliation, and mailing and phone information.

h. <u>Disclaimers:</u> Many firms routinely employ disclaimers to e-mails. Determine whether this is the case at your firm. If so, set up your electronic signature to include the firm disclaimer.

d. Attachments: You may need to include an attachment with your e-mail. While most e-mail servers can accommodate large attachments, for exceptionally large or multiple attachments, you may want to first confirm that the recipient's inbox can receive the attachment. For e-mail attachments you may also want to ask the recipient to confirm that he has received the attachment and can open it.

e. Final Thoughts

Always read your e-mail message one time through before you send it. Check the recipients in the To, CC, and BCC options. Check the content in the e-mail, including any forwarded content from the prior exchanges. Check all attachments. Be confident that you have crafted a professional, thorough e-mail before you hit the send button.

Chapter 4

PREDICTIVE MEMORANDA

Even an office memo gives you a chance to establish a respected reputation. Integrity and good judgment come together when you write about how the law applies to a particular situation. Integrity always starts with yourself — with telling yourself the truth. You must have the courage to tell yourself the truth about the most likely outcome, even when the truth is not what you, your client, or the other lawyers in your firm want to hear.

> — Terrill Pollman, Ralph Denton Professor of Law and Director of Legal Research and Writing, William S. Boyd School of Law, University of Nevada at Las Vegas

Interoffice, or predictive, memoranda are informal documents used by lawyers to memorialize their analysis of a legal issue. Because they are informal and typically not disseminated outside the lawyer's practice, they are not the subject of direct regulation by ethical rules. Memoranda are frequently prepared at the beginning of representation in order to determine whether a client should proceed with a legal matter. Memoranda are also prepared during the representation of a client in order to determine how to proceed with a claim or issue. Because they provide a written record of the lawyer's analysis, they establish the basis for the lawyer's advice, whether that advice is delivered in written or oral form. To this extent they invoke the obligation of the lawyer as advisor. In addition, lawyers use these informal documents to prepare documents that are formally filed in court or sent as correspondence. To the extent that predictive memoranda provide the basis for lawyering activities, including the preparation of documents that are formally regulated, there are a variety of ethical rules that should be considered when preparing them.

I. CONTENT-BASED CONSIDERATIONS

A. Overview

i. Competence

Model Rule 1.1 provides that "A lawyer shall provide competent representation to a client. Competent representation requires the legal knowledge, skill, thoroughness and preparation reasonably necessary for the representation." The Rule's first comment helps to describe how a lawyer should evaluate whether she can provide competent representation in a particular matter:

> In determining whether a lawyer employs the requisite knowledge and skill in a particular matter, relevant factors include the relative complexity and specialized nature of the matter, the lawyer's general experience, the lawyer's training and experience in the field in question, the preparation

and study the lawyer is able to give the matter and whether it is feasible to refer the matter to, or associate or consult with, a lawyer of established competence in the field in question.

Model Rules of Prof'l Conduct R. 1.1 cmt. 1 (2008). Competence requires that a lawyer be reasonably familiar with well-settled principles of law applicable to her client's case or, if unfamiliar, to perform research necessary to acquire that knowledge or to associate with a lawyer who does have competence in the field. The lawyer must be familiar not only with the substantive law, but with the procedural requirements of a client's position and any applicable court rules.

With regard to predictive memoranda, comment 2 to Rule 1.1 notes that "[s]ome important legal skills, such as the analysis of precedent, the evaluation of evidence and legal drafting, are required in all legal problems. Perhaps the most fundamental legal skill consists of determining what kind of legal problems a situation may involve, a skill that necessarily transcends any particular specialized knowledge." Model Rules of Prof'l Conduct 1.1 R. cmt. 2 (2008). Further, the Rule's requirement that a lawyer prepare properly and handle client matters thoroughly requires inquiry "into and analysis of the factual and legal elements of the problem, and use of methods and procedures meeting the standards of competent practitioners." Model Rules of Prof'l Conduct R. 1.1 cmt. 5 (2008).

Competence is addressed in the Model Code under Canon 6, which requires lawyers to represent their clients competently. DR 6-101(A)(1) prohibits a lawyer from handling a matter "which he knows or should know that he is not competent to handle, without associating himself with a lawyer who is competent to handle [the matter]." DR 6-102(A)(2) requires a lawyer to be adequately prepared under the circumstances of representation. Therefore, under both the Model Code and Model Rules, a lawyer has a basic obligation to be able to identify legal issues that are raised in the context of a client matter and, once identified, research, analyze, and understand the law applicable to those issues. A failure in this regard would become evident in memoranda preparation.

ii.   Communication and Advice

The other prevailing ethical consideration in the context of memo preparation involves the lawyer's role as advisor. Model Rule 2.1 provides: "In representing a client, a lawyer shall exercise independent professional judgment and render candid advice." Interoffice memoranda are prepared to memorialize the lawyer's *objective*, or *predictive*, analysis. In other words, the analysis may conclude that the client's claim will fail. The lawyer then has the obligation to communicate that opinion to the client, notwithstanding the client's likely disappointment. The comment to Model Rule 2.1 illustrates this obligation:

> A client is entitled to straightforward advice expressing the lawyer's honest assessment. Legal advice often involves unpleasant facts and alternatives that a client may be disinclined to confront. In presenting advice, a lawyer endeavors to sustain the client's morale and may put advice in as acceptable a form as honesty permits. However, a lawyer should not be deterred from giving candid advice by the prospect that the advice will be unpalatable to the client.

Model Rules of Prof'l Conduct R. 2.1 cmt. 1 (2008). Consequently, in memo preparation, the lawyer should perform comprehensive research and evaluate applicable law objectively, in order to appropriately advise the client of the viability of her claim.

B.   Competence

i.   Identification of Issues and Identifying the Facts

As an initial matter in memo preparation, the lawyer must evaluate what issues are presented by the client's factual situation. Typically, a lawyer first meets with the client to go over the facts. Once the lawyer begins her analysis, she may have to follow up with the client and/or independently investigate facts that become relevant to the client's case in light of the applicable law. As the following cases illustrate, competent handling of a client matter begins with the lawyer's obligation to have an understanding of the facts that are relevant to the client's issue. It is only after the lawyer has a decent understanding of the facts that she can begin to determine what legal issues are presented by those facts.

UNITED STATES v. RUSSELL
221 F.3d 615 (4th Cir. 2000)

Richard Deon Russell appeals his convictions by a jury in the Eastern District of Virginia for possession of heroin with intent to distribute, in violation of 21 U.S.C. § 841(a)(1), and for prisoner possession of heroin, in violation of 18 U.S.C. § 13 (assimilating Va.Code Ann. § 53.1- 203(5)). Because we conclude that the district court erred in denying Russell's motion for a new trial, we must vacate his convictions and remand for further proceedings.

*   *   *

Russell was charged and tried for possession with intent to distribute heroin, and for prisoner possession of heroin. The trial was conducted in the district court in Alexandria on September 23, 1998, and the jury found Russell guilty on both counts. Following the verdict, Russell timely filed a Rule 33 motion for a new trial, which was denied. He now appeals his convictions and sentence. . . . Russell asserts that the district court erroneously denied his motion for a new trial, which was based on two theories: (1) newly discovered evidence; and (2) ineffective assistance of counsel.

*   *   *

[During the criminal trial] [i]f the jury had found Russell's explanation plausible and had credited his testimony, the Government's case would have undoubtedly failed. However, Russell's credibility was all but destroyed when he was mistakenly impeached on the basis of three felony convictions — two of which had been vacated before trial. After weighing the evidence, including Russell's testimony and his impeachment, the jury rejected Russell's explanation and convicted him on both counts of the indictment.

*   *   *

In order to establish ineffective assistance of his trial counsel, Russell must satisfy the two-pronged test articulated by the Supreme Court in *Strickland v. Washington*, 466 U.S. 668, 687, 104 S.Ct. 2052, 80 L.Ed.2d 674 (1984). First, Russell must show that counsel's performance was deficient. Second, Russell must demonstrate that this deficient performance prejudiced his defense. The first prong of the *Strickland* test is satisfied if counsel's performance "fell below an objective standard of reasonableness." If "counsel's errors were so serious as to deprive the defendant of a fair trial, a trial whose result is reliable," then the second prong is also satisfied.

An attorney is obligated to provide competent representation to his client. To satisfy this basic obligation, counsel must exercise the "legal knowledge, skill, thoroughness and preparation reasonably necessary for the representation." *Model Rules of Professional Conduct* Rule 1.1 (1999). Thus, an attorney has a duty to adequately examine the law and facts relevant to the representation of his client: "[C]ounsel has a duty to make reasonable investigations or to make a reasonable decision that makes particular investigations unnecessary." As the ABA Standards for Criminal Justice provide:

> Defense counsel should conduct a prompt investigation of the circumstances of the case and explore all avenues leading to facts relevant to the merits of the case and the penalty in the event of conviction. The investigation should include efforts to secure information in the possession of the prosecution and law enforcement authorities. . . .

When representing a criminal client, the obligation to conduct an adequate investigation will often include verifying the status of the client's criminal record, and the failure to do so may support a finding of ineffective assistance of counsel. *See Tolliver v. United States*, 563 F.2d 1117, 1120–21 (4th Cir.1977) (holding defense attorneys' apparent unawareness of the potential invalidation of defendant's prior convictions by a Supreme Court decision, even after defendant informed counsel of the decision, to constitute ineffective assistance).

Here, we find that defense counsel's failure to confirm the status of two of Russell's three prior convictions to be unreasonable. Prior to trial, Russell informed his lawyer that the District of Columbia convictions had been "overturned" and were therefore invalid. And counsel acknowledged that, rather than confirming Russell's assertion before advising him that he must acknowledge and testify to *three* prior convictions, counsel simply "relied on the representations of the government that these convictions were in fact still valid at the time of trial." The necessary investigation was minimal: a simple check of the District of Columbia Superior Court records would have verified that Russell's convictions had been vacated.

In the context of this case, it was critical for Russell to accurately portray his criminal record. Given the ease with which such information could have been obtained, we are constrained to conclude that his trial counsel's failure to verify the accuracy of the District of Columbia convictions fell below an objective standard of reasonableness.

* * *

Having determined that Russell's counsel breached his obligation of competent representation, we must also analyze whether Russell was prejudiced by this breach. To establish prejudice under *Strickland*, Russell must show there is a "reasonable probability that, but for counsel's unprofessional errors, the result of the proceeding would have been different. . . ."

* * *

Given the marginal nature of the Government's case, an accurate presentation of Russell's prior criminal record was critical to his credibility and to his defense. As the Supreme Court recognized in *United States v. Agurs*, 427 U.S. 97, 113, 96 S.Ct. 2392, 49 L.Ed.2d 342 (1976), "[I]f the verdict is already of questionable validity, additional evidence of relatively minor importance might be sufficient to create a reasonable doubt." We recognize that the fate of a criminal defendant often depends on the jury's credibility determination. Indeed, "[t]he jury's estimate of the truthfulness and reliability of a given witness may well be determinative of guilt or innocence. . . ."

In this case, Russell's defense rose or fell based on the credibility of a single witness: himself. While Russell's credibility was paramount in the jury's deliberations, it was irrevocably undermined by his improper impeachment with the two vacated convictions. The inaccurate presentation of Russell's criminal record, particularly where his credibility as a witness is in issue, cannot be said to be an insubstantial error. And, as we recognized in *Foster v. Barbour*, 613 F.2d 59 (4th Cir.1980), where the defendant's veracity was also critical, the "repeated assertions that [the defendant] had been convicted of other crimes . . . *when those assertions were untrue* . . . destroyed the fairness of [the defendant's] trial and denied him due process of law." Moreover, we find it significant that the jury necessarily knew that Russell possessed at least one conviction. . . . It is axiomatic that the use of a single conviction for impeachment of a prisoner witness is of little evidentiary value. On the other hand, the use of three convictions for impeachment was devastating to Russell's credibility.

We also recognize that, as a practical matter, evidence of previous convictions often has a prejudicial impact beyond its proper purpose of impeachment. As the Fifth Circuit acknowledged in *United States v. Holloway*, 1 F.3d 307, 311 (5th Cir.1993), admitting evidence of a defendant's prior conviction carries with it the "inherent danger that a jury may convict a defendant because he is a 'bad person' instead of because the evidence of the crime with which he is charged proves him guilty." Similarly, the Court of Appeals for the District of Columbia has noted that admitting a defendant's prior convictions may "divert[ ] the attention of the jury from the question of the defendant's responsibility for the crime charged to the improper issue of his bad character." In this case, we conclude that there is a reasonable probability that the jury's attention was diverted from the crimes charged to the issue of Russell's bad character.

NOTES

1. In *Russell* the court concluded that Russell's attorney had provided incompetent representation. Why? How could the lawyer have avoided this finding?

2. The lawyer's failing in *Russell* occurred during the course of a criminal trial. How does the ruling relate to objective memo preparation?

3. In *Russell*, the lawyer was expected to verify the existence of prior convictions. Similarly, in *Attorney Grievance Comm'n of Maryland v. Chasnoff*, 783 A.2d 224 (Md. 2001), a lawyer was sanctioned for misconduct related to incompetence for failing to adequately investigate claims related to a personal injury. Chasnoff, the lawyer, represented a client, Errera, who was injured due to a fall at a construction area at an airport. *Id.* at 229. In order to establish liability, the lawyer had an obligation to review the site of the injury to document the conditions related

to Errera's fall. The court noted that proof of liability would be problematic, but that Chasnoff "had the duty to proceed competently and with diligence." *Id.* at 231. With regard to Chasnoff's failings in preserving and assessing the relevant facts, the court noted:

> [Chasnoff] did not act with the skill, thoroughness and preparation reasonably necessary to represent Errera. Indeed, [Chasnoff] did not even visit the scene of the accident until some two years after the fact. He did not attempt to locate the employee who assisted Errera on the night of the accident. He did not attempt to preserve the testimony of Mrs. Errera and Dr. Thorp. He did not see to it that Errera have his medical condition monitored in order to document that it was not improving. [Chasnoff] did not even act with the diligence necessary to ensure that the witnesses he did name were able to testify at trial. There is no question that [Chasnoff] violated both Rule 1.1 [duty to act with competence] and Rule 1.3 [duty to act diligently].

Id.

4.   The standard for pretrial investigation by defense counsel in a criminal matter was discussed in *United States v. Roane*, 378 F.3d 382 (4th Cir. 2004). The court explained that the extent of investigation must be that which is reasonable under the circumstances and that it is not the job of the court to play "Monday-morning quarterback and second-guess" the efforts of counsel in hindsight. *Id.* at 411. Distinguishing *Russell* as a situation in which counsel performed no investigation, the *Roane* court concluded that the lawyer, Baugh,

> was diligent and highly effective in his representation of [the criminal defendant] Roane during this litigation — he conferred with Roane, he investigated the crime scene, he located an eyewitness to the Moody murder who provided a physical description of a murderer dissimilar to Roane, he learned that Moody's mother had advised the police that another man had been searching for Moody hours before his murder, and he aggressively and professionally cross-examined the Government's witnesses. Mr. Baugh investigated the possible Moody alibi — a weak one at that — but when the investigation proved unfruitful, he put on a strong misidentification defense. According a "heavy measure of deference" to Mr. Baugh, as we must, his representation of Roane was not constitutionally ineffective.

Id.

5.   Can a lawyer not rely on the representations of fact offered by her client? How far does the duty of factual investigation extend? What obligation does a lawyer have when she discovers that her client has provided inaccurate or misleading information?

ii.   Sufficiency of Research

Once the lawyer has a basic understanding of the facts that give rise to a legal issue, he must properly research the law in order to predict a result. This requires the lawyer to have some basic level of competence with regard to locating and evaluating the applicable law. Indeed, the comments to Model Rule 1.1 make clear that "competent handling of a particular matter includes inquiry into and analysis of the factual and legal elements of the problem, and use of methods and procedures meeting the standards of competent practitioners." Model Rule Prof'l Conduct 1.1 cmt. 5 (2008). The lawyer's obligation to adequately research and analyze the law is imposed under the Federal Rules of Civil Procedure as well. A lawyer must personally sign most documents submitted to court. Rule 11 addresses the assurance given by the lawyer by virtue of that signature. It provides:

> By presenting to the court (whether by signing, filing, submitting, or later advocating) a pleading, written motion, or other paper, an attorney or unrepresented party is certifying that to the best of the person's knowledge, information, and belief, formed after an inquiry reasonable under the circumstances, . . . the claims, defenses, and other legal contentions therein are warranted by existing law or by a nonfrivolous argument for the extension, modification, or reversal of existing law or the establishment of new law; [and] the allegations and other factual contentions have evidentiary support or, if specifically so identified, are likely to have evidentiary support after a reasonable opportunity for further investigation or discovery. . . .

Fed. R. Civ. Pro. 11(B) (2), (3).

Interoffice memoranda, as informal documents, are not submitted to court and do not require signature. To the extent that memos memorialize the research and analysis of a claim that will later appear in a formal document, however, lawyers who prepare memos should be cognizant of the obligations related to research and analysis imposed by Rule 11.

IN RE TCI LTD.
769 F.2d 441 (7th Cir. 1985)

Lawyers sometimes file first and think later. This may impose on the other party the costs of deciphering the pleading, running down the cases, informing the court, and putting things right. One of the premises of the legal system, however, is that each party should bear its own expenses and not fob them off on the other side.

A court may order an attorney who "multiplies the proceedings . . . unreasonably and vexatiously" to bear the adversary's costs and attorneys' fees personally. William L. Needler & Associates, Ltd., filed unjustified pleadings in this bankruptcy suit. When its adversaries demonstrated that the pleadings were without substance, Needler's firm revised them slightly and filed them twice more. The district judge awarded costs and fees for the second and third filings.

[TCI Ltd. leased a building from Marathon Oil Co. TCI borrowed money from a bank to refurbish the building, and the loan was secured by the lease and the fixtures and furnishings of the restaurant. Tassos and Georgene Chronopoulos guaranteed the loan. TCI fell behind in its rental, and Marathon obtained an order of eviction from a state court. Before TCI was evicted, it filed a petition in bankruptcy, which stayed the eviction. However, in September 1981, one year after TCI stopped paying rent, Marathon obtained an order from the bankruptcy court which released Marathon from the bankruptcy stay and allowed Marathon to sell the building. In 1982, Marathon sold the building to Constantine Drugas. The sale was subject to the rights of the bank which had provided TCI the loan.]

* * *

[W]eeks later Jeffrey P. White of William L. Needler & Associates, Ltd. . . . filed an adversary proceeding on behalf of TCI and the Chronopouloses against Marathon, Drugas, and the bank. The complaint alleges that Marathon and the bank "were to act in good faith and use their best efforts to get a satisfactory disposition of the property" yet had not done so. The complaint objected to their "failure . . . to follow the order of this court by failing to sell the property in good faith and to give notice to all interested parties . . . and also giving an opportunity to said parties to purchase." White also asserted in a second count that the fixtures of the restaurant were still the property of TCI. The complaint requested damages together with an order annulling the sale, extinguishing the bank's claims against the Chronopouloses on the guarantees, and requiring Marathon to account for its profits.

Marathon and Drugas filed motions to dismiss and motions for costs under 28 U.S.C. § 1927. They observed that the order of September 1981 was unconditional and that Marathon, as the owner of the building and real estate, was free to do with the property what it pleased. After several continuances, Judge Hertz heard the motions. Marathon and Drugas orally represented that they had been trying without success to get TCI to take the restaurant's fixtures and any other property off their hands. The judge orally dismissed the complaint for failure to state a claim.

Thirteen days later White filed an amended complaint. The amended complaint repeated all of the contentions of the first and added the assertion that the order of September 1981 had not abandoned TCI's interest in the building.

* * *

New motions to dismiss followed, as did a new hearing. When it became clear that the bankruptcy judge thought the amended complaint no better than the first, White voluntarily dismissed it. Judge Hertz asked whether there was any allegation of fraud in obtaining the order of September 1981 and volunteered the advice that fraud would be about the only thing entitling TCI and the Chronopouloses to relief. White asked for leave to file still another amendment, which Judge Hertz granted with the ominous note that "there are certain risks you are going to run."

The second amended complaint was not long in coming. This document contained five counts instead of the two in the earlier pleadings. But nothing of substance changed. Every assertion in this complaint had been in an earlier one. It did not mention fraud. Still another hearing on the complaint, and still another dismissal was its fate. Judge Hertz denied the requests [and later] . . . transferred the case to Judge Robert D. Martin.. . . Judge Martin held a new hearing, at which Needler explained that his firm had filed the complaints at the insistence of the Chronopouloses, who feared liability on their guarantees to the bank. Judge Martin found that White had "responded to the urgings of the debtor's principal to stop or undo the sale by whatever means possible. The matter was viewed as urgent and the pressure from the client was no doubt intense."

Judge Martin concluded that the conduct of the Needler firm had been unreasonable. "Desperate problems are said to call for desperate measures. However, the measures available to counsel are not unlimited." Once the automatic stay has been lifted, only proof of fraud or changed circumstances will allow alteration. The three complaints filed here did not allege either. "Mr. White filed a complaint which made only vague claims under general powers of equity. Rather than present a sound legal theory, the complaint recited remedies for which there was no precedent nor statutory authority." Judge Martin conceded that counsel must have room for creative endeavors, but here "[w]hat was actually pleaded- . . . does not demonstrate imagination, but rather a lack of care, scrutiny and serious intention to put forth any bona fide claims."

Judge Martin concluded that White had framed and prosecuted the complaint without any effort to ascertain whether it had a basis in law. He did not grant the request for fees in full, however, but awarded only the expenses Marathon and Drugas incurred in defending against the amendments. "The initial attempt may well be deemed creative. Subsequent efforts to plead the case, however, lacked the real or imagined urgency which may have justified Mr. White's first effort. . . . [A]rguing the same claims after repeated rejections is not creative. It is harassing, frivolous and in bad faith. Creativity does not demonstrate itself in slight variations on a theory previously and emphatically rejected." The bankruptcy judge awarded fees aggregating some $8,000.

*   *   *

All three parties appeal. The Needler firm contends that it should pay nothing; Marathon and Drugas seek fees for resisting the first complaint.

*   *   *

A lawyer has a duty, which the recent amendment to Rule 11 emphasizes, to limit litigation to contentions "well grounded in fact and . . . warranted by existing law or a good faith argument for the extension, modification, or reversal of existing law." If a lawyer pursues a path that a reasonably careful attorney would have known, after appropriate inquiry, to be unsound, the conduct is objectively unreasonable and vexatious. To put this a little differently, a lawyer engages in bad faith by acting recklessly or with indifference to the law, as well as by acting in the teeth of what he knows to be the law. Our court has long treated reckless and intentional conduct as similar. . . . A lawyer's reckless indifference to the law may impose substantial costs on the adverse party. Section 1927 permits a court to insist that the attorney bear the costs of his own lack of care.

*   *   *

The principle underlying § 1927, Rule 11, and the bad faith exception to the American Rule is that in a system requiring each party to bear its own fees and costs, courts will ensure that each party really *does* bear the costs and does not foist expenses off on its adversaries. One cost of a lawsuit is research. An attorney must ascertain the facts and review the law to determine whether the facts fit within a recognized entitlement to relief. This may be a costly endeavor. Defense against a colorable claim also may be very costly. It would warp the system if a lawyer for a would-be claimant could simply file a complaint and require the adversary to do both the basic research to identify the claim and then the further work needed to craft a response. Suits are easy to file and hard to defend. Litigation gives lawyers opportunities to impose on their adversaries costs much greater than they impose on their own clients. The greater the disparity, the more litigation becomes a predatory instrument rather than a method of resolving honest disputes.

*   *   *

Needler's second argument is that White did nothing out of the ordinary. Much bankruptcy practice in Chicago is a high-volume, low-margin practice. Lawyers with such a practice must do the best they can, and if this means filing pleadings in advance of doing legal research, it is an incident of the press of business. We agree with the implicit position that not all pleadings must (or should) be handcrafted. Short deadlines may lead to filings that are not fully formed. It is also folly to spend $2,000 worth of time researching and writing the complaint in a $2,000 case. One of the innovations in legal practice is the "legal clinic," which specializes in routine cases that lawyers can handle at low fees precisely because they need not research every case from scratch. A bankruptcy practice — like many other specialized practices may be handled in large part with complaints and arguments pulled off the rack of documents suited to the task. The lawyer may rely on memory or seasoned intuition in place of fresh research.

The premise of routinized legal service, however, is precisely the routine nature of the claims. A lawyer may handle a large number of cases quickly by applying standard legal principles to each one. This does not support a complaint that proffers a new theory — not only in the sense that there is no precedent but also in the sense that it cuts against much precedent. Such a complaint is not a routine part of a busy practice. Rule 11 now requires a lawyer to undertake research before filing such a complaint. The rule was not in effect when Needler's firm filed the complaints, and its requirement of prior research is novel, but the principle that the suit must have an objective foundation is familiar. An attorney who wants to strike off on a new path in the law must make an effort to determine the nature of the principles he is applying (or challenging); he may not impose the expense of doing this on his adversaries — who are likely to be just as busy and will not be amused by a claim that the rigors of daily practice excuse legal research.

Needler contends that the application of § 1927 to a case such as this will stultify creativity and dampen the zeal an attorney owes his client. As we emphasized in *Knorr*, courts must be careful not to undercut the orderly development of the law and ethical representation. But the "bad faith" standard serves this function. . . . The amended Rule 11 sets out a standard that we think applies equally to § 1927: a complaint must be "warranted by existing law or a good faith argument for the extension, modification, or reversal of existing law." If a competent attorney would find no basis for a legal argument, then it does not interfere with zealous advocacy to penalize the repetitious assertion of that argument.

*   *   *

The legal work that we review cannot be characterized as a good faith application of the law or even a good faith request for a change in the law. . . . We are therefore not worried about "chilling" the sort of "creativity" demonstrated by these pleadings. Chilling *this* sort of "creativity" is the central function of § 1927.

NOTES

1. *TCI Ltd.* underscores the importance of thorough research. In the case, a portion of the research and analysis was farmed out to an external source. Does the case stand for the proposition that such routinized legal research is inappropriate? Does the case mean that a lawyer can never rely on materials generated previously

in practice? Does *TCI Ltd.* stand for the proposition that an attorney can never amend a complaint to remedy errors made?

2.   In *TCI Ltd.*, the lawyer argued that the sanction on his conduct would chill creative analysis of client claims. Should this argument have prevailed?

3.   Interoffice memoranda memorialize the lawyer's analysis of a client's legal matter and therefore serve to document the work performed by the lawyer on behalf of a client. In practice, memos serve another function — they preserve the analysis of particular issues for later use by the lawyer. In order to provide efficient service to the client, lawyers should strive to utilize prior experience. However, when a lawyer reviews an analysis previously performed, she must be cognizant of the temporal limitations of that analysis. To the extent the law may have changed, the lawyer has the obligation to update research so that the advice given on the basis of predictive analysis is accurate. In *Salahuddin v. Coughlin*, 999 F.Supp. 526, 539–40 (S.D.N.Y. 1998), the court criticized a lawyer's failure to update law cited in an appellate brief:

> The Court cannot fathom how defense counsel . . . an Assistant Attorney General . . . submitted the brief that he did. Defense counsel argued that the law regarding keeplocked prisoner's access to congregate religious services was unclear in 1985 without citing Judge Jones' contrary opinion earlier in this case or the Second Circuit's *Mawhinney* decision. Even assuming that defense counsel somehow did not find Judge Jones' decision in his file, his Shepardization of the Second Circuit's *Salahuddin* decision would have uncovered it. But even without Judge Jones' opinion, the Court cannot fathom how defense counsel could find (and cite) *LaReau* and *Smith*, but not *Mawhinney* and *Leon*. The Court notes that *Mawhinney* and/or *Leon* would have been uncovered by any of the following: Shepardization of *LaReau*, a keynote search based on keynotes gleaned from the Second Circuit's *Salahuddin* opinion, or any word search the Court can conceive that results in finding *LaReau* and *Smith*. Moreover, defense counsel did find *Mawhinney* — he cited it in a different section of his brief. . . .

4.   The duty to update the law was also noted by the court in *Gosnell v. Rentokil, Inc.*, 175 F.R.D. 508 (N.D.Ill. 1997). In *Gosnell*, a lawyer had prepared a motion in which he relied on a case that had been expressly overruled. The court noted, "It is really inexcusable for any lawyer to fail, as a matter of routine, to Shepardize all cited cases (a process that has been made much simpler today than it was in the past, given the facility for doing so under Westlaw or Lexis). Shepardization would of course have revealed that the "precedent" no longer qualified as such." *Id.* at 510, n. 1.

5.   In *TCI Ltd.*, the lawyers were sanctioned for failing to perform adequate research. What is the lawyer's obligation in case in which the results of her research reveal unsettled law? Can the lawyer be sanctioned if she predicts a result that later turns out to be inaccurate?

6.   *TCI Ltd.* has also been cited as a reminder to lawyers of their role as advisor to clients. In *Bailey v. Bicknell Minerals, Inc.*, 819 F.2d 690 (7th Cir. 1987), the court, citing *TCI Ltd.*, noted that "Telling would-be litigants that the law is against them is an essential part of a lawyer's job." *Id.* at 693. Similarly, in *Visoly v.*

Security Pac. Credit Corp., 768 So. 2d 482 (Fla. Dist. Ct. App. 3d Dist. 2000), the court noted:

> [W]hen an attorney is solicited to pursue an appeal that is devoid of merit, he or she has a duty to advise the client of the potential for sanctions, and that it would be unethical for the attorney to go forward with frivolous appellate proceedings. As officers of the court and members of the bar, attorneys have an ethical and professional responsibility to withdraw from representation rather than to pursue a frivolous appeal.
>
> Since unprofessionalism can exist only to the extent it is tolerated by the courts, we emphasize that attorney's fees will be assessed as a sanction against appellate counsel to deter members of the bar from pursuing appeals which clearly lack merit. Our further purpose is to achieve the just result of compensating the nonappealing party for the expense of having to defend spurious appeals, and to preserve the appellate calendar for cases truly worthy of consideration.

Id. at 493.

As *TCI Ltd.* makes clear, lawyers can be sanctioned under Rule 11 for failing to conduct adequate research to support a claim. Moreover, a lawyer who fails to perform adequate research on a client matter could be subject to a claim by the client for malpractice. However, be aware that the law that relates to a client matter is not always clear, and lawyers do not guarantee legal predictions. There is therefore a limit to what a client can demand in the way of an assurance that a particular course of action will prevail, as the following case explains.

WOOD v. MCGRATH, NORTH, MULLIN & KRATZ, P.C.
589 N.W.2d 103 (Neb. 1999)

We granted the appellant, Beverly J. Wood's petition for further review of the Nebraska Court of Appeals' decision. The Court of Appeals concluded that as a matter of law, Timothy J. Pugh, an attorney with the appellee, the law firm of McGrath, North, Mullin & Kratz, P.C. (McGrath), did not breach the standard of care or commit legal malpractice by failing to inform Wood that the law relating to two issues relevant to a divorce settlement was unsettled and that the settlement resolved those issues against her. We reverse the Court of Appeals' decision and conclude that the doctrine of judgmental immunity does not apply to an attorney's failure to inform a client of unsettled legal issues relevant to a settlement agreement.

* * *

Wood brought a legal malpractice action against McGrath, alleging that Pugh had negligently represented her in a dissolution action. The underlying dissolution action was concluded by settlement and decree. In her petition against McGrath, Wood alleged that Pugh allowed her to accept less than her share of the marital estate and was negligent by, inter alia, failing to inform her that (1) the settlement reflected a distribution which excluded all rights to then unvested stock options which her husband held through his employment at Werner Enterprises, Inc.; (2) the state of the law indicated that a trial court could likely include all such stock options within the marital estate; (3) the settlement reflected a distribution which excluded approximately $210,489 from the marital estate to account for potential capital gains tax on the stock that the couple owned; and (4) the state of the law indicated that a trial court could likely value the Werner stock without deducting any potential capital gains tax.

At trial, Wood testified that Pugh told her the settlement awarded her 40 percent of the marital estate and that when she asked if that was appropriate, she said Pugh told her a judge would award her anywhere from 35 to 50 percent — that she could do better or worse than the settlement by going to trial. However, Wood testified that Pugh never discussed the different terms of the settlement, never mentioned any alternatives to settling, never provided any reasons to reject the settlement, and never discussed the potential outcome of a trial. She stated that she would not have signed the agreement if Pugh had told her that a trial court might include the unvested stock options as part of the marital estate and that a trial court might prohibit the deduction of potential capital gains tax when valuing the stock, contrary to what the settlement proposed.

Two attorneys testified as expert witnesses for Wood. David Domina stated that when a property settlement raises the issue of unvested stock options, the decision is the client's whether to pursue the issue to trial or to nonetheless settle the issue and that a lawyer breaches the applicable standard of care by failing to inform the client of the existence of the issue and the related law. Domina testified that when a settlement agreement deducts potential capital gains taxes from the value of a marital estate, a lawyer breaches the applicable standard of care by failing to inform a client of the effect of the deduction and the related law. Paul Galter testified that given the terms of the settlement agreement presented to Wood, Pugh breached the standard of care because Pugh did not give Wood sufficient information on the unvested stock options and capital gains tax issues. Galter stated that Pugh had a duty to tell Wood that the agreement raised the issues; to explain their effects to Wood; and to explain what the relevant law on the issues was, including what courts in other jurisdictions had held, before permitting her to sign the agreement.

At the close of Wood's evidence, McGrath moved for a directed verdict, which the court sustained on the issues of the stock valuation and the exclusion of unvested stock options.

On appeal, Wood asserted, inter alia, that the trial court erred in granting McGrath's directed verdict, arguing that Pugh breached the standard of care by failing to properly advise her in regard to the settlement agreement.

The Court of Appeals noted that the law on both the inclusion of unvested stock options in the marital estate and the consideration of potential capital gains taxes in valuing the estate were unsettled in Nebraska at the time the parties entered into the agreement. Accordingly, the court held that the judgmental immunity rule applied and concluded that Pugh's acts and omissions relating to the issues were not negligent as a matter of law. The court then stated that "Pugh, upon exercise of informed judgment, was not obligated to give additional advice regarding the unsettled nature of relevant legal principles."

*   *   *

[On appeal] Wood argues that the doctrine of judgmental immunity does not apply to Pugh's failure to inform her of the law relating to the unvested stock options and capital gains tax deduction issues; that the settlement resolved those issues against her; and that given the body of law on the issues at the time, a trial judge might have resolved those issues in her favor. McGrath notes that the law regarding those issues was unsettled in Nebraska when Pugh represented Wood and argues that the doctrine of judgmental immunity applies to an attorney's decision regarding unsettled law. McGrath thus contends that when presenting a client with a settlement, an attorney has no duty to inform a client of possible options when the law relating to a relevant issue is unsettled.

In *Baker, supra*, this court held that an attorney is not liable for an error in judgment on a point of law which has not been settled by this court and on which reasonable doubt may be entertained by well-informed lawyers. Thus, an attorney's judgment or recommendation on an unsettled point of law is immune from suit, and the attorney has no duty to accurately predict the future course of unsettled law. This immunity rule encourages practicing attorneys in this state to predict, in a professional manner, the outcome of legal issues relevant to their clients' cases. However, Pugh's recommendations (or lack thereof) on the unvested stock options and capital gains tax issues are not before us. Rather, the issue is whether the doctrine of judgmental immunity applies to Pugh's failure to inform Wood that the law relating to unvested stock options and potential capital gains tax issues, while unsettled in Nebraska, were settled in other jurisdictions in a manner which would have been favorable to Wood. The question of whether an attorney owes a duty to inform a client of the unsettled nature of relevant law was not addressed in *Baker*. Thus, we must determine whether to extend the *Baker* judgmental immunity rule to an attorney's failure to inform a client of unsettled legal issues relevant to a settlement agreement.

"[W]e insist that lawyers . . . advise clients with respect to settlements with the same skill, knowledge, and diligence with which they pursue all other legal tasks." We decline[] " 'to adopt a rule that insulates attorneys from exposure to malpractice claims arising from their negligence in settled cases if the attorney's conduct has damaged the client.' ". . .

The decision to settle a controversy is the client's. If a client is to meaningfully make that decision, he or she needs to have the information necessary to assess the risks and benefits of either settling or proceeding to trial. "A lawyer should exert his or her best efforts to ensure that decisions of a client are made only after the client has been informed of relevant considerations." The desire is that a client's decision to settle is an informed one.

The attorney's research efforts may not resolve doubts or may lead to the conclusion that only hindsight or future judicial decisions will provide accurate answers. The attorney's responsibilities to the client may not be satisfied concerning a material issue simply by determining that a proposition is doubtful or by unilaterally deciding the issue. Where there are reasonable alternatives, the attorney should inform the client that the issue is uncertain, unsettled or debatable and allow the client to make the decision.

Additionally, an allegation that an attorney is negligent by failing to inform a client of an unsettled legal issue relevant to a settlement does not demand that an attorney accurately predict the future course of unsettled law. Thus, an allegation that an attorney did not properly inform a client of relevant unsettled legal issues does not provide the same need for immunity from suit as does an attorney's judgment or recommendation in an area of unsettled law.

In *Williams v. Ely*, 423 Mass. 467, 668 N.E.2d 799 (1996), lawyers affiliated with a law firm prepared disclaimers for clients in which the clients renounced their remainder and contingent interests in a family trust. In affirming the lower court's ruling that a competent estate planning attorney would have advised that the law was unsettled regarding the appropriate time to file the disclaimers, the *Williams* court recognized the difference between alleging negligence for a recommendation based upon an area of unsettled law and alleging negligence for failing to inform a client of relevant unsettled law.

> It does not matter that the opinion that the disclaimers would generate no adverse gift tax consequences was a reasonable view of the law in 1975. The problem is not that Gaston Snow gave reasonable advice that in time proved to be wrong. The problem is that the apparent certainty of the opinion given, at a time when the issue was not conclusively resolved, denied the plaintiffs the opportunity to assess the risk and to elect to follow alternative estate planning options.

In *Crosby v. Jones*, 705 So.2d 1356 (Fla.1998), which the Court of Appeals relied upon, the *Crosby* court addressed whether an attorney must inform a client of the unsettled law relevant to the client's case. In the underlying case, Crosby advised Jones to settle with one of two tort-feasors, but in doing so, Crosby did not advise Jones that a decision from a Florida appellate district court had determined that settling in such a situation would be adverse to her interests. On appeal in her suit against the second tort-feasor, Jones' appellate district court ruled adversely to her. Jones sued Crosby for malpractice, and on appeal, the *Crosby* court held that the attorney had no duty to inform the client of the unsettled nature of the law. However, the court's decision was based upon the fact that at the time of Crosby's recommendation, (1) a statute and a Florida Supreme Court decision appeared to be on point and supported Crosby's recommendation, (2) two prior decisions issued by Jones' own appellate district court, the same court that ruled adversely in the underlying case, also supported Crosby's recommendation to settle.

In *Crosby*, 705 So.2d at 1359, the court noted that its decision "does not mean that an attorney should never be required to inform a client regarding a conflict in the law; however, when an interpretation has been made as to the state of the law in a given district and that interpretation has a proper basis of support," an attorney need not advise his or her client of case law from other jurisdictions. Indeed, the facts and the holding in *Crosby* indicate that that case involved the failure to advise a client in an area of *apparently settled* law, rather than *unsettled* law. . . . In the instant case, however, Pugh had no case law from this jurisdiction which supported the settlement agreement's determinations on the unvested employee stock options or capital gains tax issues.

In *Davis v. Damrell*, 119 Cal.App.3d 883, 174 Cal.Rptr. 257 (1981), which the Court of Appeals also cited for support, the *Davis* court held that under the circumstances, the doctrine of judgmental immunity applied to the attorney's failure to inform the client of the unsettled nature of the law relating to a settlement agreement. "As a matter of policy," the court stated that an attorney should not be required to compromise his or her good faith and informed judgment by advising the client of the unsettled nature of relevant legal principles.

The fallacy in the *Davis* court's reasoning is that when determining whether to settle a dispute, it is the client, not the attorney, who bears the risk. Because the client bears the risk, it is the client who should assess whether the risk is acceptable, not the attorney.

Ultimately, we cannot support what would be the clear result of extending the judgmental immunity rule in the instant case. If we conclude that the judgmental immunity rule applies to an attorney's failure to inform a client of unsettled legal issues relevant to a settlement, an attorney could forgo conducting research or providing a client with information on a relevant legal issue once he or she determined that the legal issue at hand was unsettled in this state. We fail to see how this result promotes the settlement of disputes in a client's best interests.

We conclude that the doctrine of judgmental immunity does not apply to an attorney's failure to inform a client of unsettled legal issues relevant to a settlement. Our conclusion makes no judgment as to whether Pugh was negligent. It imposes no additional duty as a matter of law to research or inform a client on unsettled legal matters. Rather, it simply directs that . . . whether an attorney is negligent for such a failure is determined by whether the attorney exercised the same skill, knowledge, and diligence as attorneys of ordinary skill and capacity commonly possess and exercise in the performance of all other legal tasks. At the same time, an attorney's ultimate recommendation in an area of unsettled law is immune from suit. Such a result gives the client the benefit of both professional advice and the information necessary to make an informed decision whether to settle a dispute.

CONCLUSION

The Court of Appeals erred in concluding that Pugh was not negligent as a matter of law in failing to inform Wood of the unsettled nature of the law regarding whether unvested stock options were part of the marital estate and whether the marital estate's unvested stock options should have been valued without deducting potential capital gains tax. Accordingly, we reverse the Court of Appeals' decision and remand the cause to the Court of Appeals with directions to remand the cause to the district court for a new trial.

NOTES

1. The *McGrath* court clarifies that a lawyer is responsible for informing a client when the law is unclear. In a legal memorandum, because the analysis is presented objectively, arguments and the supporting law for each side of the issue are presented. Indeed, in *McGrath*, Pugh's interoffice memo exploring the treatment of unvested stock options should have noted the unsettled nature of the issue and identified the alternative ways the court might treat the options.

2. Would the result in *McGrath* have been different if the lawyer had failed to consider the competing law? What if the lawyer had never located the law? What would have been an effective way to locate the competing law?

C. Communication and Advice

A lawyer has the duty to communicate with the client so that the client can be involved in the representation. Indeed, Model Rule 1.2 identifies the allocation of authority between the lawyer and client and requires that the client decide the objectives of the representation. In order for the client to provide such direction, the lawyer has the responsibility to keep the client informed and to communicate effectively with the client so that the client can give such direction. Comment 5 to Model Rule 1.4 provides:

> The client should have sufficient information to participate intelligently in decisions concerning the objectives of the representation and the means by which they are to be pursued, to the extent the client is willing and able to do so. Adequacy of communication depends in part on the kind of advice or assistance that is involved.

Model Rules of Prof'l Conduct R. 1.4 cmt. 5 (2008). Similarly, EC 7–8 notes that

> [a] lawyer should exert his best efforts to insure that decisions of his client are made only after the client has been informed of relevant considerations. . . . Advice of a lawyer to his client need not be confined to purely legal considerations. A lawyer should advise his client of the possible effect of each legal alternative. . . . In the final analysis, however, the lawyer should always remember that the decision whether to forego legally available objectives or methods because of non-legal factors is ultimately for the client. . . .

Thus, to communicate properly under the ethical rules, the lawyer must keep the client informed about the status of the case, about any important information relating to the case, and about settlement offers. Further, in providing advice and guidance to clients, the lawyer must inform the client about ethical and legal limitations on the lawyer's conduct. The lawyer must also explain the law and the benefits and risks of alternate courses of action. To the extent that these admonitions might arise as a result of analysis in a memorandum, a lawyer should keep them in mind as he engages in predictive analysis.

Related to the lawyer's duty to communicate with her clients is the lawyer's duty as an advisor. Model Rule 2.1 provides: "In representing a client, a lawyer shall exercise independent professional judgment and render candid advice. In rendering advice, a lawyer may refer not only to law but to other considerations such as moral, economic, social and political factors, which may be relevant to the client's situation." Particularly with regard to predictive memoranda, a lawyer has the duty to give candid advice, even though the advice may involve "unpleasant facts and alternatives that a client may be disinclined to confront.'" Model Rules of Prof'l Conduct R. 2.1 cmt. 1 (2008). It is further noteworthy that the lawyer's obligation as an advisor specifically condones the lawyer's reference to nonlegal considerations, such as the moral, economic, social, and political considerations associated with the client's situation. The advice given by an attorney may be given to the client in person during a meeting or may be provided by the lawyer in a letter. A failure by the lawyer to adequately explain the law to a client, as well as the legal options available to the client, can give rise to sanctions under the ethical rules. Such a failure can also subject the lawyer to a claim of legal malpractice, as the following case explores. In reviewing the opinion, pay particular attention to the court's discussion of the scope of the lawyer's obligation to provide advice.

NICHOLS v. KELLER

19 Cal. Rptr. 2d 601 (Cal. App. 5 Dist. 1993)

* * *

[In December, 1987, Plaintiff was injured on a construction worksite.] On February 24, 1988, plaintiff and his wife met with defendant E. Paul Fulfer, an attorney with the defendant firm of Fulfer & Fulfer, to discuss plaintiff's accident and legal rights and remedies. At the conclusion of the meeting, defendant Fulfer had plaintiff sign a workers' compensation application for adjudication of claim. Fulfer executed the form as "applicant's attorney" and filed the application on plaintiff's behalf with the Stockton office of the Division of Industrial Accidents/ California Department of Industrial Relations. The Stockton office received the document on February 26. Defendant Fulfer then associated defendant Edward Keller, an attorney with defendant firm of LaCoste, Keller, Mello & Land, to prosecute the workers' compensation claim. Fulfer signed a formal pleading bearing the caption "association of attorneys" on January 20, 1989.

Defendant Keller met with plaintiff on March 28, 1988, and said he would represent plaintiff in his pending workers' compensation matter against Zurn Industries and Aetna Casualty and Surety Company. Defendant Keller continued to represent plaintiff in the workers' compensation proceeding until July 1989.

* * *

On July 7, 1989, plaintiff and his wife met with [another] attorney [by the name of] Butler. According to plaintiff, "At this meeting I learned for the first time that a third-party claim could and very likely should have been brought in regards to my industrial injury in December 1987, and that my wife and I may have a legal claim against Edward C. Keller and Elbert Paul Fulfer, attorneys, who had failed to advise or inform us of these facts."

On March 21, 1990, plaintiff filed a complaint for damages in Stanislaus County Superior Court. Plaintiff named attorneys Keller, Fulfer, and their respective law firms as defendants. He alleged causes of action for legal malpractice and negligent spoliation of evidence against all defendants. He also alleged a cause of action for negligent referral against defendant Fulfer and his law firm.

* * *

I. DID DEFENDANTS OWE PLAINTIFF A DUTY TO ADVISE HIM OF THE POSSIBILITY OF A THIRD-PARTY CIVIL LAWSUIT AND THE APPLICABLE STATUTE OF LIMITATIONS?

Plaintiff contends:

> [A]n attorney does have a duty to provide sound advice in furtherance of the client's best interests. Mr. Nichols, a man of limited education . . . went to respondents seeking legal advice and representation from members of the Bar of California regarding any and all legal remedies he might be eligible for arising from his work injury. Respondents' failure to advise appellant that he may have a third party claim; respondents' failure to advise appellant regarding the applicable statute of limitations; and respondents' failure to refer appellant to an attorney experienced in third

party actions was a breach of that duty." . . . In the instant case, the state of the law concerning the peculiar risk of harm and safe place to work doctrines was solidified and 'discoverable'. Appellant suffered fractures of his cervical vertebrae and brain damage when he was injured at the cogeneration plant construction site. There was a general contractor on site who, by all reports, was solvent, knew or should have known of the special risks presented by workers performing tasks in close vertical proximity to each other and who failed to take adequate and special precautions against this foreseeable risk of injury.

*   *   *

Actionable legal malpractice is compounded of the same basic elements as other kinds of actionable negligence: duty, breach of duty, causation, and damage. The elements of a cause of action for professional negligence are (1) the duty of the professional to use such skill, prudence and diligence as other members of the profession commonly possess and exercise; (2) breach of that duty; (3) a causal connection between the negligent conduct and the resulting injury; and (4) actual loss or damage resulting from the professional negligence. When these elements coexist, they constitute actionable negligence. On the other hand, absence of, or failure to prove, any of them is fatal to recovery. An attorney, by accepting employment to give legal advice or render legal services, impliedly agrees to use ordinary judgment, care, skill, and diligence in the performance of the tasks he or she undertakes.

The question of the existence of a legal duty of care in a given factual situation presents a question of law which is to be determined by the courts alone.

*   *   *

One legal scholar has noted:

An attorney advising or representing an injured employee concerning workers' compensation benefits must consider whether the employee should also pursue a lawsuit for civil damages against (1) a third party . . . or (2) the employee's employer or coworker, or the employer's workers' compensation insurer. . . . For comparable injuries, damages recoveries often greatly exceed workers' compensation recoveries.

The compensation attorney should either personally conduct a skilled and careful inquiry into the prospects for obtaining damages for the client that would exceed recoverable workers' compensation benefits or refer the client to an attorney who is competent to determine the prospects for such a recovery. . . .

A workers' compensation attorney's failure to file and pursue a timely lawsuit for civil damages, or to refer the client to another lawyer for that purpose, can be the basis for a legal malpractice action. . . .

Often, it is prudent to initiate both a compensation claim and a civil action, and to pursue both until it is determined that one of them will provide a full recovery. There are, of course, situations in which workers' compensation clearly provides the worker a complete remedy. It is not helpful to pursue a lawsuit for an injured worker when, e.g.: (1) A tort cause of action cannot be stated against any identifiable defendant; (2) A trier of fact is unlikely to assign liability to a defendant who could pay the judgment; or (3) The injured employee's own fault seems likely to reduce the amount of recoverable damages to less than the value of recoverable workers' compensation benefits.

A significant area of exposure for the workers' compensation attorney concerns that attorney's responsibility for counseling regarding a potential third-party action. One of an attorney's basic functions is to advise. Liability can exist because the attorney failed to provide advice. Not only should an attorney furnish advice when requested, but he or she should also volunteer opinions when necessary to further the client's objectives. The attorney need not advise and caution of every possible alternative, but only of those that may result in adverse consequences if not considered. Generally speaking, a workers' compensation attorney should be able to limit the retention to the compensation claim if the client is cautioned (1) there may be other remedies which the attorney will not investigate and (2) other counsel should be consulted on such matters. However, even when a retention is expressly limited, the attorney may still have a duty to alert the client to legal problems which are reasonably apparent, even though they fall outside the scope of the retention. The rationale is that, as between the lay client and the attorney, the latter is more qualified to recognize and analyze the client's legal needs. The attorney need not represent the client on such matters. Nevertheless, the attorney should inform the client of the limitations of the attorney's representation and of the possible need for other counsel.

An attorney's duty to his or her client depends on the existence of an attorney-client relationship. If that relationship does not exist, the fiduciary duty to a client does not arise.

*　*　*

In their motions for summary judgment, defendant attorneys maintained they agreed to undertake only a limited employment. Attorney Fulfer asserted he agreed to represent plaintiff in the workers' compensation matter only and, even then, for two specific purposes: (1) to file a workers' compensation application on plaintiff's behalf and (2) to refer plaintiff to defendant Keller, so the latter could actually prosecute the workers' compensation claim on plaintiff's behalf. Attorney Keller argued the attorney-client relationship between the plaintiff and himself was solely for the purpose of representation in the workers' compensation claim. Keller claimed he owed only a duty to prosecute that claim and not to prosecute any possible third-party claim or to advise plaintiff as to the prosecution of such a claim. Defendants reiterate these positions on appeal.

In his opposition to the motions for summary judgment, plaintiff attached the declaration of attorney Yale Jones, a certified specialist in workers' compensation law. Jones declared attorney Fulfer acted below the standard of care of an attorney in the Stockton area by failing to (1) advise plaintiff of the different remedies available through the Workers' Compensation Appeal Board and through a civil action; (2) advise plaintiff of the statute of limitations applicable to plaintiff's third-party action; (3) advise plaintiff to consult another attorney concerning any available rights and remedies plaintiff might have against third parties; and (4) provide plaintiff with written advice regarding which rights defendant Fulfer would protect or which needed to be reviewed by other competent attorneys and what would happen in the event plaintiff did not protect those rights. Attorney Jones also declared defendant Keller acted below the standard of care for the same reasons. Declarant's opinion as to defendant Keller was based on a set of hypothetical facts.

Thus, defendants maintained they undertook limited duties to plaintiff and, as a matter of law, they owed him no duty to advise about possible third-party claims, while plaintiff's expert, Yale Jones, declared their duties were far more expansive and required both counsel to advise plaintiff about various workers' compensation and civil remedies, the applicable statute of limitations for a third-party action, the propriety of obtaining a "second opinion" as to available rights and remedies, and the precise scope of defendants' representation. The lower court's minute order concluded: "[I]t is undisputed that the representation was undertaken for the limited purpose of the workman's compensation claim. Furthermore, an attorney's obligation does not include a duty to advise on all possible alternatives no matter how remote or tenuous.

A determination that defendants owe plaintiff no duty of care would negate an essential element of plaintiff's cause of action for negligence and would constitute a complete defense. Whether a duty of care exists is a question of law for the court and is reviewable de novo. All persons are required to use ordinary care to prevent injury to others from their conduct. A professional has a duty to use such skill, prudence and diligence as other members of the profession commonly possess and exercise. Legal duties are not discoverable facts of nature. Rather, they are merely conclusory expressions that, in cases of a particular type, liability should be imposed for damage done.

Foreseeability of harm, though not determinative, has become the chief factor in duty analysis. Confusion has arisen over the concept of foreseeability and the variety of roles it plays in tort law. Foreseeability is a question of fact for the jury in many contexts. However, in defining the boundaries of duty, foreseeability is a question of law for the court. The question of foreseeability in a "duty" context is a limited one for the court and is readily contrasted with the fact-specific foreseeability questions bearing on negligence (breach of duty) and causation posed to the jury or trier of fact.

It seems to us the foreseeability factor compels a finding of duty in cases of this type. A trained attorney is more qualified to recognize and analyze legal needs than a lay client, and, at least in part, this is the reason a party seeks out and retains an attorney to represent and advise him or her in legal matters. As Justice Brandeis observed a century ago:

> The duty of a lawyer today is not that of a solver of legal conundrums: he is indeed a counsellor at law. Knowledge of the law is of course essential to his efficiency, but the law bears to his profession a relation very similar to that which medicine does to that of the physicians. The apothecary can prepare the dose, the more intelligent one even knows the specific for most common diseases. It requires but a mediocre physician to administer the proper drug for the patient who correctly and fully describes his ailment. The great physicians are those who in addition to that knowledge of therapeutics which is open to all, know not merely the human body but the human mind and emotions, so as to make themselves the proper diagnosis — to know the truth which their patients fail to disclose. . . .

What was true in 1893 is certainly true today in this increasingly complex and technologically advanced society in which we live. In the context of personal injury consultations between lawyer and layperson, it is reasonably foreseeable the latter will offer a selective or incomplete recitation of the facts underlying the claim; request legal assistance by employing such everyday terms as "workers' compensation," "disability," and "unemployment"; and rely upon the consulting lawyer to describe the array of legal remedies available, alert the layperson to any apparent legal problems, and, if appropriate, indicate limitations on the retention of counsel and the need for other counsel. In the event the lawyer fails to so advise the layperson, it is also reasonably foreseeable the layperson will fail to ask relevant questions regarding the existence of other remedies and be deprived of relief through a combination of ignorance and lack or failure of understanding. And, if counsel elects to limit or prescribe his representation of the client, i.e., to a workers' compensation claim only without reference or regard to any third party or collateral claims which the client might pursue if adequately advised, then counsel must make such limitations in representation very clear to his client. Thus, a lawyer who signs an application for adjudication of a workers' compensation claim and a lawyer who accepts a referral to prosecute the claim owe the claimant a duty of care to advise on available remedies, including third-party actions.

*   *   *

NOTES

1. *Nichols* addresses the obligations imposed upon a lawyer with special expertise in the workers' compensation area. The court concludes that such a specialized practice imposes some minimum standard on the attorney. This is consistent with the Model Rule's requirement of competence. For a lawyer with a more general practice, what is the lawyer's obligation with regard to explanation?

2. The lawyer's duty to provide advice to a client is not without limits. In *Lamb v. Barbour*, 455 A.2d 1122 (N.J. Super. Ct. 1982), a lawyer represented clients in the acquisition of a bakery business. The plaintiff, Lamb, was a 23-year-old high school graduate with limited business experience. *Id.* at 1124. When the business failed two months after the sale, Lamb sued his lawyer. The trial court found the lawyer negligent, ruling that the lawyer failed in his obligation to advise the clients that they were not adequately trained or educated to manage the business and that he failed to highlight that the business's records suggested that failure was "inevitable." *Id.* at 1124–1125. The appellate court reversed. The court noted that "an attorney is required to exercise on his client's behalf the knowledge, skill and ability ordinarily possessed and exercised by members of the legal profession similarly situated and to employ reasonable care and prudence in connection therewith." *Id.* at 1125. Notwithstanding, the court concluded:

> We disagree with the trial judge's conclusion that the nature of the relationship between the parties imposed a duty upon defendant to advise plaintiffs that they lacked the experience needed to run the businesses and that they should not therefore make the purchase. The extent of a lawyer's liability to his client "necessarily depends upon the nature of the undertaking." Although plaintiffs may have been dependent on defendant for financial and legal guidance, under the facts shown it would have been presumptuous for defendant to have tendered such a recommendation. Plaintiffs' reliance on defendant's background in tax law and accounting did not justify the expectation of counselling as to the prudence of the course

they had chosen. This decision was properly left to the exercise of plaintiffs' business judgment. To hold defendant answerable for his failure to discourage the transaction we would have to speculate about his possible liability had he succeeded and the businesses were later operated successfully by another buyer.

Id. at 1126.

3.   Model Rule 2.1 indicates that a lawyer's advice may refer to "moral, political, economic, social and political factors." What obligations does that impose in terms of representation and advice? In *Matter of Marriage of Foran*, 834 P.2d 1081 (Wash. App. Div. 1 1992), the court referenced this obligation in the context of advice relating to a prenuptial agreement. The court invalidated the agreement as economically unfair and warned that lawyers who handle prenuptial contracts "should seriously consider the implications of RPC 2.1.. . . A client is not well served by an unenforceable contract. Marital tranquility is not achieved by a contract which is economically unfair or achieved by unfair means." *Id.* at 1089, n. 14. While lawyers are rarely sanctioned for failing to advise clients with respect to non-legal consequences, the court in *Friedman v. Commr. of Public Safety*, 473 N.W.2d 828 (Minn. 1991) addressed this responsibility. The lawyer in *Friedman* represented a client charged with repeated DWI offenses. The court noted:

> If the objective of DWI prosecution is to get drunk drivers off the highways, into treatment, and on the way to sobriety, an attorney can play a very important role. A good lawyer is not only interested in protecting the client's legal rights, but also in the well-being and mental and physical health of the client. A lawyer has an affirmative duty to be a counselor to his client. *See* Minn.R.Prof.Conduct 2.1 (1985) ("In rendering advice, a lawyer may refer not only to law but to other considerations such as moral, economic, social and political factors, that may be relevant to the client's situation.") The lawyer may be able to persuade a problem drinker to seek treatment . . .

Id. at 834–835.

II.   FORMAT AND PRACTICE CONSIDERATIONS

The format for a memo generally includes the issue or question presented, a short answer or conclusion, a statement of the facts, and the legal analysis or discussion of the issue. Because interoffice, predictive memoranda are not submitted to a court and, typically, are not distributed to clients, the ethical rules do not impact the format of the document. However, as noted previously, because the analytical section of a memo is often used to prepare documents that are provided to clients such as advice letters, or are submitted to a court in the form of a motion, lawyers are well-served to have properly researched the issue in the memo and provided appropriate citation. Moreover, lawyers should carefully prepare the facts section of predictive memoranda, as the facts establish the basis upon which the prediction is ultimately made. To the extent that discovery or further discussion with the client reveals additional information, an accurate facts section preserves the basis upon which the advice was rendered.

Chapter 5

CLIENT LETTERS

As a lawyer, you will write to a number of audiences, including clients, supervisors, opposing counsel, and judges. Those audiences do not expect to be entertained by your writing; they expect to be educated and informed. Accordingly, to meet your audience's expectations, your writing must be well-organized, clear, and precise.

— Alison Julien, Associate Professor of Legal Writing,
Marquette University School of Law

Lawyers write letters to their clients for a variety of reasons. They may communicate the results of their research in the form of an advice letter. They may send status letters to apprise clients of the status of their cases. While the content and tone of these documents vary, a variety of ethical and professional considerations come into play in the context of this form of written communication.

The following cases illustrate attorney misconduct in connection with the ethical rules that impact letter writing, but they do not involve situations in which attorneys were cited for lapses in letter writing. Because client letters are informal correspondence, lawyers are not frequently sanctioned for the material they transmit (or fail to transmit) via letters. Notwithstanding, there are ethical rules that impact communications made by lawyers in letters to clients. Consequently, although the following opinions do not illustrate discipline for improper letters, they do illustrate attorney lapses that could have been prevented with more effective communication, the evidence of which could have been produced in the form of client letters

I. CONTENT-BASED CONSIDERATIONS

A. Overview

i. Communication and Diligence

A lawyer has the obligation under Model Rule 1.4 to keep the client advised as to the status of her matter and to respond to client requests for information. Similarly, under the Model Code, EC 9-2 notes that "a lawyer should fully and promptly inform his client of material developments in the matters being handled for the client." In the context of letter writing, a lawyer also has the obligation to represent the client diligently. Model Rule 1.3 requires that the lawyer act with reasonable diligence and promptness in representing a client and DR 6-101(A)(3) requires that a lawyer not "[n]eglect a matter entrusted to him."

ii.   Explanation

The allocation of responsibility between client and lawyer vests responsibility for objectives of representation with the client. The lawyer generally has responsibility for advising the client regarding those objectives and directing the client as to the means to pursuing those objectives. Model Rule 1.2 provides that "A lawyer shall abide by a client's decisions concerning the objectives of representation . . . and shall consult with the client as to the means by which they are to be pursued." Similarly, EC 7-7 states that "In certain areas of legal representation not affecting the merits of the cause or substantially prejudicing the rights of a client, a lawyer is entitled to make decisions on his own. But otherwise the authority to make decisions is exclusively that of the client."

To the extent the client is able to make decisions regarding the objectives of representation, the lawyer must fully explain the alternatives to the client. To that end, Model Rule 1.4 provides that the lawyer has the responsibility to "explain a matter to the extent reasonably necessary to permit the client to make informed decisions regarding the representation." Consequently, in letter writing, a lawyer should strive to keep the client informed on a regular basis and to communicate in a manner that facilitates the representation — in other words, in a style and format that the client understands.

When the lawyer is handling a matter for a client with a disability, Model Rule 1.14 advises that "[w]hen a client's capacity to make adequately considered decisions in connection with a representation is diminished, whether because of minority, mental impairment or for some other reason, the lawyer shall, as far as reasonably possible, maintain a normal client-lawyer relationship with the client." Likewise, under the Model Code, EC 7-11 advises that the "responsibilities of a lawyer may vary according to the intelligence, experience, mental condition or age of a client. . . ." EC 7-12 adds that "[a]ny mental or physical condition of a client that renders him incapable of making a considered judgment on his own behalf casts additional responsibilities upon his lawyer." In advising clients with physical or mental impairments, EC 7-12 further provides that "[i]f the client is capable of understanding the matter in question or of contributing to the advancement of his interests . . . the lawyer should obtain from him all possible aid. . . . But obviously a lawyer cannot perform any act or make any decision which the law requires his client to perform or make. . . ."

iii.   Candor

In rendering advice in the form of a letter, the lawyer has a duty of candor to the client. Model Rule 2.1 sets forth the lawyer's role as advisor and provides: "In representing a client, a lawyer shall exercise independent professional judgment and render candid advice. In rendering advice, a lawyer may refer not only to law but to other considerations such as moral, economic, social and political factors, that may be relevant to the client's situation." Further, the lawyer's obligation of candor requires that the lawyer communicate bad news. "[A] lawyer should not be deterred from giving candid advice by the prospect that the advice will be unpalatable to the client." Model Rules of Prof'l Conduct R. 2.1 cmt. 1 (2008).

iv.   Client Confidences

Model Rule 1.6 requires that a lawyer maintain the confidentiality of client information. The comments to the rule require that the lawyer "take reasonable precautions to prevent [confidential] information from coming into the hands of unintended recipients" when transmitting information related to a client matter. Model Rules of Prof'l Conduct R. 1.6 cmt. 17 (2086). When a lawyer transmits advice or other information to a client regarding her matter in the form of a letter, the lawyer should be cognizant of the fact that letters do often fall into the hands of unintended recipients. To that end, and while the rule "does not require that the lawyer use special security measures if the method of communication affords a reasonable expectation of privacy," the lawyer should carefully consider the sensitivity of material communicated to the client and evaluate whether it would be preferable to transmit the information to the client orally as opposed to in writing. *Id.* The duty to preserve client confidences under the Model Code is addressed under Canon 4, which requires lawyers to preserve the confidences and secrets of clients. As noted in EC 4-1, "The observance of the ethical obligation of a lawyer to hold inviolate the confidences and secrets of his client not only facilitates the full development of facts essential to the proper representation of the client but also encourages laymen to seek early legal assistance." Model Code of Prof'l Responsibility EC 4-1 (1981).

B.   Letter Writing: Diligent Communication

The obligations to keep a client reasonably informed about the status of a matter under Model Rule 1.4, and to represent a client diligently under Model Rule 1.3, impact letter writing. "Reasonable communication between the lawyer and the client is necessary for the client to participate in the representation." Model Rules of Prof'l Conduct R. 1.4 cmt. 1 (2008). Lack of communication, coupled with neglect of client matters, can give rise to sanctions even where the client's claim is not undermined. "Even where the client's interests are not affected in substance,. . . unreasonable delay can cause a client needless anxiety and undermine confidence in the lawyer's trustworthiness." Model Rules of Prof'l Conduct R. 1.3 cmt. 3 (2008). These rules should particularly encourage lawyers to keep in communication with their clients in the form of providing status letters to the client at reasonable intervals. There may be a period of time during which little transpires on the client's matter. Nonetheless, clients resent a lack of communication, particularly when they continue to receive billing statements from their lawyers. Lawyers can be sanctioned for neglecting a client matter when the client raises a legitimate claim regarding a lack of communication from the lawyer. Moreover, a failure to respond to client requests for information either by status letter or phone call can amount to client neglect.

IN RE DISCIPLINARY ACTION AGAINST PETERS
474 N.W.2d 164 (Minn. 1991)

Respondent William A. Peters is before the court on a petition for disciplinary action alleging six counts of professional misconduct issued January 28, 1991, by the Director of the Office of Professional Responsibility. In 1983 this court suspended respondent indefinitely with leave to apply for reinstatement in three years if he met certain specified conditions. On January 12, 1987, we ordered respondent's reinstatement to practice conditioned upon three years unsupervised probation and a three year restriction against solo practice. On January 12, 1990, on the expiration of his three year probation, respondent resumed solo practice. We now order his disbarment.

* * *

The current petition was issued on January 28, 1991, and on February 13, 1991, served by publication because respondent had abandoned his law practice without leaving a forwarding address. On February 20, 1991, the director was appointed trustee over respondent's law practice, and has since been attempting to return all client files. Respondent appeared at the director's office on March 18, 1991, and personally accepted service of the petition but provided no current address.

* * *

Backelin Matter. Susan Backelin hired respondent in August 1989 to handle a post-dissolution motion. While respondent promised Backelin that prompt action would be taken, a court date for the motion was not scheduled until March 1990, and the hearing was eventually postponed to May 2, 1990.

Backelin learned that the May 2 hearing date was also going to be postponed because respondent had not given the opposing party sufficient notice of the hearing date. Backelin then discharged respondent by letter on April 25, 1990, requesting return of her file and the unearned portion of her advance fee. Although Backelin made repeated phone calls and left messages, respondent did not return Backelin's file until September 1990, after she had hired a new attorney, and, to date, has not provided Backelin with either a refund or an accounting. Respondent's failure to return Backelin's phone calls, her file and her refund violated Rules 1.4(a) (duty to keep client reasonably informed and to comply with reasonable requests for information); 1.15(b)(3) (duty to maintain complete records of all client funds and to render appropriate accounting to the client), and (b)(4) (duty to promptly pay client's funds when requested), 1.16(d) (duty to surrender client's papers and property upon termination), Minn.R.Prof.Conduct.

Dimmer Matter. Respondent represented Betty Dimmer in a December 1989 bank dispute. Respondent had three meetings with either Dimmer or bank personnel, but was unable to resolve the dispute. From that point until August 1990, Dimmer left more than forty phone messages with respondent which he failed to return. On August 23, 1990, Dimmer complained about the lack of communication by letter, and on September 1, she fired respondent and hired a new attorney. Respondent's conduct violated Rule 1.4(a) (duty to keep client reasonably informed and to comply with reasonable requests for information).

* * *

The purpose of attorney discipline is to guard the administration of justice; to protect the courts, the legal profession and the public; and to deter future misconduct. When determining appropriate disciplinary sanctions the court weighs four factors: (1) the nature of the misconduct; (2) the cumulative weight of the rules violations; (3) the harm to the public; and (4) the harm to the legal profession. Although prior cases may be helpful by analogy, each disciplinary case is decided on its own facts together with any aggravating or mitigating circumstances.

The only issue to be decided in this matter is the disciplinary sanction to be imposed. The public must be protected and similar misconduct deterred. Respondent was afforded leniency in the 1983 proceeding. Upon reinstatement to practice, however, he immediately resumed his pattern of neglect without any evidence of the renewed commitment to ethical and professional behavior we expect after a disciplinary proceeding. Respondent offers no evidence in explanation or mitigation of his repeated pattern of misconduct. There is no alternative to disbarment.

NOTES

1.   Note the *Peters* court's explanation of the purposes of attorney discipline. How are those purposes advanced by disciplining an attorney who fails to communicate effectively with his client?

2.   Managing a law practice and multiple client matters is a demanding process. Are there circumstances that could justify a lapse in communication? Are there circumstances that could mitigate the discipline imposed on a lawyer who has failed to communicate effectively with clients? The following case discusses one lawyer's proffered defense to a claim of client neglect.

STATE EX REL. OKLAHOMA BAR ASS'N v. SCHRAEDER
51 P.3d 570 (Okla. 2002)

In this disciplinary proceeding against a lawyer, the issues to be decided are: [1] Does the record submitted for our examination provide sufficient evidence for a meaningful *de novo* consideration of the complaint and of its disposition? and [2] Is a license suspension for thirty (30) days an appropriate disciplinary sanction for respondent's breach of professional ethics? We answer both questions in the affirmative.

At the commencement of its hearing on 16 May 2001 a trial panel of the Professional Responsibility Tribunal [panel or PRT] recognized for the record the admission of the parties' stipulations of fact, conclusions of law and an agreed disciplinary recommendation. As for mitigation, the parties agreed that respondent had never before been disciplined (by the Professional Responsibility Commission or by this court) or been the subject of a formal investigation by the Bar's counsel. The parties submit *professional burnout syndrome* as a factor to be considered in mitigation of respondent's culpability.

Upon completion of the hearing and consideration of the stipulations and testimony on file, the trial panel issued its report (which incorporates the parties' stipulations). The panel recommended that respondent receive a private reprimand and be directed to pay the costs of this proceeding.

*   *   *

Count I — *The McMinn Grievance*

Count one is predicated upon a grievance by Perry A. McMinn. McMinn hired respondent to assist in a criminal appeal filed in the United States District Court for the Northern District of Oklahoma. He paid respondent on 4 September 1997 the sum of $2,000 by cashier's check as part of the agreed fee of $10,000 and gave Schraeder an additional $800 on 21 January 1998.

After writing McMinn in February, March and May of 1998, respondent ceased communicating with his client and failed to file any motions or briefs in his appeal. Following respondent's inactivity, McMinn filed a motion on his own behalf and wrote respondent a letter, dated 5 May 1999, asking him to review and revise the document. When respondent failed to reply, McMinn wrote him again on 2 June 1999 and enclosed copies of several cases that he wanted him to review. Respondent did not answer the June 2 letter; he claims that he never received the letter or the enclosed cases. By letter dated 27 September 1999 McMinn requested a detailed accounting of all costs and legal services expended on his behalf and a refund of the unearned portion of the $2,800 fee. Respondent failed to answer the September 27 letter.

Schraeder insists (1) that he filed no briefs or pleadings in the McMinn case because he was waiting to receive pertinent information from McMinn's family to proceed with the appeal and claims (2) that he neither responded to the September 27 letter nor provided the requested accounting because he believed that he had earned the $2,800 fee by (a) *researching* the various issues in the McMinn appeal, (b) *speaking* on several occasions to members of McMinn's family and (c) *traveling* twice to visit McMinn at the Adult Detention Center in Tulsa, Oklahoma.

The Bar and respondent agree that the latter's misconduct violates the mandatory provisions of ORPC Rules 1.4 (failure promptly to communicate with his client's request for information), 1.5 (failure to charge reasonable fees), 1.15(b) (failure promptly to account for and return any unearned fees), 1.16(b)(2) and (d) (failure promptly to notify McMinn of his withdrawal from the appeal), 8.4(a) (misconduct) and RGDP Rule 1.3 (bringing discredit upon the legal profession). Upon *de novo* review of the record, we hold the charges are supported by clear and convincing proof that respondent's conduct warrants the imposition of discipline.

Count III — *The Parsons Grievance*

In Count three of the complaint the Bar charged respondent with failure to communicate with a client and to perform the work for which he was hired. Around 13 February 1999 Loretta Parsons retained Schraeder to represent her grandchildren's interest in her deceased daughter's estate. He was also to represent another granddaughter in both a criminal and a domestic matter. Parsons paid him $1,500.00. She also delivered to him several documents relevant to the estate as well as to possible civil litigation pertaining to her daughter's death. Respondent claims that Parsons paid him the fee to represent two of Parsons' adult children in three legal matters but that he never agreed to represent her in any wrongful death or other civil action. He insists that he completed the criminal and domestic matters for one granddaughter and performed work in the probate case.

The record is replete with letters from Parsons to respondent in which she insists that her efforts to communicate with respondent and to retrieve from him personal documents relating to a wrongful death suit proved unsuccessful. Schraeder takes the position that he terminated all communications with Parsons because his representation ended after the conclusion of the estate matters for her grandchildren and another family member's criminal case and annulment.

A constant flow of communication between an attorney and client constitutes a vital part of a lawyer's professional undertaking.[22] When a client seeks information from one who is retained for representation, prompt responsive action should be forthcoming. *Prolonged and willful silence by the lawyer's failure to return calls or answer letters is the very kind of neglect that destroys the public's confidence in the lawyer's integrity.*

Both the Bar and respondent agree that the latter's actions *violate* the mandatory provisions of ORPC Rules 1.4, 1.15(b), and 8.4(a) and RGDP Rule 1.3 and constitute grounds for the imposition of professional discipline. On *de novo* review of the record, we hold there is clear and convincing probative support in the record for a breach of professional ethics and that the imposition of discipline is warranted.

[The court then addressed the lawyer's failure to communicate with the Bar regarding the allegations of and investigation into ethical violations.]

IV. FACTORS TO BE CONSIDERED IN MITIGATION OF DISCIPLINE

Mitigating circumstances may be considered in the process of assessing the appropriate quantum of discipline. Respondent has raised several factors in mitigation

Respondent submits medical proof that he suffered from *occupational burnout*[40] diagnosed by his physician during the time of the breach. When the condition is

---

[22] "Professional competence — *i.e.*, acting promptly in pending matters and communicating with a client — is a *mandatory obligation* imposed upon licensed practitioners. Albeit onerous, this obligation is the *very minimum* to be expected from a lawyer. It epitomizes professionalism. Anything less is a breach of a lawyer's duty to serve the client."

[40] *Professional burnout syndrome* has been used in bar disciplinary matters either as a defense or as a mitigating factor. *See State ex rel. Okla. Bar Ass'n v. Wolfe*, 919 P.2d 427 (lawyer's license to practice law was suspended for two years and one day despite the use of *burnout* as a defense); *In re Conduct of Loew*, 642 P.2d 1171 (Ore. 1982) (a lawyer's license was suspended for thirty days despite the court's recognition of burnout as mitigating factor for neglect of a legal matter and for misrepresentation to a client); *In re Ontell*, 593 A.2d 1038, 1042 (D.C. 1991) (a lawyer's license was suspended for thirty days for two instances of neglect of legal matters coupled with misrepresentation to clients despite the court's recognition of *burnout* as a mitigating factor). In *Loew, supra*, 642 P.2d at 1173, the respondent's psychiatrist described the condition as follows:

> A number of things occur when somebody has reached this so[-]called burn out point. They feel fatigue all the time, they have difficulty sleeping, they feel drained, may have an array of physical ailments which occur which are quite real, maybe hospitalized as you were, have memory lapses, impaired concentration, frequently miss deadlines, backlog of work, financial problems, begin to view patients or clients or whatever people you're working with, or you begin to view your work as the enemy and 'Oh, my God, here comes another patient, another client,' and so on. Rather than someone who is a team member, it's an opponent.

In Judith L. Maute, *Balanced Lives in a Stressful Profession: an Impossible Dream?* 21 Cap. U. L. Rev. 797, 812 n. 54 (1992), the author observes that in many discipline cases evidence of burnout results in neglect, citing in footnote 54:

> *In re Sullivan*, 530 A.2d 1115 (Del. 1987) (lawyer disbarred for pattern of serious misconduct; court rejected claim of mental incompetence); *Colorado v. Heilbrunn*, 814 P.2d 819 (Colo. 1991) (repeated instances of neglect related to lawyer's severe chronic depression which led to drug and alcohol abuse). A number of articles have been written on the subject. *See, e.g.,* Michael J. Sweeney, *Stress, Anxiety & Burnout*, Practical Skills Seminar (1989); Thomas L. Cory, *Stress: How it Affects Trial Lawyers and Their Clients*, 24 TRIAL 54–57 (May 1988); Sarah B. Singer, *Stress and the Sole Practitioner Hard Times for Lawyers*, Boston B. J., Nov-Dec. 1987 at 16; Stress Takes Heavy Toll on Profession . . . [B. Leader

tendered as a mitigating factor for assessment of one's culpability there must be a causal relationship between a medical condition and the professional charged. *Yet emotional or psychological disability, though it may serve to reduce the actor's ethical culpability, does not immunize one from imposition of disciplinary measures that are necessary to protect the public.* The record provides a sufficient causal connection between respondent's ethical lapses and his professional burnout syndrome. His condition is now believed by his physician to have been arrested. Respondent continues to be seen once a week as part of an ongoing counseling program.

Shortly after he became aware of his inability fully to serve his clients respondent sought to correct certain deficiencies in the way his office was managed by closing out his private practice and joining an assemblage of practitioners who can assist him.

Respondent has been a member of the bar for over 19 years and his professional record reflects neither previous blemishes nor a pattern of misconduct.[43] He has acknowledged and accepted responsibility for his professional derelictions. The record shows that respondent's actions caused no grave economic harm. We note that respondent's dealings with the Bar, *albeit* dilatory during the initial investigative stages, were characterized by candor and cooperation during the latter stages and in the PRT proceedings.

V. RESPONDENT'S MISCONDUCT WARRANTS A LICENSE SUSPENSION FOR THIRTY (30) DAYS TOGETHER WITH PAYMENT OF THE COSTS OF THIS PROCEEDING

A bar disciplinary process, including that for imposition of a disciplinary sanction, is designed not to punish the delinquent lawyer, but to safeguard the interests of the public, of the judiciary, and of the legal profession. Neglect of a lawyer's responsibilities compromises the independence of the profession and the public interest which that independence serves. A license to practice law is not conferred for the benefit of an individual, but for that of the public. The disciplinary measure imposed upon an offending lawyer should be consistent with the discipline imposed upon other practitioners for similar acts of professional misconduct.

A lawyer's failure to respond to the bar's investigative inquiries is a serious offense. This court in *State ex rel. Oklahoma Bar Association v. Robb* imposed a suspension of two years and one day for a lawyer's *failure to respond to three client*

Sept.–Oct. 1990, at 19]; Marion R. Frank, *How to Avoid Burnout*, Penn. L.J. Rep., March 7, 1988, at § 2.

In Charles J. Ogletree, Jr. *Beyond Justifications: Seeking Motivations to Sustain Public Defenders*, 106 Harv. L. Rev. 1239, 1241 n.9 (1993), the author states:

> Burnout has been studied empirically in various contexts. *See, e.g.*, Deborah L. Arron, RUNNING FROM THE LAW: WHY GOOD LAWYERS ARE GETTING OUT OF THE LEGAL PROFESSION 2-3 (1989); Barry A. Farber, CRISIS IN EDUCATION: STRESS AND BURNOUT IN THE AMERICAN TEACHER 24 (1991) ("Burnout is a work related syndrome that stems from an individual's perceptions of a significant discrepancy between effort (input) and reward (output).. . . . It occurs most often in those who work face to face with troubled or needy *clients.. . .*" *(emphasis omitted))*; Paul Ligda, *Work Overload and Defender Burnout*, 35 NLADA Briefcase 5, 5 (1977) (noting the effects of working environment on public defender performance).. . .

[43] A lawyer's good character, reputation and exemplary professional standing are factors to be considered in mitigation of charges.

grievances or appear for depositions in response to subpoenas and for failure to respond to the disciplinary complaint.

The trial panel recommends a private reprimand as a fit discipline for respondent's breach of professional ethics. After a review of the record and the court's acceptance of the tendered mitigating factors, we hold that the appropriate disciplinary measure to be imposed is a thirty-day suspension of license to practice law. Today's decision is based upon the cumulative effect of the following factors: (1) respondent's utter failure *promptly* to respond to the bar's investigative inquires, (2) his lack of concern for a client's economic interest by *refusal promptly* to account for and restore the unearned portion of fees for nearly a three-year period and (3) his *disregard* for a client's right to know the status of her case. Although we take note that upon his own initiative respondent sought to determine if there was an underlying cause for his apathy and lost sense of career satisfaction and now seeks professional counseling on a continual basis, the standards to be followed are those that best protect the public and not those that shield the offending lawyer.

* * *

NOTES

1.   Note the *Schraeder* court's characterization of the effect of one lawyer's neglect of a client matter on the "independence of the profession." There is a relationship between society's impression of lawyers and the ability of the profession to maintain the law as an institution. As one scholar notes:

> The large gulf between society's respect for the law as an institution and society's growing disrespect for lawyers threatens the very institution of law itself. Undoubtedly, unethical and unprofessional conduct has led to a serious decline in public respect for the legal profession. Public respect for the legal system is necessary for the acceptance of judicial decisions; in order to maintain public respect, it is essential to maintain high standards of lawyer conduct.

Allen K. Harris, *The Professionalism Crisis — The 'Z' Word and Other Rambo Tactics: The Conference of Chief Justices' Solution*, 53 S.C. L. Rev. 549, 558–559 (2002) (citations omitted). Given these characterizations, the profession as a whole would be well-served by a renewed, collective sense of responsibility to the client and the ethical obligations associated with serving those clients.

2.   The *Schraeder* court acknowledges professional burnout syndrome and the fact that Schraeder affirmatively sought assistance for this condition. Did the existence of the condition mitigate Schraeder's discipline?

3.   What type of circumstances do warrant mitigation in disciplinary proceedings based on a failure to communicate? Courts have favorably recognized an otherwise unblemished professional record, an appropriate response to disciplinary proceedings, significant ill health and/or personal and financial problems, and the youth of the attorney as factors favoring mitigation of sanctions. *See generally Failure to Communicate with Client as Basis for Disciplinary Action Against Attorney*, 80 A.L.R.3d 1240 (1977).

However, many courts reject ill health, depression, and drug and alcohol dependencies as excusing client neglect. For example, in *Grove v State Bar of*

California, 427 P.2d 164 (1967) the court rejected a lawyer's argument that his failure to communicate with clients was mitigated by psychological problems. The court stated:

> While we sympathize with petitioner's psychological difficulties and commend him on his frankness in recognizing his problems, we cannot find that the psychiatric report states any grounds for excusing him from observation of at least the minimum standards of professional conduct. We realize that in many cases psychoneurotic problems may underlie professional misconduct and moral turpitude. In this area our duty lies in the assurance that the public will be protected in the performance of the high duties of the attorney rather than in an analysis of the reasons for his delinquency. Our primary concern must be the fulfillment of proper professional standards, whatever the unfortunate cause, emotional or otherwise, for the attorney's failure to do so.

Id. at 167. Similarly, in *Stark County Bar Asso. v Lukens*, 357 N.E.2d 1083 (1976), the court rejected a lawyer's contention that physical and emotional problems justified mitigation in a disciplinary proceeding. Noting that the argument "gives rise to the basic question of whether a member of the legal profession should continue to hold himself out as an attorney in general practice, undertaking new and possibly complicated cases, when he has full knowledge of his condition and its attendant problems," the court concluded "If a lawyer cannot stand the rigors of an active general practice due to his health problems, he should not be permitted to maintain a posture of competency and availability as regards the general public." *Id.* at 1089.

4. What is the lawyer's obligation when a demanding client makes repeated requests for information? Model Rule 1.4(a)(4) requires that the lawyer "promptly comply with reasonable requests for information." Some clients can be particularly demanding. In *In re Schoeneman*, 777 A.2d 259 (D.C. 2001), the court considered a client complaint that her lawyer had not returned her phone calls for a period of three weeks. The court concluded:

> An attorney need not communicate with a client as often as the client would like, as long as the attorney's conduct was reasonable under the circumstances. . . . [The lawyer] had been keeping [the client] informed of the status of her case over an extended period of time. Given the nature of the matter — a long-term, complex fraud investigation coupled with extended negotiations — monthly conversations are not *prima facie* unreasonable. Nothing in the record points to any events or circumstances that would have required [the lawyer] to communicate with [the client] during the time that she was trying to reach him, or that she was not adequately informed of his efforts.

Id. at 264.

5. How often should the lawyer communicate with the client, particularly when little has happened with respect to the client's matter? In *In re Hallmark*, 831 A.2d 366 (D.C. 2003), the court explained the lawyer's obligation under the Model Rules as follows: "The guiding principle for evaluating conduct under Rule 1.4(a) 'is whether the lawyer fulfilled the client's 'reasonable . . . expectations for information.' . . . To meet that expectation, a lawyer not only must respond to client inquiries but also must initiate communications to provide information when

needed." *See* Model Rules of Prof'l Conduct R. 1.4(a) cmt. 1 (2008).

C.   Letter Writing: The Duty of Explanation and Candor

The Model Rules allocate authority between lawyer and client such that the client has authority over the objectives of the representation, while the lawyer is largely responsible for the means to that objective. In order for this interchange to be meaningful, the lawyer must adequately explain matters to the client. The rules explain:

> The client should have sufficient information to participate intelligently in decisions concerning the objectives of the representation and the means by which they are to be pursued, to the extent the client is willing and able to do so. Adequacy of communication depends in part on the kind of advice or assistance that is involved. . . . The guiding principle is that the lawyer should fulfill reasonable client expectations for information consistent with the duty to act in the client's best interests, and the client's overall requirements as to the character of representation.

Model Rules of Prof'l Conduct R. 1.4 cmt. 5 (2008). The duty of explanation may be modified in situations in which the client has a disability or is otherwise unable to understand the communication. Under Model Rule 1.4, "the information to be provided is that appropriate for a client who is a comprehending and responsible adult. However, fully informing the client according to this standard may be impracticable, for example, where the client is a child or suffers from diminished capacity." Model Rules of Prof'l Conduct R. 1.4 cmt. 6 (2008).

Further, in rendering advice, the lawyer has the obligation of candor to the client. This obligation includes the requirements that the lawyer deliver unpleasant news and that the lawyer explain matters so that the client can understand them. Model Rule 2.1 explains:

> Legal advice often involves unpleasant facts and alternatives that a client may be disinclined to confront. In presenting advice, a lawyer endeavors to sustain the client's morale and may put advice in as acceptable a form as honesty permits. However, a lawyer should not be deterred from giving candid advice by the prospect that the advice will be unpalatable to the client. . . . Advice couched in narrow legal terms may be of little value to a client, especially where practical considerations, such as cost or effects on other people, are predominant. Purely technical legal advice, therefore, can sometimes be inadequate. It is proper for a lawyer to refer to relevant moral and ethical considerations in giving advice. Although a lawyer is not a moral advisor as such, moral and ethical considerations impinge upon most legal questions and may decisively influence how the law will be applied.

Model Rules of Prof'l Conduct R. 2.1 cmts. 1-2 (2008). Thus, in preparing an advice letter, the lawyer should be cognizant of her responsibility to explain the advice adequately and to communicate deficiencies in the client's matter.

i.   Explanation

The Model Rules make clear that a lawyer has an obligation to explain matters to a client to the extent necessary to enable the client to participate in the representation. The duty to explain matters will vary depending upon the complexity of the matter and the level of understanding of the client.

Note that a failure with regard to the obligation to explain can give rise to sanctions under the ethical rules, and can also give rise to a claim of attorney malpractice. The court's analysis of an ethical violation differs distinctly, however, from its analysis of whether an attorney is liable for malpractice. Consider how the two claims differ. The following case outlines some differences between these two types of claims.

IN RE DISCIPLINARY ACTION AGAINST MCKECHNIE
656 N.W.2d 661 (N.D. 2003)

William E. McKechnie and Disciplinary Counsel have filed objections to a hearing panel's report and order of discipline suspending McKechnie from the practice of law for 30 days and ordering he pay costs of the disciplinary proceedings. . . . We conclude there is clear and convincing evidence McKechnie violated N.D.R. Prof. Conduct 1.4(b), and we order that he be publicly reprimanded and pay the costs of the disciplinary proceedings in the amount of $5,375.59.

McKechnie was admitted to practice law in North Dakota on October 5, 1981. On January 5, 1996, Dennis Follman retained McKechnie to investigate a possible discrimination or sexual harassment lawsuit he might have against his former employer, Upper Valley Special Education Unit ("Upper Valley"). McKechnie told Follman the statute of limitations on his claim would be three years from the date of Follman's June 2, 1995 resignation from Upper Valley. McKechnie had Follman sign an authorization so McKechnie could obtain Follman's personnel file from Upper Valley. At that time, Follman paid McKechnie $1,500, which McKechnie categorized in his records as $500 for costs and $1,000 for a retainer. No written fee agreement between McKechnie and Follman was executed.

McKechnie met with Follman in February 1996 and again told him he had three years from the date of his resignation to commence the lawsuit. Follman told McKechnie he was not ready to file the lawsuit at that time because "I wanted to take a look at some medical concerns . . . and I didn't want to have a conflict between the sexual harassment claim and the medical one at the time."

On October 10, 1996, McKechnie sent Follman a $500 check noted "retainer refund," but the check was unaccompanied by an explanatory letter. On January 17, 1997, Follman sent a letter to McKechnie requesting an itemized billing for the $1,000 he had paid in 1996. Follman also informed McKechnie he anticipated that McKechnie could still represent him in his lawsuit against his former employer and that he had not hired another attorney. Following the April 1997 Grand Forks flood, McKechnie wrote Follman a letter on June 16, 1997, stating: It has been several months since we heard from you and I would like to touch base with you with regard to representation of your claim. We have now reach [sic] a sense of normalcy in Grand Forks and I am ready to proceed on your behalf. Please contact me at your earliest convenience to discuss.

In May 1998, Follman wrote a letter to McKechnie advising him that he wanted to resume his case against Upper Valley. McKechnie and Follman then entered into a written fee agreement providing for a contingent fee if a recovery was obtained in the sexual harassment case.

In late May 1998, Follman sued Upper Valley. The trial court dismissed the lawsuit, concluding Follman's claims were barred by the three-year statute of limitations because Follman discovered the facts which formed the basis of his claim in January 1995. This Court affirmed.

A petition for discipline was filed against McKechnie in June 2001. Following a hearing, the hearing panel found McKechnie violated N.D.R. Prof. Conduct 1.1, which states that a lawyer shall provide competent representation, and N.D.R. Prof. Conduct 1.4(b), which states that a lawyer shall explain matters related to the representation to the extent reasonably necessary to permit the client to make informed decisions. The panel recommended that McKechnie be suspended from the practice of law for 30 days and that he pay the costs of the disciplinary proceedings. McKechnie and Disciplinary Counsel filed objections with this Court.

*   *   *

McKechnie argues there is no evidence that McKechnie violated any of the ethical rules in this case because Disciplinary Counsel presented no expert evidence of the applicable standard of care to support the charges. McKechnie presented expert testimony of a trial attorney who opined that McKechnie's actions in accepting $1,500 to investigate the claim during the initial consultation, in advising Follman about the statute of limitations, and in his response to Follman's correspondence, met the applicable standard of care under the circumstances. The expert witness also testified an attorney-client relationship did not exist until the written fee agreement was executed in May 1998. Disciplinary Counsel argues the hearing panel should not have admitted this testimony.

We have said that expert testimony regarding the interpretation of the rules of professional conduct and whether a rule has been violated is inappropriate in a disciplinary proceeding. Interpretation of the rules of professional conduct, like interpretation of statutes, is a question of law for a court to decide. . . .

Although expert testimony is generally necessary in a legal malpractice action to establish the professional's standard of care and whether the professional's conduct in a particular case deviated from that standard of care, expert testimony on the standard of care required in a malpractice action is not required to aid the trier of fact in determining whether an attorney's actions violate the rules of professional conduct. Disciplinary proceedings differ significantly, both procedurally and substantively, from civil legal malpractice actions. *See Olson v. Fraase*, 421 N.W.2d 820, 828 (N.D.1988) (holding although conduct proscribed by a rule of professional conduct may also be relevant in determining whether an attorney has breached a civil duty an attorney owes a client, a violation of the rules does not itself form the basis for a claim for relief against a wrongdoing attorney). Whereas the rules of professional conduct set a minimum level of conduct with the consequence of disciplinary action, malpractice liability is premised upon the conduct of the reasonable lawyer under the particular circumstances. *See Matter of Disciplinary Action Against Jaynes*, 267 N.W.2d 782, 784 (N.D.1978) (stating the "fact that an injured party may recover from a lawyer in a malpractice action is in itself not sufficient to maintain the necessary high standard"). In *In re Disciplinary Action*

Against Howe, 621 N.W.2d 361, we rejected an argument that expert evidence of the standard of care is necessary to support charges in a disciplinary proceeding and quoted the hearing panel's resolution of the issue with approval: In this case the standard of care is set forth in the rules themselves. There is no issue as to what the standard of care is. There is no dispute as to the interpretation of the standard of care, nor is the standard that of what a reasonably competent attorney might do under the same or similar circumstances.

As the court stated in *In re Conduct of Leonard*, 784 P.2d 95, 100 (1989), expert witness testimony under these circumstances "amount[s] to nothing more than an oral brief as to why one particular construction of the governing disciplinary rule would not be violated by a particular hypothetical set of facts. . . ."

We conclude Disciplinary Counsel was not required to present expert testimony of the standard of care to support the charges in this case. We further conclude the expert testimony presented by McKechnie was not necessary to "assist the trier of fact to understand the evidence or to determine a fact in issue." . . .

* * *

McKechnie argues there is no clear and convincing evidence that he violated N.D.R. Prof. Conduct 1.1, which provides: A lawyer shall provide competent representation to a client. Competent representation requires the legal knowledge, skill, thoroughness and preparation reasonably necessary for the representation.

Disciplinary Counsel's theory for the violation is straightforward. McKechnie advised Follman in 1996 that Follman had three years from the date he resigned from Upper Valley to file the suit under the North Dakota Human Rights Act, N.D.C.C. ch. 14-02.4. However, under the Act, Follman's suit had to be filed within three years of the last discriminatory incident. Because McKechnie gave Follman incorrect legal advice about the statute of limitations, which resulted in Follman's case being dismissed, Disciplinary Counsel argues McKechnie violated N.D.R. Prof. Conduct 1.1.

We note the California Supreme Court's concern over "the problems inherent in using disciplinary proceedings to punish attorneys for negligence, mistakes in judgment, or lack of experience or legal knowledge." We share that concern. In C. Wolfram, *Modern Legal Ethics* § 5.1, the author states: To date, the enforcement of competence standards has been generally limited to relatively exotic, blatant, or repeated cases of lawyer bungling. Lawyers who make some showing of effort, and who do nothing other than perform badly, rarely appear in the appellate reports in discipline cases. The lawyers who are disciplined for incompetence have usually aggravated their situation. For example, several cases involve lawyers who, after their incompetent work, concocted elaborate schemes or lies to deceive a client whose case was mishandled. Most decisions and official ABA policy insist that a single instance of "ordinary negligence" is usually not a disciplinary violation, although some decisions hold a lawyer to a standard of ordinary care that is similar to that required in malpractice cases . . . or discipline a lawyer for a single instance of neglect. Consistent with that position, courts will discipline lawyers when the neglect is accompanied by some other violation, as an impermissible conflict of interest, or when the acts of negligence are repeated.

We agree with the observation of the Arizona Supreme Court in *Matter of Curtis*, 908 P.2d 472, 477–78 (1995): Neither failure to achieve a successful result nor mere negligence in the handling of a case will necessarily constitute an ER 1.1 violation. We recognize the important distinction between conduct by an attorney that is simply negligent and conduct that rises to the level of an ethical violation. Clearly, the Bar must be vigilant in guarding the rights of clients, "but care should be taken to avoid the use of disciplinary action . . . as a substitute for what is essentially a malpractice action." Thus, although not every negligent act violates an ethical rule, neglect in investigating the facts and law necessary to present a client's claim crosses the fine line between simple neglect and conduct warranting discipline. *See also The Florida Bar v. Neale*, 384 So.2d 1264, 1265 (Fla.1980) (stating the "rights of clients should be zealously guarded by the bar, but care should be taken to avoid the use of disciplinary action . . . as a substitute for what is essentially a malpractice action"); *In re Complaint as to Conduct of Gygi*, 273 Or. 443, 541 P.2d 1392, 1396 (1975) (stating "we are not prepared to hold that isolated instances of ordinary negligence are alone sufficient to warrant disciplinary action"); *Committee on Legal Ethics v. Mullins*, 159 W.Va. 647, 226 S.E.2d 427, 430 (1976) (stating "[c]harges of isolated errors of judgment or malpractice in the ordinary sense of negligence would normally not justify the intervention of the ethics committee"), *overruled on other grounds, Committee on Legal Ethics v. Cometti*, 189 W.Va. 262, 430 S.E.2d 320, 330 (1993); 1 R. Mallen and J. Smith, *Legal Malpractice* § 1.9, at p. 45 (5th ed.2000) (stating "[o]rdinary negligence should not warrant discipline").

Our caselaw accords with this view. In *In re Disciplinary Action Against Nassif*, 504 N.W.2d 311 (N.D.1993), this Court publicly reprimanded for a violation of N.D.R. Prof. Conduct 1.1 a lawyer who, among other things, allowed a statute of limitations to run on a client's claim. However, *Nassif* involved more than an isolated instance of ordinary negligence. In *Nassif*, 504 N.W.2d at 312, 315, the lawyer was "oblivious [] to the statute of limitation," was unaware of the date of the client's injury, failed to communicate with the client, and when the client sought to change representation for her claim, the lawyer told her "he was still entitled to 'my share of the money,'" and would continue to handle her claim. In *In re Disciplinary Action Against Orvik*, 549 N.W.2d 671 (N.D.1996), we accepted a stipulation for discipline where the lawyer violated N.D.R. Prof. Conduct 1.1 and other rules by failing to file an action within the time required by the applicable statute of limitations and by failing to inform the client of the legal significance of the error until almost five years after the lawyer was hired to bring the action.

In this case, McKechnie gave Follman incorrect legal advice about the statute of limitations and Follman's case was dismissed for failure to file within the limitations period. This evidence shows nothing more than an isolated instance of ordinary negligence, or error of judgment. We conclude there is no clear and convincing evidence that McKechnie violated N.D.R. Prof. Conduct 1.1.

McKechnie argues there is no clear and convincing evidence that he violated N.D.R. Prof. Conduct 1.4(b), which provides: (b) A lawyer shall explain matters related to the representation to the extent reasonably necessary to permit the client to make informed decisions.

The record shows McKechnie's contacts with Follman regarding the lawsuit were sporadic and, at times, confusing. McKechnie mailed Follman a $500 "retainer refund" without any further explanation. The advice McKechnie did provide regarding the statute of limitations was incorrect. Although Follman told McKechnie of the dates incidents of harassment occurred at Upper Valley, McKechnie did not advise Follman during the ensuing two and one-half years that an action would have to be filed within three years from the date of the alleged wrongdoing. McKechnie argues that he gave Follman a copy of the applicable statute of limitations which would have advised him of the applicable limitations period. However, Follman paid McKechnie for his legal expertise and advice, and McKechnie could not satisfy his duty to explain matters related to the representation by simply providing Follman with a copy of the applicable statute, particularly when McKechnie specifically advised Follman he had until three years after his resignation to bring suit.

We conclude there is clear and convincing evidence that McKechnie violated N.D.R. Prof. Conduct 1.4(b).

*   *   *

The violation of N.D.R. Prof. Conduct 1.4(b) is premised on McKechnie's failure to correctly advise Follman about the statute of limitations and the status of the representation. Rule 4.53, N.D. Stds. Imposing Lawyer Sanctions, provides:

> 4.53 Reprimand is generally appropriate when a lawyer: (a) demonstrates failure to understand relevant legal doctrines or procedures and causes injury or potential injury to a client.

We believe a public reprimand is an appropriate sanction under the circumstances. Although prior disciplinary offenses are aggravating factors under N.D. Stds. Imposing Lawyer Sanctions 9.22(a), we do not view McKechnie's prior admonitions as warranting a sanction more severe than a public reprimand.

*   *   *

NOTES

1. The *McKechnie* court notes that expert testimony may be relevant to determine whether an attorney deviated from an established standard of care in a malpractice action, but that such testimony is not relevant to determining whether an attorney violated an ethical rule. What is the basis for this distinction?

2. Consider the court's discussion of the distinction between lawyer mistake or negligence and a violation of an ethical standard. Which is a higher standard? Why?

3. How did McKechnie fail in his duty of communication and explanation?

ii.   Candor

Lawyers often communicate advice to clients in letters. To the extent that the Model Rules require the advice to be candid, the lawyer has the obligation to discuss potential adverse consequences. Indeed, the comments to Model Rule 2.1 make clear that the lawyer "should not be deterred from giving candid advice by the prospect that the advice will be unpalatable to the client." Model Rules of Prof'l Conduct R. 2.1 cmt. 1 (2008).

iii.   Scope of Advice

To the extent that a lawyer communicates her advice regarding a legal matter to the client, the lawyer has an obligation to be thorough and to explain matters to the client carefully so that the client can reasonably participate in the representation. Indeed, as the court explained in *McKechnie*, clients pay lawyers for their expertise and advice. The scope of advice necessary to direct a client varies with respect to the matter at issue. Model Rule 2.1 notes that a lawyer's advice may include reference to "moral, economic, social and political factors [] that may be relevant to the client's situation." With regard to the scope of advice required by the rule, the comments explain that "[p]urely technical legal advice [] may be inadequate" and that "the lawyer's responsibility as advisor may include indicating that more may be involved [in a matter] than strictly legal considerations." Model Rules of Prof'l Conduct R. 2.1 cmts. 2–3 (2008). Moreover, in terms of the lawyer's responsibility to offer advice not requested by the client, the comments explain that the rules on communication, together with rules regarding the lawyer's role as an advisor, may give rise to a duty to provide advice even where not solicited by the client, such as where the "lawyer knows that a client proposes a course of action that is likely to result in substantial adverse consequences to the client." Model Rules of Prof'l Conduct R. 2.1 cmt. 5 (2008).

The following case addresses the obligation of a lawyer to provide advice beyond that which is specifically requested by the client. The case involves a lawyer who represents a trustee in a bankruptcy proceeding. Pay particular attention to the court's discussion of the scope of advice required of the lawyer.

IN RE CONSUPAK, INC.
87 B.R. 529 (Bkrtcy. N.D. Ill. 1988)

This matter is before the Court on application of various counsel and the Trustee for fees, and on the Court's own motion to consider whether Trustee Edward Limperis (the "Trustee") should be surcharged for mismanaging part of the funds of this estate. As described below, substantial sums of money have been held in a noninterest-bearing checking account throughout the course of this case. . . . There were several issues [before the court]: (1) whether Trustee had a duty to invest the estate's idle funds; (2) whether the Trustee breached such duty; and (3) if such duty existed and was breached, whether Trustee should be surcharged for the interest lost by reason of such breach. In addition to affidavits, evidence heard, and reports filed by the Trustee, the Court has considered memoranda and argument of counsel regarding *inter alia* whether they had a duty to counsel the Trustee with regard to the investment of the estate's funds.

*   *   *

[On October 11, 1977 Consupak, Inc. ("Debtor") filed a petition for reorganization under the Bankruptcy Act (the "Act"). The proceeding was subsequently converted to a liquidation. Edward Limperis, an experienced trustee who had handled an estimated 1,200 to 1,500 cases, was appointed Trustee. Joseph Matz was selected as the attorney for the Trustee (the "Trustee's Attorney").

The Trustee liquidated most of the Debtor's assets in early 1979. The greater portion of sale proceeds were initially certificates of deposit ("CD's"). At the end of 1979, over 95% of the estate's cash was invested at interest.

In order to meet the estate's cash needs from 1980 to 1983, the Trustee reduced the estate's investment in CDs and moved most funds to a noninterest-bearing checking account. From 1980 to 1986, the investments at interest decreased substantially while the noninterest-bearing checking account balance grew.

The bankruptcy court conducted a status hearing in 1986 and immediately directed the Trustee to move the estate's funds from the noninterest-bearing accounts to investments at interest. The Trustee was also directed to prepare a report of all estate investments and a hearing was set on the report. In the Trustee's report he presented evidence that it was common practice of bankruptcy trustee to remove funds from interest at the time of filing the Final Report of the bankruptcy.]

At the hearing held June 18, 1987, Trustee's counsel basically reiterated the statements of the Trustee's affiants and argued that this District's local bankruptcy rules did not impose on the Trustee any duty to invest idle funds of the estate.

* * *

This Court concludes for reasons set forth below that the Trustee at all times had a duty to seek Court permission to invest all funds in excess of a reasonable reserve to meet immediate expenses and unpaid dividends due to be paid to creditors, and a duty to do so in precise obedience to our Local Bankruptcy Rule. In the interim between June 1, 1983 and the filing of the Filing Report on September 29, 1986, the Trustee breached that duty by leaving several hundreds of thousands of dollars in a noninterest-bearing account from time to time. The Trustee was entitled to rely both on the wording of the Local Bankruptcy Rule (which required investment except during the 90-day period prior to distribution of assets) and the advice of the Clerk's Office (which normally closed its cases during the same 90-day period after the Final Report was filed). However, once this unusually large and complex case was not closed after the 90 days had passed, he was under a duty to reinvest or obtain court order to excuse himself from doing so if there was any good reason not to do so. By failing to reinvest or seek court leave to withhold estate funds from investment more than 90 days after the filing of the Final Report, the Trustee further breached his duty. Trustee's duty to invest was a corollary of Trustee's duty to maximize the estate for the benefit of creditors. His breaches of that duty over the years were both deliberate and negligent.

Trustee's Attorney also had a fiduciary duty to the estate and its creditors. Trustee's Attorney was aware of the Trustee's disinvestment after the Final Report and he had a duty to counsel the Trustee regarding the duty to invest. Counsel has argued the same "practice" of disinvestment as did the Trustee. However, he had a fiduciary duty to inquire into the status of investment and to counsel Trustee to invest except during the 90 days after Final Report was filed, unless otherwise excused or directed by the Court. Breach of that duty by such counsel lessens the value of his services for which compensation may be awarded.

This opinion addresses, in turn, the duty of the Trustee and the attorney for the Trustee. . . .

* * *

DUTY OF TRUSTEE'S ATTORNEY TO ADVISE TRUSTEE REGARDING INVESTMENT OF ESTATE'S FUNDS

All parties seeking compensation from a bankruptcy estate may be held to fiduciary standards. Those performing duties in the administration of a bankrupt estate are not acting as private individuals, but as officers of the court. As such, they are expected to render loyal and disinterested service in the interest of those for whom they purport to act.

Among the fiduciaries of a bankruptcy estate are the various attorneys who may be compensated from the estate. Similarly, the fiduciary duties of counsel for a bankruptcy trustee have been held to be "equivalent" to those of the trustee.

This does not mean that counsel for a trustee is to undertake the administrative responsibilities of the trustee. An attorney may only be compensated as an attorney for services requiring legal expertise. Where counsel does not so limit his services, this Court would accordingly deny him professional compensation. Thus, while both a trustee and his attorney are fiduciaries, they do not perform the same functions in a bankruptcy case.

In this case, Trustee's Attorney stresses the distinction between the functions of a bankruptcy trustee and his attorney. He correctly asserts that a trustee has primary responsibility for administering the estate and may seek legal advice when necessary. On the other hand, Trustee's Attorney would limit his own role to rendering legal advice upon request. Under this interpretation of duty, unless a trustee takes the initiative to seek his attorney's advice, the attorney would have no duty to counsel the trustee. As applied to his own case, Trustee's Attorney argues that he had no duty to render unsolicited advice regarding the investment of funds.

Trustee's Attorney misstates his duty. Besides serving as agent of a bankruptcy trustee, counsel for a trustee is a fiduciary of the estate. As a result, the attorney's contractual obligation to respond to requests from his client for legal advice is only part of his broader fiduciary duty to the estate. The fact that counsel fulfilled the obligation to advise his client upon request does not establish satisfactory performance of his overall fiduciary duty.

The Court also takes issue with assertion by Trustee's Attorney that "counsel for trustee was under no obligation to counsel [Trustee] to act in any manner inconsistent with the practice followed by other trustees and by the Bankruptcy Court Clerk's office in this district." As earlier discussed, the existence of custom does not establish the standard of care by which trustee's actions should be judged. Certainly, counsel should never advise trustees to act with disregard for their duties to the estate regardless of what others do or don't do.

In evaluating the performance of a trustee's attorney, then, it is necessary to determine the extent of duty to advise a trustee. The lower bounds of that duty are obvious: any attorney must, at a minimum, respond to client requests for legal advice. Because a trustee's attorney also has duties to the estate and to the court, however, the duty to advise requires a more active concern for the interests of the estate and of its beneficiaries, the unsecured creditors.

A trustee's attorney cannot close his eyes to matters having legal consequences for the estate. Especially where legally adverse facts come to his attention, the attorney for a trustee must take the initiative to inform his client of the need for preventative or corrective action. In the case of uninvested funds, this means that the attorney must remind the trustee of the latter's duty to invest or seek court direction. At a minimum, the attorney should advise the trustee to consider whether investment at interest would yield a net benefit to the estate. In this case, the attorney was obliged to know of the Local Rule and to counsel the Trustee to obey it.

The principles underlying this conclusion are not set forth in bankruptcy statutes or rules. Rather, they are derived from ethical norms governing the practice of law. In particular, the Court looks to the American Bar Association Model Code of Professional Responsibility (the "ABA Code") and the American Bar Association Model Rules of Professional Conduct (the "Model Rules").

"As the profession's own expression of its ethical standards, the [ABA] Code of Professional Responsibility, Ethical Considerations, and Disciplinary Rules provide substantial guidance to federal courts in evaluating the conduct of attorneys appearing before them." "The ABA Code has long been the established norm for guiding ethical conduct in the federal courts of this district." Besides the ABA Code, a federal court may consider the Model Rules in evaluating the professional conduct of attorneys appearing before them.

Those portions of the ABA Code dealing with the duty to advise clients fall under Canon 7, which states that: "[a] lawyer should represent a client zealously within the bounds of the law." Model Code of Professional Responsibility Canon 7 (1981). At a minimum, Disciplinary Rule 7- 101(A)(1) provides that: "[a] lawyer shall not intentionally [f]ail to seek the lawful objectives of his client through reasonable means permitted by the law. . . ." Model Code of Professional Responsibility DR 7-101(A)(1) (1981).

Ideally, an attorney will take the role of active advisor, as set forth in Ethical Consideration 7–8:

> A lawyer should exert his best efforts to insure that decisions of his client are made only after the client has been informed of relevant considerations. A lawyer ought to initiate this decision-making process if the client does not do so. Advice of a lawyer to his client need not be confined to purely legal considerations. A lawyer should advise his client of the possible effect of each legal alternative. A lawyer should bring to bear upon this decision-making process the fullness of his experience as well as his objective viewpoint. In assisting his client to reach a proper decision, it is often desirable for a lawyer to point out those factors which may lead to a decision that is morally just as well as legally permissible. . . .

Model Code of Professional Responsibility EC 7–8 (1981).

The Model Rules reiterate the proposition that an attorney is to facilitate informed decision-making by his client. This obligation stems from the attorney's role as advisor and is part of the continuing obligation to communicate with clients. Although lacking authority of the Model Rules themselves, comment 5 to Rule 2.1 specifically addresses the circumstances in which an attorney should take initiative in offering advice to a client:

> In general, a lawyer is not expected to give advice until asked by the client. However, when a lawyer knows that a client proposes a course of action that is likely to result in substantial adverse legal consequences to a client, duty to a client under Rule 1.4 may require that the lawyer act if the client's course of action is related to the representation. A lawyer ordinarily has no duty to initiate investigation of a client's affairs or to give advice that

the client has indicated is unwanted, but a lawyer may initiate advice to a client when doing so appears to be in the client's interest.

Model Rules of Professional Conduct Rule 2.1, comment 5 (1983).

The foregoing suggests that an attorney should, on his own initiative, offer legal advice in two circumstances: (1) when the client is unaware of the potentially adverse legal consequences of a proposed course of action, and (2) where the offering of advice would be in the client's best interests. In so doing the attorney would further Canon 7's objective of zealous client representation. Nowhere in the above-cited standards is there any suggestion that a responsible attorney is a passive observer who can remain silent in the face of a client's legally unacceptable decisions.

These principles are applicable here because Trustee's Attorney was aware that the Trustee had removed funds from interest after September 29, 1986. Both reasons for offering advice were present. First, the Trustee was allegedly unaware of his duty to invest and the potentially adverse legal consequences of disinvestment. Second, it was certainly in the estate's best interests to maximize the estate through investment. Thus, because Trustee's Attorney knew of the Trustee's disinvestment after the Final Report was filed, he was under an ethical obligation to advise his client of the duty to re-invest or at least seek Court direction. And he certainly was under an obligation to know of the Local Rule that he now disclaims awareness of.

Violation of an ethical obligation lessens the value of an attorney's services to his client. An omission to duty may result in denial or reduction of attorney's fees. Accordingly, the Court will order an appropriate reduction in the fees to be paid Trustee's Attorney. In this case, the reduction will consist of one-half of the lost interest for the period after the Final Report was filed (one-half of $22,619) or $11,309.50.

NOTES

1.   The *Consupak* court's analysis of the lawyer's duty to advise was illustrated by the circumstances of the case and the fact that both the lawyer and the trustee had fiduciary duties to the estate. Was the lawyer's affirmative duty to advise distinct to the bankruptcy setting?

2.   Under what circumstances does a lawyer have the obligation to initiate advice that has not been solicited by the client? What is the reasonable extent of such a duty? In *Kurtenbach v. TeKippe*, 260 N.W.2d 53 (Iowa 1977), the court explained:

> In determining the scope of the attorney's duty, courts must give effect to the fiduciary role of the attorney and the heavy responsibility this imposes on him to represent and protect the client's interests with respect to the subject matter of the employment. . . . However, the attorney's duty to represent and protect his client does not extend beyond reasonable bounds. Specifically, when a question arises as in the present case about the extent of a lawyer's duty to investigate or inquire about a client's transaction, the following principles are applicable:

> Under certain circumstances it may be the duty of the lawyer to investigate the facts applicable to a transaction and report the results to the client. . . . If the attorney should have inquired concerning the facts and did not, the client cannot be said to have been negligent in failing to disclose said facts. . . . However, an attorney need not inquire into matters that do not pertain to the discharge of duties that he has undertaken. . . . Likewise, an attorney need not make inquiry where the responsibility of the matter is assumed by the client.

Id. at 56–57 (citations omitted).

II. FORMAT AND PRACTICE CONSIDERATIONS

Client letters are informal correspondence and therefore vary according to the client and the matter at issue. Notwithstanding, there are a few ethical or professional considerations that influence the format, tone, and preparation of the letters. The duty of candor under Model Rule 2.1 requires that the advice rendered to a client in the form of a letter be accessible to the client. Comment 2 to Model Rule 2.1 notes that "Advice couched in narrow legal terms may be of little value to the client [and] [p]urely technical legal advice . . . can be inadequate." Model Rules of Prof'l Conduct R. 2.1 cmt. 2 (2008).

In addition, the duty to communicate in a manner accessible to the client may influence the form of a client letter. As the comments to Rule 1.4 acknowledge, "Adequacy of communication depends in part on the kind of advice or assistance that is involved." Model Rules of Prof'l Conduct R. 1.4 cmt. 5 (2008). The requirement under Model Rule 1.3 to represent clients diligently coupled with Model Rule 1.4's acknowledgement that "regular communication with clients [serves to] minimize the occasions on which a client will need to request information" suggests that lawyers would be well-served to communicate regularly with clients. Model Rules of Prof'l Conduct R. 1.4 cmt. 4 (2008). Indeed, to the extent that the client has a right to be kept informed regarding the status of her matter and has the need to be able to participate in the representation, these rules should influence the letter-writing lawyer to present material in a form that the receiving client can understand and appreciate. Where the matter is highly complex or technical, the lawyer should make every effort to use accessible language to communicate legal advice.

Chapter 6

DEMAND LETTERS

In every legal document, underneath the story of the parties, is the story of the lawyer. The carefully-crafted document tells the story of a lawyer who respects her client, who embraces her role as an advocate and an officer of the court, and who expects the system to work because everyone is doing their best. The carelessly put-together document tells the story of a lawyer who is so lost that he hopes the client's story can save them both. Sadly, it almost never does.

> — Tracy L. McGaugh, Associate Professor of Legal Process,
> Touro Law Center

Demand letters are written once a lawyer determines that the client has a viable claim. A demand letter is typically a preliminary step before initiating a formal legal claim. In drafting a demand letter, the lawyer should first determine whether the opposing party is represented by counsel. If the opposing party is represented by counsel, the demand letter should be sent to the opposing party's lawyer. The demand letter should introduce the lawyer and client making the demand, should specifically set forth the factual and legal basis for the demand, and should set forth the consequences for noncompliance with the demand. To the extent that the demand letter is correspondence, there is no general format for the tone of the letter. The tone will likely be influenced by the personality of the lawyer who writes it, by the nature of the claim, and by the relationship between the issuing lawyer and the recipient of the letter. Regardless of these considerations, the tone should be professional and civil, notwithstanding any acrimony associated with the matter at hand.

I. CONTENT-BASED CONSIDERATIONS

A.   Overview

i.   Truthfulness

A lawyer has an obligation to communicate a demand on behalf of his client in a truthful manner, both with regard to the law and the facts relating to the demand. Model Rule 4.1 specifically prohibits a lawyer from making a false statement of material fact or law to a third person. With respect to revealing deficiencies in the demand, the comments explain that "[a] lawyer is required to be truthful when dealing with others on a client's behalf, but generally has no affirmative duty to inform an opposing party of relevant facts." Model Rules of Prof'l Conduct R. 4.1 cmt. 1 (2008). The obligation of truthfulness under the Model Code arises under DR 7-102(A)(5), which prohibits a lawyer from knowingly making false statements of law or fact.

ii.   Prohibition on Threatening Criminal Process in a Civil Matter

The Model Code contains an express prohibition against threatening criminal process in a civil matter. DR 7-105(A) provides "A lawyer shall not present, participate in presenting, or threaten to present criminal charges solely to obtain an advantage in a civil matter." The Model Rules have omitted this specific prohibition, but several relevant rules caution against the use of such threats except in fairly limited circumstances. The prohibitions are generally directed at the use of threats of criminal process against the opposing party. While not expressly prohibited, threats of criminal process against opposing counsel in an effort to gain advantage in a civil suit are implicitly restricted by the Model Rules, as well as the Model Code and relevant sections of state professional codes.

B.   Truthfulness

Model Rule 4.1 imposes upon a lawyer the obligation to be truthful. False statements in a demand letter may therefore give rise to sanctions under the ethical rules. Further, false statements concerning the opposing party's conduct can give rise to a claim of defamation.

Bear in mind that demand letters are written well before any discovery has taken place. Therefore, the lawyer's knowledge of the extent of the facts is limited. For this reason there is a commonly recognized privilege that protects a lawyer's statements made in the context of litigation. However, as the following case demonstrates, that privilege is not absolute.

NGUYEN v. PROTON TECHNOLOGY CORP.
69 Cal. App. 4th 140 (Cal. App. 1999)

This appeal presents the interesting issue of the extent to which the absolute litigation privilege provided by Civil Code section 47, subdivision (b),[1] protects statements made in pre-civil litigation demand letters or telephone calls which reflect discredit on individuals and are substantially extraneous to the threatened litigation. In reversing the summary judgment granted by the trial court in favor of the respondents, we hold that reasonable limits should and do exist on the type and character of prelitigation statements which are protected by the privilege.

FACTUAL AND PROCEDURAL BACKGROUND

Appellant [Nguyen] was employed as sales representative of respondent Proton Technology Corporation (Proton) from approximately August 1995 until March 1996. Proton is a Fremont-based manufacturer of printed circuit boards. At least as of December 1995, appellant was employed by Proton through the Santa Clara County Probation Department's Work Furlough Program. The only communication in the record to Proton from that department does not recite any offense committed by appellant which brought him to that probationary status, but respondents' appendix includes material establishing that appellant had, in 1995, pled guilty to shooting a gun at an unoccupied vehicle.

---

[1] Hereafter referred to simply as "section 47(b)."

In March 1996, appellant, along with several others, left Proton and became employed by a San Jose-based printed circuit board manufacturer, Excelsior Manufacturing, Inc. (Excelsior). Proton became concerned that Excelsior was improperly soliciting its employees and customers, and consulted its attorneys, respondent Pahl & Gosselin, about filing a lawsuit to stop Excelsior from so doing. Accordingly, respondent Fenn Horton III, a litigation attorney with Pahl & Gosselin, sent a fax letter to Manny Lee, the chief executive officer of Excelsior. Insofar as pertinent to this litigation, the letter read:

> This law firm represents Proton Technology Corporation on a continu-ing basis in matters involving litigation. This letter is to provide clear warning to you that your company's recent acts of unfair competition will not be tolerated. Specifically, your employee, Tam Le Ta, has been raiding Proton's employees to induce them to go to work for Excelsior. Tam began his raiding activities while he was still employed by Proton. The day after Tam began working for your company, approximately 20 of Proton's production employees left to follow Tam in going to work for your company. In addition, a former Proton sales representative, Vinh Phuc Nguyen, who recently began working for Excelsior, has been soliciting Proton's custom-ers to induce them to switch their business to Excelsior. Vinh also began his wrongful solicitations while he was still an employee of Proton. We think you should be aware that Vinh was working for Proton under a work furlough program sponsored by the Santa Clara County Probation Depart-ment. Vinh was in prison for repeatedly and violently assaulting his wife. . . . We have information to prove that Excelsior and these three former Proton employees were involved in a conspiracy to injure Proton's business in violation of California Business & Professions Code. Excelsior's complic-ity in the conduct of Tam and Vinh also gives rise to tort liability under various common law causes of action. Unless Excelsior's recent acts of unfair competition and misappropriation of trade secrets stops immedi-ately, Proton intends to take full advantage of all of its legal rights in filing a lawsuit against Excelsior and obtaining injunctive relief, compensatory damages, as well as punitive damages and the reimbursement of its attorney's fees. We trust that this warning will be sufficient to stop these recent acts of unfair competition.

This letter had been approved in advance by Proton's chief executive officer, Tony Wang. Indeed, it was Wang who advised Horton that appellant's conviction had been "for beating his wife."

On April 2, Excelsior's attorneys briefly responded to Horton's letter. This response recited an unfamiliarity with the details alleged by Horton, but generally denied his allegations of wrongdoing and requested that further communications to either Excelsior or any of its current employees be via them.

*   *   *

Also early in April, Horton received a report on appellant's criminal record. In the process, he learned that he had been mistaken regarding the crimes for which appellant had been convicted. Several weeks later, on April 22, he wrote Excelsior's attorneys as follows:

> This letter is to correct an error made in my letter to Manny Lee dated March 29, 1996, concerning Proton Technology's accusations of unfair

competition. Although it is true that Vinh Phuc Nguyen was in the county jail when he was released to work at Proton Technology under a work furlough program in December 1995, Vinh Nguyen's conviction was for shooting a gun at an unoccupied motor vehicle and vandalism. Vinh Nguyen pled guilty to these felonies on October 31, 1995. If you have any questions, or wish to see the record of the conviction, please feel free to contact me.

On July 24, 1996, appellant filed a six count complaint in Alameda County Superior Court. Included in the complaint were causes of action for libel, slander, invasion of privacy, intentional infliction of emotional distress, and interference with economic relationship. The complaint was directed entirely to the March 29 letter to Excelsior and the telephone conversation or conversations Horton had with appellant's probation officer, Martinez. A demurrer was sustained without leave to amend as to the two causes of action for invasion of privacy; it was overruled as to the other four causes of action.

After discovery, respondents filed motions for summary judgment in November 1997. These motions asserted that Horton's several communications were either absolutely protected by the litigation privilege of section 47(b) or, alternatively, qualifiedly privileged under Civil Code section 47, subdivision (c). The court granted both motions on the basis of the section 47(b) privilege.

Appellant filed a timely notice of appeal.[7]

DISCUSSION

Section 47(b) provides that a communication made "[i]n any . . . (2) judicial proceeding" is privileged. This privilege is absolute, not qualified, even when pre-litigation communications are implicated.

Twice in this decade, our Supreme Court has explored both the purposes served and sorts of communications protected by the litigation privilege. In the leading case of *Silberg v. Anderson* (1990) 786 P.2d 365 (*Silberg*), the court explained the rationale of the privilege — then codified as section 47(2) — as follows:

> The principal purpose of section 47(2) is to afford litigants and witnesses the utmost freedom of access to the courts without fear of being harassed subsequently by derivative tort actions. Section 47(2) promotes the effectiveness of judicial proceedings by encouraging "open channels of communication and the presentation of evidence" in judicial proceedings. A further purpose of the privilege "is to assure utmost freedom of communication between citizens and public authorities whose responsibility is to investigate and remedy wrongdoing." Such open communication is "a fundamental adjunct to the right of access to judicial and quasi-judicial proceedings." Since the "external threat of liability is destructive of this fundamental right and inconsistent with the effective administration of justice' courts

---

[7] Appellant's attorney did not, however, include the same in the Appellant's Appendix, as is required by California Rules of Court, rules 5.1(b) and 5.1(c), hence leading respondents to suggest it had not been supplied to us. And, as respondents point out, he failed to comply in many meaningful ways with other portions of those same rules, e.g., regarding what should be included in an appendix and how the same is to be organized and paginated. However, because of the importance of the issue raised by this appeal, we have reluctantly determined to rule on its merits rather than striking appellant's opening brief (no reply brief was filed on his behalf) and appendix.

have applied the privilege to eliminate the threat of liability for communications made during all kinds of truth-seeking proceedings: judicial, quasi-judicial, legislative and other official proceedings. . . . Section 47(2) further promotes the effectiveness of judicial proceedings by encouraging attorneys to zealously protect their clients' interests. "[I]t is desirable to create an absolute privilege . . . not because we desire to protect the shady practitioner, but because we do not want the honest one to have to be concerned with [subsequent derivative] actions. . . ." Finally, in immunizing participants from liability for torts arising from communications made during judicial proceedings, the law places upon litigants the burden of exposing during trial the bias of witnesses and the falsity of evidence, thereby enhancing the finality of judgments and avoiding an unending roundelay of litigation, an evil far worse than an occasional unfair result. For our justice system to function, it is necessary that litigants assume responsibility for the complete litigation of their cause during the proceedings. To allow a litigant to attack the integrity of evidence after the proceedings have concluded, except in the most narrowly circumscribed situations, such as extrinsic fraud, would impermissibly burden, if not inundate, our justice system . . . Given the importance to our justice system of ensuring free access to the courts, promoting complete and truthful testimony, encouraging zealous advocacy, giving finality to judgments, and avoiding unending litigation, it is not surprising that section 47(2), the litigation privilege, has been referred to as "the backbone to an effective and smoothly operating judicial system."

The court also addressed the nature of the communications protected by the privilege: "The usual formulation is that the privilege applies to any communication (1) made in judicial or quasi-judicial proceedings; (2) by litigants or other participants authorized by law; (3) to achieve the objects of the litigation; and (4) that have some connection or logical relation to the action." Later in this opinion, however, the court effectively conflated the last two factors into one: "The requirement that the communication be in furtherance of the objects of the litigation is, in essence, simply part of the requirement that the communication be connected with, or have some logical relation to, the action, i.e., that it not be extraneous to the action. A good example of an application of the principle is found in the cases holding that a statement made in a judicial proceeding is not privileged unless it has some reasonable relevancy to the subject matter of the action." Only this last "combined" *Silberg* factor is pertinent to this appeal, and we shall shortly return to it.

It is clear that whether a given communication is within the privilege is an issue of law, and not fact. "[W]here the facts and circumstances under which a defamatory publication was made are undisputed, the question of privilege is a matter of law." . . .

The Supreme Court's most recent venture into the litigation privilege was in *Rubin v. Green* (1993) 847 P.2d 1044 (*Rubin*). There, it made clear that the "litigation privilege" applies to pre-litigation communications as well as those occurring during the course of actual litigation. In that case, Green, a resident of a San Bernadino County mobile home park, had addressed a written "notice of intention to commence action," purportedly written on behalf of the several hundred residents of the park, to Rubin, one of its owners. In it, she listed 23 alleged defects in the operation of the park and asserted the availability of various federal and state law remedies. After two more pieces of correspondence between the attorneys for Rubin and Green, Rubin sued both Green and her attorneys alleging, inter alia, unlawful interference with contractual relations via the solicitation of the park's residents. The Supreme Court's opinion was directed to the limited issue of whether "a defendant in an impending civil action may sue the attorneys for the opposing party on the ground that they wrongfully 'solicited' the litigation against him." It unanimously held that, as to Rubin's suit for damages, the answer was in the negative; the basis of the ruling was section 47(b).

In the course of its opinion, the court noted that "[f]or well over a century, communications with 'some relation' to judicial proceedings have been absolutely immune from tort liability" by section 47(b). It then went on to note, as it had three years earlier in *Silberg*, the policy reasons underlying the rule, principally protecting access to the courts. It then addressed the issue of whether the privilege protected *prelitigation* activities, and confirmed that it well could: "In light of this extensive history, it is late in the day to contend that communications with 'some relation' to an *anticipated* lawsuit are not within the privilege."[8]

More specifically, both before and after *Rubin*, several cases have held that prelitigation demand letters of the sort involved here may be privileged under the section.

However, the privilege obviously cannot extend to *anything* that is written just because it is contained in a pre-litigation demand letter, a point which brings us back to the passage in *Silberg* in which the two tenets regarding the relationship of the statements to the litigation are fused into one. The court's language, again, was that "the communication be connected with, or have some logical relation to, the action, i.e., that it not be extraneous to the action." A few lines later, it restated the requirement as being that the statement have some "reasonable relevancy to the subject matter of the action."

This was not always the principle applied by our appellate courts. Pre-*Silberg*, there are several reported cases in which a very loose and general relationship between the statement and the putative litigation was deemed sufficient. Thus, in *Pettitt v. Levy* (1972) 28 Cal. App. 3d 484, 489, the court wrote: "The publication need not be pertinent, relevant or material in a technical sense to any issue if it has some connection or relation to the proceedings." After quoting that sentence, the court in *Profile Structures, Inc. v. Long Beach Bldg. Material Co.* (1986) 181 Cal. App. 3d 437, 442, added: "Any doubt as to whether such relationship or connection existed must be resolved in favor of a finding of privilege." Finally, in *Cayley v. Nunn* (1987) 190 Cal.App.3d 300, a case relied upon in the trial court's orders here, the court summarized the applicable rule to be: "The privilege is denied to any participant in legal proceedings only when the matter is so palpably irrelevant to

---

[8] Recently, our colleagues in Division Three of this district have refined the *Rubin* principle by holding that it applies only where the privileged communication has "some relation to an imminent lawsuit or judicial proceeding which is *actually* contemplated seriously and in good faith to resolve a dispute, and not simply as a tactical ploy to negotiate a bargain." We do not reach the interesting question of whether the principle articulated in *Edwards* applies here because (1) the trial court apparently did not consider it and we decline to do so in the first instance and (2) at least superficially the record suggests that Proton was seriously considering suing Excelsior. We do, however, suggest that it is an issue that may well be relevant on remand.

the subject matter that no reasonable man can doubt its irrelevancy and impropriety."

Whatever the pre-*Silberg* merits of these expansive views, we think they are clearly outdated in view of the limitations we have quoted from that case. Additionally, even pre-*Silberg*, the appellate courts often found superficially litigation-related statements not protected by the privilege. *Younger v. Solomon* (1974) 38 Cal. App. 3d 289 is perhaps the most interesting such case. It was an action brought by one Kern County attorney against another. The respondent was one of ten attorneys who had filed ethics charges against the appellant with the State Bar of California. Later, respondent filed a civil action against the appellant on behalf of one of the alleged victims of the latter's conduct. In the course of that action, the respondent filed extensive interrogatories, including one specifically referencing and incorporating the "ambulance chasing" State Bar charges. The appellant filed a cross-complaint seeking damages, contending that the publication via the interrogatory of the State Bar charges was tortious on several theories. The superior court granted summary judgment against the appellant on the basis of section 47(b). The court of appeal reversed, holding that "[p]ublication of these matters has no logical relation or connection with Mrs. Jenkins' action. . . . The terms 'related to' or 'connected with' necessarily require more than a remote relationship or common factual genesis between two otherwise unconnected subjects. To come within the privilege, the fact communicated itself must have some bearing on or connection with the subject matter of the litigation."

Similarly, in *Kinnamon v. Staitman & Snyder* (1977) 66 Cal. App. 3d 893, disapproved on other grounds in *Silberg*, the court ruled that the privilege could not be invoked to foreclose an action for infliction of emotional distress against a collection attorney. In an effort to collect a later-dishonored check given his client, the attorney had written the plaintiff a demand letter which, among other things, threatened to file a criminal complaint. Noting that such action contravened the Rules of Professional Conduct, the court distinguished *Lerette, supra,* 60 Cal.App.3d 573, and held that the "threat . . . cannot serve the purpose of litigation" because it could be a cause for professional discipline.

Finally, in *Carney v. Rotkin, Schmerin & McIntyre* (1988) 206 Cal. App. 3d 1513, the court disallowed another claim of litigation privilege asserted by yet another firm of collection attorneys. These attorneys had advised the plaintiff, once via telephone and again by a confirming letter, that a "bench warrant" had been issued for her because of her failure to appear at a judgment-debtor examination, and had demanded immediate partial payment of the judgment before they would "recall the Bench Warrant." Of course, no bench warrant had issued. Justice Kennard, writing for a unanimous panel, reversed a grant of a demurrer based on the section 47(b) privilege. Noting that the threats of the attorneys might, themselves, well be a misdemeanor she observed that the apparent "purpose of defendant attorney's extrajudicial statements was to deceive plaintiff and thus obtain an advantage over her." As a consequence of both that and the lack of any apparent intention to effect a settlement, the court ruled the statements were not made "to achieve a purpose of the litigation. . . ."

We think these cases, and several others discussed earlier, establish an important point for both litigants and attorneys concerning prelitigation demands and the like. That point is that section 47(b) does not prop the barn door wide open for any and every sort of prelitigation charge or innuendo, especially concerning individuals. Indeed, the court of appeal in *Lerette* anticipated exactly the problem which this case highlights when it cautioned: "We recognize that the fact that a suit eventually is filed does not protect all defamatory communications made prior to the filing. *But most potential abuse of this privilege for prelitigation communications can be prevented by enforcement of the relevancy requirement. . . .*"

Or, as our colleagues in Division Three of this district recently noted (lifting ever so gently from the language of *Rubin* in the process): "It is not too late in the day to establish the appropriate standards for extending the litigation privilege to communications made in anticipation of litigation."

This case presents facts eminently befitting that goal. We have no difficulty in holding that the inclusion in Horton's demand letter to Excelsior of references to appellant's criminal record falls outside of the section 47(b) privilege. In the first place, Horton's particularization of appellant's criminal history was simply incorrect. It was alleged that he had been "in prison for repeatedly and violently assaulting his wife." It turned out that he wasn't in prison, but only county jail, and then for convictions for shooting at an unoccupied car and vandalism.

More importantly, we think any "connection" between such a conviction and the civil unfair competition focus of Horton's demand letter is, to be charitable about it, tenuous. Respondents attempt to "connect" the statements regarding appellant's criminal record with the dispute by arguing that the former "may have persuaded Excelsior that [appellant] was more than capable of committing unfair business practices since he had been convicted of more serious crimes in the past." This contention borders on the specious. First, the "unfair business practices" of which Proton and its attorneys complained in their March 29 letter are not "crimes." Second, one's proclivity to engage in such practices is in no way, shape or form predictable by whether he (a) beats his wife (b) shoots at unoccupied cars, or (c) commits vandalism.

The only other "connection" respondents offer is equally attenuated: they contend that, "if Proton decided to pursue litigation," appellant's convictions would be relevant because, if he became a witness, such would be admissible to impeach him . . . Thus, informing Excelsior of this fact in advance might achieve the goal of "avoiding litigation." First of all, respondents overlook the fact that admission of a prior felony conviction in a civil action is very much subject to the exercise of a court's discretion . . . Second, it simply stretches credulity to the breaking point to believe that any part of respondents' motivation for including a reference to appellant's alleged wife beating was a desire to advise Excelsior that he might be subject to impeachment if used as a witness in a civil unfair competition action.

Rather, we think the reaction of Excelsior's Lee to the letter, i.e., that it was essentially "vindictive" behavior on the part of Proton and its attorneys, is not only reasonable but possibly the only reasonable interpretation. This is corroborated by the fact that only *after* writing it did Horton undertake to investigate appellant's criminal history.

Two of the pre-*Silberg* cases discussed above, *Kinnamon* and *Carney*, involved civil law disputes in which the challenged communication implicated, in one way or another, criminal law issues. In both, overly-aggressive collection attorneys sent demand letters which, in one case threatened to initiate, and in the other misrepresented the existence of, criminal proceedings. In both, the courts denied application of the privilege. We think the broader import of these holdings is that the use of the criminal records of individuals in purely civil disputes such as that between Proton and Excelsior is and should be fraught with peril. That is, surely, why our Rules of Professional Conduct send this warning shot across attorneys' bows: "A member shall not threaten to present criminal . . . charges to obtain an advantage in a civil dispute."[11]. . .

For the foregoing reasons, we hold that the prelitigation demand letter's reference to appellant's prior criminal history was not privileged under section 47(b).

*   *   *

NOTES

1.   The *Nguyen* court found that the attorney who prepared the demand letter that referred to Nguyen's alleged criminal conduct could be sued for defamation. What was the primary rationale for this conclusion? How does this ruling relate to the attorney's obligation under Model Rule 4.1? When are statements made in demand letters protected under the litigation privilege?

2.   Note that the *Nguyen* court alluded to the prohibition against threatening criminal process in a civil matter, stating "the use of the criminal records of individuals in purely civil disputes . . . is and should be fraught with peril." *Nguyen*, 69 Cal. App. 4th at 152.

3.   Note the *Nguyen* court's criticism of the attorney's failure to conform to the local appellate rules in footnote 7. The court specifically criticizes the brief's failure to employ proper organization and pagination. Lawyers should recognize the potential consequences of such failures to conform to local rules, including the possibility that the court will strike the document and dismiss the matter. Indeed, the *Nguyen* court acknowledges its "reluctance" to proceed with the appeal, notwithstanding the deficiencies in the lawyer's appeal.

4.   The litigation privilege protects a lawyer at the initial stages of litigation, while facts and related legal claims are still being investigated. In fact, at the demand letter stage, a lawyer will not likely have engaged in discovery to investigate all facts fully. Moreover, a lawsuit filed against the opposing counsel who writes a demand letter would likely sound in defamation or tortious interference rather than negligence, in part because the opposing attorney owes no duty to the receiving party. As the court noted in *McKenna Long & Aldridge, LLP v. Keller*, 598 S.E.2d 892, 895 (Ga. App. 2004), "[i]f an attorney owes no legal duty sounding in negligence to an adversary to investigate a client's claim prior to filing suit or to avoid filing a potentially frivolous suit, . . . certainly the attorney owed no duty to investigate before merely sending a demand letter on behalf of a client." Given the limited obligation of investigation at the demand letter stage, is it fair to assess whether comments made in the demand letter are related to the subject of the action when such an assessment will invariably be made in hindsight?

5.   Regarding the litigation privilege for statements made in demand letters, audience is also a consideration. Courts have held that although the privilege

---

[11] By this reference, we are not suggesting that Horton's letter violated this rule, but only that the rule exemplifies the principle that adverting to criminal law matters in the course of purely civil disputes is strongly discouraged.

applies to alleged defamatory statements in letters when sent to the other party and counsel, the privilege does not provide protection where the letter is sent to other interested non-parties. In *Troutman v. Erlandson*, 593 P.2d 793 (Or. 1979) the court considered whether the litigation privilege applied to an allegedly defamatory letter sent by an individual, acting as an attorney on his own behalf, to an opposing party. The letter related to a series of debt and business disputes between the parties. A potential investor, Fackrell, was copied on the letter. When a defamation suit was filed, the court concluded that the letter to Fackrell was not privileged, because he was not sufficiently connected to the judicial proceeding. Noting that the rationale for the privilege considers that "the defendant is acting in furtherance of some interest of social importance, which is entitled to protection even at the expense of uncompensated harm to the plaintiff's reputation," the court concluded that Fackell's relationship to the matter was sufficiently attenuated to deny application of the privilege. *Id.* at 794–5. Fackrell's indirect involvement as a potential investor, "important to defendant as [it] might be . . . [was not] so important to society that defendant, or any person in his position, should be granted immunity from malicious, untruthful statements, if they be such." *Id.* at 795.

6. For a summary of privilege issues relevant to attorney demand letters, *see* Thomas Goger, *Libel and Slander — Out-of-Court Statements between Attorneys Made Preparatory To, or in the Course of, or Aftermath of, Civil Judicial Proceedings as Privileged*, 36 A.L.R.3d 1328 (1971).

C. Prohibition on Threatening Criminal Process in a Civil Matter

i. Threats of Criminal Process against the Opposing Party

The Model Rules do not expressly prohibit an attorney from threatening criminal process in a civil matter. However, the Model Code of Professional Responsibility does contain such a restriction. Disciplinary Rule 7-105(A) provides that "[a] lawyer shall not present, participate in presenting, or threaten to present criminal charges solely to obtain advantage in a civil matter."

When the Model Rules of Professional Conduct were drafted, the rules deliberately omitted a counterpart to DR 7-105(A). The drafters concluded that such a restriction was "redundant or overbroad or both" and that "extortionate, fraudulent, or otherwise abusive threats were covered by other, more general prohibitions in the Model Rules and thus . . . there was no need to outlaw such threats specifically." ABA Comm. on Ethics and Prof'l Responsibility, Formal Op. 92-363 (1992). In addressing the use of threats of prosecution in connection with a civil matter, the ABA concluded:

> [T]he Model Rules do not prohibit a lawyer from using the possibility of presenting criminal charges against the opposing party in a civil matter to gain relief for her client, provided that the criminal matter is related to the civil claim, the lawyer has a well founded belief that both the civil claim and the possible criminal charges are warranted by the law and the facts, and the lawyer does not attempt to exert or suggest improper influence over the criminal process. It follows also that the Model Rules do not prohibit a lawyer from agreeing, or having the lawyer's client agree, in return for

satisfaction of the client's civil claim for relief, to refrain from pursuing criminal charges against the opposing party as part of a settlement agreement, so long as such agreement is not itself in violation of law.

Id. However, notwithstanding the lack of formal prohibition in the Model Rules, lawyers who draft demand letters should carefully consider whether to threaten criminal process in connection with the demand contained in the letter. As the following cases illustrate, where such threats are not warranted, courts will not hesitate to criticize lawyers who resort to such arguably abusive tactics.

MATTER OF GLAVIN
484 N.Y.S.2d 933 (N.Y. App. Div. 3 Dept. 1985)

In this disciplinary proceeding respondent, an Albany attorney admitted to practice in this Department in 1929, is charged with one count of misconduct arising out of an April 6, 1984 letter which he sent to an individual who had apparently done some unsatisfactory repair work at the home of one of his clients. The petition charges respondent with violating several provisions of the Code of Professional Responsibility in that his letter, *inter alia*, threatens the recipient with arrest and/or jail in an effort to obtain a refund of moneys paid by the client and implies that respondent possessed the authority to impose or withhold these criminal sanctions.

Following the filing of respondent's answer, we vacated his demand for a bill of particulars and denied petitioner's motion for a reference noting that respondent did not deny sending the letter and no other factual issues of any substance were presented. In accordance with 22 NYCRR 806.5 of our rules, respondent was permitted to appear and be heard in mitigation.

Respondent's one-page letter, written on behalf of his client, charges the recipient with having "conned her out of $1,000 before you did a lick of work." The letter further informs the recipient, *inter alia*, that "you will return the money or go to jail", "you will be arrested", and "I will have a warrant issued for your arrest." In addition, the letter advises the recipient that "If you return her money and just don't do any work *then I will tell the City not to punish you*" (emphasis added). We conclude that these statements, read together, could be construed as suggesting that respondent possessed authority to impose or withhold criminal sanctions and thus constituted misrepresentation in violation of the Code of Professional Responsibility, DR 1-102(A)(4). We also find respondent's letter to be improper in that it threatens to use the criminal process to coerce the adjustment of a private civil claim.

Although respondent believed he was justified in sending the correspondence in question, his behavior constituted unprofessional conduct for which, considering all of the circumstances, censure is the appropriate sanction.

Respondent censured.

IN RE CONDUCT OF MCCURDY
681 P.2d 131 (Or. 1984)

In this disciplinary proceeding, the Oregon State Bar charges the accused with violating Disciplinary Rule 7-105(A) of the Code of Professional Responsibility. It provides: "A lawyer shall not present, participate in presenting, or threaten to present criminal charges solely to obtain an advantage in a civil matter."

We find: A car owned by Chuck Krening, 21, was struck by another car on September 5, 1982, while it was parked. The driver of the other car, a young woman named Kathy Fluaitt, left the scene claiming to be unaware that she had struck Krening's car. Witnesses took down her license number, and Krening later traced the license number to David Fluaitt, Kathy Fluaitt's father. Krening went to the Fluaitt home and spoke with Kathy Fluaitt, who denied knowledge of striking Krening's car.

Krening later returned when David Fluaitt was home. After comparing Krening's car with the Fluaitt car, it was determined that the Fluaitt car had struck Krening's car. Mr. Fluaitt then referred Krening to D & J Body Shop. Mr. Fluaitt agreed to pay the repair figure given by that shop. D & J Body Shop gave Krening an estimate of $70. Krening previously had obtained estimates from two other body shops for $267 and $276. Mr. Fluaitt refused to consider payment of either of those estimates or of any compromise between those figures and the D & J Body Shop figure.

Krening then consulted the accused. On September 29, 1982, the accused sent a letter to David and Kathy Fluaitt. The first paragraph of the letter demanded payment of $267 for the damages to Krening's car, and stated that if such payment was not received within ten days, Krening would file suit. The second paragraph of the letter reads:

> I am taking up this case because your daughter is clearly at fault and because you gave Mr. Krening such a hard time when he came over to your house. Mr. Krening had the courtesy to seek your daughter out, even though she had hit and run. She is guilty of a class A Misdemeanor for which she can receive a jail sentence of one year and a fine of $2,500. I am not telling you what the penalty is to threaten you, but I am telling you this to illustrate the kind of person that Mr. Krening is. He is giving you a break and is entitled to be paid for the damage to his car. Find enclosed two estimates for the damage.

Krening subsequently recovered a small claims judgment of $150 against the Fluaitts. Krening paid the accused $15 for his assistance.

The threat of criminal prosecution to enforce a claim is contrary to the accepted precepts of "fair play" and is proscribed by the lawyer's code of ethics. The purpose of DR 7-105(A) is expressed in Ethical Consideration 7–21:

> The civil adjudicative process is primarily designed for the settlement of disputes between parties, while the criminal process is designed for the protection of society as a whole. Threatening to use, or using, the criminal process to coerce adjustment of private civil claims or controversies is a subversion of that process; further, the person against whom the criminal process is so misused may be deterred from asserting his legal rights and thus the usefulness of the civil process in settling private disputes is impaired. As in all cases of abuse of judicial process, the improper use of criminal process tends to diminish public confidence in our legal system.

The Bar takes the position that the mention of criminal penalties in the context of a demand letter implies a threat of criminal prosecution which constitutes a per se violation of DR 7-105(A). We disagree, and hold that DR 7-105(A) requires evidence of a specific intent to threaten to present criminal charges to obtain an advantage in a civil matter.[1]

The letter in this case sets out possible criminal penalties, but follows with a disclaimer of intent to prosecute ("I am not telling you what the penalty is to threaten you"). Although the Bar and the accused stipulated that the Fluaitts interpreted the letter as a threat of criminal prosecution if the sum was not paid, Mr. Fluaitt testified that he also understood the meaning of the clause in which the accused disclaimed an intent to prosecute.

The accused states that his letter is not a model of draftsmanship and that he prepared and mailed the letter in haste. He testified that he mentioned criminal penalties not to threaten criminal prosecution but to contrast his client's "reasonable efforts" to resolve the matter with the conduct of Mr. Fluaitt. The accused also testified that he thought his client had given the Fluaitts "a break" by not bringing criminal charges and that he thought Mr. Fluaitt had tried to use his greater age and experience to give Krening a "hard time."

We are not convinced that the accused threatened to present criminal charges to obtain an advantage in a civil matter. Accordingly, we dismiss the complaint. Costs to accused.

NOTES

1.   Are the decisions in *Glavin* and *McCurdy* consistent?

2.   Note the *McCurdy* court's reference to the rationale behind the prohibition that is set forth in the Model Code of Professional Responsibility, EC 7-21. Threats of criminal process to gain advantage in a civil matter undermine the civil process as well as diminish confidence in the legal system. If this is indeed a compelling justification, why did the drafters of the Model Rules choose to reject an express prohibition against the threat of criminal process in a civil matter? Refer to the following case for an explanation.

COMMITTEE ON LEGAL ETHICS OF THE WEST VIRGINIA STATE BAR v. PRINTZ
416 S.E.2d 720 (W. Va. 1992)

In this attorney disciplinary proceeding, the Committee on Legal Ethics of the West Virginia State Bar recommends that this Court publicly reprimand Charles F. Printz, Jr., for violation of Disciplinary Rule 7-105(A) of the Code of Professional Responsibility (1978) for his role in negotiations between his father and an embezzler formerly employed by his father. After independently examining the record, we disagree with the Board's recommendations, and we find that the complaint against Mr. Printz should be dismissed.

[Charles F. Printz, Jr. represented his father, Charles F. Printz, Sr., in an action against Charles Sr.'s former employee, Mr. Kesecker. Mr. Kesecker admitted to having embezzled $395,515 from Charles Sr.'s business. Following a

---

[1] Additionally, the determination of whether a violation of DR 7-105(A) occurs in any given case may require inquiry into whether an accused threatened criminal prosecution *solely* to obtain an advantage in a civil matter, which necessarily requires evaluation of an accused's [lawyer's] intent.

series of negotiations made in an effort to settle the matter, Charles Jr. sent Larry Kesecker a "final demand" letter. In this letter he gave Mr. Kesecker the choice of agreeing to a strict financial arrangement for repayment of the embezzled money or criminal prosecution. Mr. Kesecker responded with a letter accepting the financial arrangement set out by Charles Jr. However, Mr. Kesecker then retained a lawyer and the negotiations broke down. Mr. Printz, Sr. ultimately notified law enforcement authorities of the embezzlement. Mr. Kesecker pleaded guilty to embezzlement, was required to make restitution, and received five years probation.]

*   *   *

In 1989, West Virginia replaced the *Code of Professional Responsibility* with the *Rules of Professional Conduct*. The Committee is correct that the replacement of the *Code* by the *Rules* does not absolve lawyers' actions in 1987 from the ethical guidelines set forth in the *Code*. However, we have taken into consideration the reasons for the omission of a counterpart to DR 7-105(A) in the new *Rules*. As stated by Professors Hazard and Hodes:

> Rule 4.4 does *not* incorporate the prohibition originally found in DR 7-105(A) of the Code of Professional Responsibility, which provided that "a lawyer shall not present, participate in presenting, or threaten to present criminal charges solely to obtain an advantage in a civil matter." Nor does this prohibition appear elsewhere in the Rules of Professional Conduct; *it was deliberately omitted as redundant or overbroad or both.*

> The ethical ban on threatening criminal prosecution is redundant because in some jurisdictions it covers much the same ground as the crimes of extortion and compounding crime, and Rule 8.4 makes it a disciplinary offense for a lawyer to commit such crimes. . . .

> Of course in many jurisdictions (and in the Model Penal Code), even overt threats are not criminally punishable if they are based on a claim of right, or if there is an honest belief that the charges are well founded. In those jurisdictions, the lawyer's actions could be a crime only if the lawyer sought more of the other party's property than he believed his client was entitled to. With respect to compounding crime, many jurisdictions excuse the victims of crime who seek restitution in exchange for an agreement not to report.

> But these exceptions only point toward the second defect of rules like DR 7-105(A): *they are overbroad because they prohibit legitimate pressure tactics and negotiation strategies.* DR 7-105(A) evidently meant to push beyond extortion and compounding crime, but without any coherent limit.

> In reality, many situations arise in which a lawyer's communications on behalf of a client cannot avoid addressing conduct by another party that is both criminal and tortious. Inevitably, the question of which remedial routes will be taken must also be addressed. An example is where a lawyer for a financial corporation must deal with an employee who has been discovered in embezzlement. In general, the client corporation is interested in recovering as much of its money as possible, and there is also a public interest in enforcement of the criminal law. These interests are not always compatible, however, for it may well be in the interest of the company to

have the employee pay back the money and quietly resign, without the adverse publicity that a criminal trial would bring to the corporation as well as to the employee. Lurking near the surface is [sic] this calculus can be uncertainty about whether the employee's crime can be proved beyond a reasonable doubt, and the risk that the employee might sue for wrongful discharge or defamation if the employer does file a criminal accusation.

In these circumstances it is counterproductive to prohibit the lawyer from discussing with the employee, or the employee's counsel, the possibilities noted above. *Indeed, competent representation would seem to require the lawyer to press ahead with such full-ranging negotiations.* Yet, so long as DR 7-105(A) was on the books, the lawyer had to worry whether she would commit professional misconduct if she even mentioned these possibilities. Indeed, the situation can degenerate into implicit or even explicit blackmail *against the lawyer*, to pressure the lawyer into recommending to her client that criminal prosecution not even be considered or discussed. Faced with such restrictions (even without the added factor of blackmail), some lawyers might simply avoid the issue, while others might resort to code words and euphemisms. In either event, the client corporation in the example could be seriously disserved.

We find this reasoning persuasive. The rules of legal ethics should not prohibit lawyers from engaging in otherwise legitimate negotiations. However, there are limits as Rule 4.4 of the *West Virginia Rules of Professional Conduct* provides the appropriate standards to guide a lawyer's conduct in these matters. Rule 4.4 states:

In representing a client, a lawyer shall not use means that have no substantial purpose other than to embarrass, delay, or burden a third person, or use methods of obtaining evidence that violate the legal rights of such a person.

All parties to this case might have been served better if the negotiations had continued and a prosecution had never ensued. However, this finding does not exonerate Mr. Printz completely. It exonerates him *only* if his actions were *otherwise legitimate.*

* * *

[The West Virginia bar committee had challenged Printz's actions under *W.Va.Code*, 61-5-19 [1923], which prohibited a person or his agent from seeking restitution in lieu of a criminal prosecution. The court, in a lengthy discussion, ultimately invalidated the code section in part under the theory of desuetude, which is a judicial doctrine that allows a court to reject the legal effect of an existing statute because of the historical lack of enforcement of the statute.]

* * *

Accordingly, we find *W.Va.Code*, 61-5-19 [1923], to the extent that it prohibits a victim or his agent from seeking restitution in lieu of a criminal prosecution, void under the doctrine of desuetude. Seeking payment beyond restitution in exchange for foregoing a criminal prosecution or seeking any payments in exchange for not testifying at a criminal trial, however, are still clearly prohibited.

Because DR 7-105(A) has proven to be unworkable and because Mr. Printz did not have fair notice that he might be subject to prosecution under *W.Va.Code*,

61-5-19 (1923) we find that he did not act inappropriately. Accordingly, we dismiss the charges against Mr. Printz.

NOTES

1. What justifications does the *Printz* court give for rejecting the prohibition against threatening criminal process in a civil matter? Are these justifications valid? How do they relate to the rationale behind the prohibition that was set forth in *McCurdy*?

2. The concept of professionalism has historically included the notion that members of a profession — lawyers, physicians, clergy — provide a valuable service to society and are therefore deserving of the public's trust and confidence. Does this characterization remain accurate today? If not, why? How does the prohibition against threatening criminal process relate to this issue?

ii.   Threats of Criminal Process against Opposing Counsel

While there is no express prohibition on threatening criminal process against opposing counsel in a civil matter in the Model Rules or the Model Code of Professional Responsibility, such action is implicitly prohibited. In an ABA formal ethics opinion, ABA Commission on Ethics and Professional Responsibility noted:

> A lawyer's use of the threat of filing a disciplinary complaint or report against opposing counsel, to obtain an advantage in a civil case, is constrained by the Model Rules, despite the absence of an express prohibition on the subject. Such a threat may not be used as a bargaining point when the subject misconduct raises a substantial question as to opposing counsel's honesty, trustworthiness or fitness as a lawyer, because in these circumstances, the lawyer is ethically required to report such misconduct. Such a threat would also be improper if the professional misconduct is unrelated to the civil claim, if the disciplinary charges are not well founded in fact and in law, or if the threat has no substantial purpose or effect other than embarrassing, delaying or burdening the opposing counsel or his client, or prejudicing the administration of justice.

ABA Comm. on Ethics and Prof'l Responsibility, Formal Op. 94-383 (1994).

Because the lawyer has an affirmative obligation under Model Rule 8.3(a) to report another lawyer's violation of the Rules of Professional Conduct, a threat related to an ethical violation made by a lawyer against another lawyer to gain advantage in a civil matter would subject the threatening lawyer to an ethical violation under Model Rule 8.3. Moreover, "[a] threat by counsel to file disciplinary charges against opposing counsel to coerce settlement in a civil case would appear to come under the Model Penal Code's definition of criminal extortion unless it concerns the lawyer's conduct in the very case in which the threat is made, or conduct which is the subject of the case in which the threat is made." *Id.* To the extent the threat is not well founded, the rules that prohibit lawyers from filing frivolous claims and from using means to merely embarrass or burden a third party restrict the lawyer's ability to threaten criminal process. *See* Model Rules of Prof'l Conduct R. 3.1, 4.1, 4.4 (2008). The ABA has noted a limited instance in which such a threat may not run afoul of the Model Rules:

There may be circumstances in which a threat to file a disciplinary complaint or report as a means of advancing a client's interests in a civil case would avoid the constraints posed by criminal law and the . . . Model Rules. . . . A lawyer who becomes aware of professional misconduct that raises a substantial question as to a lawyer's honesty, trustworthiness or fitness as a lawyer in other respects should report that misconduct promptly, to the extent required by Rule 8.3(a) . . . and not use it as a bargaining chip in the civil case. On the other hand, a well-founded report of misconduct which is not required by Rule 8.3(a) to be reported, and which is not within the jurisdiction of the trial court where the civil matter is pending, usually can and should be postponed to the conclusion of the civil proceeding.

Id.

II.   FORMAT AND PRACTICE CONSIDERATIONS

A.   Overview

i.   Communication with Someone Represented by Counsel

Model Rule 4.2 prohibits a lawyer from communicating directly with a person the lawyer knows to be represented by counsel. This rule "contributes to the proper functioning of the legal system by protecting a person who has chosen to be represented by a lawyer in a matter against overreaching by other lawyers who are participating in the matter. . . ." Model Rules of Prof'l Conduct R. 4.2 cmt. 1 (2008). For purposes of a demand letter, which is typically prepared at the onset of the matter, the prohibition applies only in cases in which the lawyer knows that the opposing party is represented by counsel in the matter that is the subject of the demand. The comments note that such representation can be inferred from the circumstances. Model Rules of Prof'l Conduct R. 4.2 cmt. 8 (2008). "In the event the person with whom the lawyer communicates is not known to be represented by counsel in the matter, the lawyer's communications are subject to [Model Rule] 4.3," which requires that the lawyer explain his role in the representation, specifically with regard to his duty of loyalty to his own client. Model Rules of Prof'l Conduct R. 4.2 cmt. 9 (2008).

ii.   Diligence

A lawyer charged with the responsibility of representing a client has an obligation to provide that representation diligently. Model Rules of Prof'l Conduct R. 1.3 (2008). This obligation is apparent in the context of demand letters, particularly where the lawyer has represented to the client his intention to forward the client's demand to the opposing party.

iii.   Civility and Professionalism

While neither the Model Rules nor the Model Code expressly require that lawyers play nicely with one another, a lack of civility may give rise to sanctions for a failure in professionalism. Many states have adopted codes of professionalism that have specific civility obligations. For example, Standard 2 of the Utah

Standards of Professionalism and Civility provides: "Lawyers shall advise their clients that civility, courtesy and fair dealing are expected. They are tools of effective advocacy and not signs of weakness. Clients have no right to demand that lawyers abuse anyone or engage in any offensive or improper conduct." In addition, the Lawyer's Creed of Professionalism of the State Bar of Arizona requires its members to "be courteous and civil, both in written and oral communication" to opposing parties and their counsel. To the extent that a lawyer uses abusive or disrespectful language in a demand letter, she may be subject to disapproval or sanctions under applicable professionalism codes.

B. Communication with Someone Represented by Counsel

Model Rule 4.2 flatly prohibits a lawyer from communicating directly with someone the lawyer knows to be represented by counsel unless the lawyer has the consent of the other lawyer or is authorized to communicate with the other party by law or court order. Where the lawyer's communication is with members of a represented organization, the rule prohibits the lawyer from communicating with

> a constituent of the organization who supervises, directs or regularly consults with the organization's lawyer concerning the matter or has authority to obligate the organization with respect to the matter or whose act or omission in connection with the matter may be imputed to the organization for purposes of civil or criminal liability.

Model Rules of Prof'l Conduct R. 4.2 cmt. 7 (2008). The comments to the rule also make clear that the prohibition applies only where the lawyer knows that the opposing party is represented by counsel with regard to the matter that is the subject of the representation. Where there is such knowledge, there is no defense to an allegation of a violation of the prohibition.

IN RE CONDUCT OF HEDRICK
822 P.2d 1187 (Or. 1991)

In this lawyer discipline case, the accused was charged with violations of five sections of the Code of Professional Responsibility in connection with litigation concerning an estate. A trial panel found the accused guilty of violating four sections of the Code and recommended that he be suspended from the practice of law for 180 days. On automatic *de novo* review we find the accused guilty of all five charges. We suspend the accused from the practice of law for two years.

* * *

Finally, we conclude that the accused violated DR 7-104(A)(1) (a lawyer shall not communicate on a subject on which the lawyer represents a client with another person known to be represented by another lawyer, unless the other lawyer consents to such communication). On January 13, 1988, the accused sent a demand letter to Anne Winkler requesting that she return certain funds from her husband's estate and that she provide an accounting. At the time, the accused knew that Anne Winkler had counsel — the accused sent counsel a copy of the demand letter. Counsel had not consented to the communication.

The accused argues that he is not guilty of violating DR 7-104(A)(1), because he sent a copy of his letter to Mrs. Winkler's lawyer, because the letter did not ask her to take any action without consulting counsel, and because no harm was caused by the communication. None of the foregoing arguments recognizes the categorical nature of the rule: communication in the manner covered by the rule is forbidden, period. A lawyer is not permitted to ignore the plain words of the rule and then escape responsibility for violating it because no harm was caused, or because counsel for the party receiving the communication was alerted that it had been made. *See, e.g., In re McCaffrey*, 275 Or. 23, 28, 549 P.2d 666 (1976) (communications of this type are apt to cause [a] party to act without advice of counsel, and it is that danger that the rule guards against; proof of harm to represented person not required for violation of rule).

* * *

MATTER OF HOHN
832 P.2d 192 (Ariz. 1992)

* * *

On October 1, 1985, Respondent hired [a] married couple as resident managers of [his] Quartzsite mobile home park for a total of $1,000 per month. Respondent terminated the managers' employment on October 29, 1985, after paying them only $500. The managers retained an attorney to collect the remaining $500 of compensation from Respondent. On December 23, 1985, that attorney sent Respondent a demand letter by certified mail. Respondent's wife received the letter on December 26.

Mrs. Hohn testified that she occasionally acted as Respondent's legal secretary. She testified that she did not open the lawyer's demand letter until January 6, 1986, and that she had no knowledge of its contents. Respondent earlier told Mrs. Hohn to handle the payment matter with the managers, but he testified that he was inclined not to pay them.

On January 3, 1986, before opening the demand letter, Mrs. Hohn sent the managers a check for $200, which they accepted as full settlement of their claim. Both Respondent and his wife testified that, at that time, neither of them knew that the managers were represented by counsel. The State Bar charged Respondent with engaging in settlement negotiations directly with a party represented by counsel, in violation of ER 4.2.

ER 4.2 provides that "[i]n representing a client, a lawyer shall not communicate about the subject of the representation with a party the lawyer *knows* to be represented by another lawyer in the matter, unless the lawyer has the consent of the other lawyer or is authorized by law to do so." ER 4.2 (emphasis added). The State Bar argued that Respondent's disregard of the certified letter from the managers' attorney should constitute imputed knowledge of its contents. The Committee concluded that were this a civil matter involving the claimed compensation, the Committee would hold Respondent accountable for the contents of the envelope admittedly received and intentionally not opened. However, the burden of the State Bar is that a violation of Rule 42 be established by clear and convincing evidence. The Committee finds that a violation [of ER 4.2] was not established by clear and convincing evidence, and therefore Count Four should be dismissed. The Commission, however, rejected the Committee's conclusion, stating that the Respondent is accountable for the contents of the envelope admittedly received and intentionally unopened. The State Bar has met its burden of proof in establishing a violation of Rule 42, ER 4.2. We agree with the Committee's conclusion. While we do not approve of a lawyer's intentional delay or failure to adopt a system of opening letters from other lawyers, on this record we do not believe there is clear and convincing evidence that Respondent *himself* either knew the managers were represented by counsel or knew he had received a letter pertaining to the managers' legal matter. While Respondent's wife occasionally acted as his legal secretary, she testified that she did not know the contents of the letter received at the couple's residence and put it aside until after their holiday vacation. Respondent's wife then handled the matter, which involved the couple's personal business dealings, before opening the letter and showing it to Respondent. We believe that this evidence is insufficient to establish a violation of ER 4.2.

* * *

NOTES

1. The *Hedrick* court makes clear that there is no defense to the ethical violation of communicating with someone known to be represented by counsel. This principle is true even where there is no harm caused by the communication. What is the basis for such a ruling?

2. The prohibition applies only where the lawyer knows that the party is represented by counsel with regard to the matter at issue. Knowledge is defined under Model Rule 1.0(f) as actual knowledge, although the comments to Model Rule 4.2 make clear that knowledge can be inferred from the circumstances. In *Humco, Inc. v. Noble*, 31 S.W.3d 916 (Ky. 2000), the court concluded that a lawyer did not have actual knowledge that a hospital corporation was represented by counsel with regard to an employment discrimination matter. The lawyer whose conduct was questioned sent a letter to the hospital administrator about her client's employment discrimination claims. *Id.* at 918. The administrator responded to the letter in writing, copying her response to the hospital's legal counsel. *Id.* Subsequently, the lawyer spoke with other hospital employees regarding the discrimination claims. *Id.* When the client eventually filed suit against the hospital, counsel for the hospital sought to disqualify the plaintiff's lawyer on the basis of a violation of the prohibition against communications with persons represented by counsel. *Id.* The court concluded that the lawyer did not have actual knowledge that the hospital was represented by counsel with regard to the discrimination claim: "Individuals often copy 'their attorney' on letters, but that fact alone does not establish that the attorney is representing the letter-writer nor does this record reveal any such representation." *Id.* at 919.

3. Though the rule requires that an attorney have actual knowledge that the recipient has retained counsel, courts hold that where such knowledge exists, the rule requires strict application. Thus, in a situation in which the court agreed that an attorney had negligently rather than intentionally contacted a party he knew to be represented by counsel, the court nonetheless upheld disciplinary action against the attorney, noting "The purpose of the rule is to prevent a person from being deprived of the advice of retained counsel by bypassing retained counsel. It is immaterial whether the direct communication is an intentional or negligent violation of the rule." *In re Conduct of McCaffrey*, 549 P.2d 666, 668 (Or. 1976).

4. What is the lawyer's responsibility when he is contacted by a potential client? Can the protection afforded to a represented party by the prohibitions on contact

in Rule 4.2 be waived by a party initiating contact with an attorney? In considering such a situation, the Iowa Supreme Court held that a party cannot unilaterally waive her Rule 4.2 protection. *Iowa Supreme Ct. Disc. Bd. v. Box*, 715 N.W.2d 758 (Iowa 2006). In rendering its decision, court referenced a comment to the Iowa Rule of Professional Conduct 4.2 which provides, "The rule applies even though the represented person initiates or consents to the communication. A lawyer must immediately terminate communication with a person if, after commencing communication, the lawyer learns that the person is one with whom communication is not permitted by this rule." The court therefore concluded that "lawyers should independently verify that opposing parties wishing to communicate directly with them are in fact not represented by counsel. . . ." *Id.* at 763 (citing *In re Capper*, 757 N.E.2d 138, 140 (Ind. 2001)).

C.   Diligence in Letter Writing

Model Rule 1.3 provides "A lawyer shall act with reasonable diligence and promptness in representing a client." When a client meets with a lawyer and determines to make a demand against an opposing party, there is an expectation that the lawyer will prepare and send the letter in a timely fashion. A failure by the lawyer in this regard causes the client stress and undermines the relationship between the lawyer and client. As the comments to Model Rule 1.3 acknowledge:

> Perhaps no professional shortcoming is more widely resented than procrastination. A client's interests often can be adversely affected by the passage of time or change in conditions; in extreme instances, as when a lawyer overlooks a statute of limitations, the client's legal position may be destroyed. Even when the client's interests are not affected in substance, however, unreasonable delay can cause a client needless anxiety and undermine confidence in the lawyer's trustworthiness.

Model Rules of Prof'l Conduct R. 1.3 cmt. 3 (2008). In *In re Schaffner*, 939 P.2d 39 (Or. 1997), a lawyer was sanctioned under the Model Code of Professional Responsibility in part for failing to send a demand letter on behalf of the client. The court held that such a failure constituted neglect of the client's matter under the applicable ethical rules. *Id.* at 40 (noting that, "in failing to prepare and send the demand letter or take any other significant action" in the client's case, the attorney had neglected the client and violated the applicable ethical rule).

D.   Civility in Letter Writing

Many state supreme courts and state and local bar associations have adopted codes of professionalism and/or civility that apply to lawyers practicing in those jurisdictions. Some codes expressly acknowledge that provisions do not supersede existing ethical rules and are aspirational in nature. However, in some instances, acts of incivility can give rise to enforcement with litigation sanctions. In any event, courts are increasingly willing to comment on bad behavior by lawyers, as the following cases illustrate.

IN RE GERSHATER
17 P.3d 929 (Kan. 2001)

* * *

On May 29, 1998, Gershater [an attorney] mailed a letter to [her lawyer] Vleisides. Her letter was vicious, offensive, and extremely unprofessional. Her letter employed a number of vile and unprintable epithets referring to both Vleisides and Donnelly.

* * *

Suffice it to say that the correspondence to Vleisides is conduct that adversely reflects on Gershater's fitness to practice law. A lawyer should be able to write a letter to an opposing party or a party with an adverse interest and intelligently communicate his or her position without the use of profane, offensive, or derogatory language. "[A]ttorneys are required to act with common courtesy and civility at all times in their dealings with those concerned with the legal process." "Vilification, intimidation, abuse and threats have no place in the legal arsenal." "An attorney who exhibits the lack of civility, good manners and common courtesy . . . tarnishes the entire image of what the bar stands for."

We agree with the Ohio Supreme Court in *Columbus Bar Assn. v. Riebel*, 69 Ohio St.2d 290, 292, 432 N.E.2d 165 (1982), when it discussed civility and the duty of attorneys to treat others with respect. It stated:

> It is within the real meaning and intent of our Code of Professional Responsibility that lawyers should always be cognizant of the necessity for good manners, courtesy and discourse, both to client and other practitioners, as being part of our professional ethics. The zeal employed by an attorney in guarding the interests of his clients [and in communicating with adverse parties] must always be tempered so as not to inject his personal feelings or display a demeanor that subjects parties to a proceeding or opposing counsel to certain indignities.

Gershater's correspondence to Vleisides, although of minor importance in our consideration of the violations committed by Gershater and the discipline to be imposed upon her, is without doubt, lacking in courtesy and civility. The abusive and threatening nature of the language has no place in the legal world.

* * *

NOTES

1. The consequences for a lack of civility may vary. In *Revson v. Cinque & Cinque*, 70 F. Supp. 2d 415 (S.D.N.Y. 1999), *vacated in part, rev'd in part by*, 221 F.3d 71 (2d Cir. 2000), Burstein, a lawyer, represented an individual who was suing the law firm of Cinque & Cinque over a fee dispute. *Id.* at 73–74. Burstein wrote a demand letter to Robert Cinque, noting that the demand was "one last effort to avoid litigation that [would] inevitably tarnish [Cinque's] reputation." In the letter Burstein stated, "I apologize in advance for the harshness of this letter. I have no desire to fan the flames of an emotional dispute. Nor do I have the desire to conduct the legal equivalent of a proctology exam on your finances and billing practices. Yet, I will not hesitate to do so unless you begin to act in a responsible manner." *Id.* at 75. The district court invoked its inherent authority under 28 U.S.C. § 1927 to sanction Burstein. The Second Circuit reversed the sanction of Burstein. *Id.* at 77. With regard to the letter, the court wrote:

Despite the harshness of the rest of the letter, we doubt that it would have been given much attention had it referred not to proctology but, for example, to an X-ray, a CAT scan, or an MRI. Further, though the reference to proctology was offensive and distinctly lacking in grace and civility, it is, regrettably, reflective of a general decline in the decorum level of even polite public discourse. Although we, like the district court, find the reference to proctology repugnant, . . . we cannot conclude that that reference was sanctionable.

Id. at 79.

2.　Civility in letter writing is implicitly required by many state bar codes of professionalism. It is also clear that incivility undermines the lawyer's ability to establish productive relationships with other lawyers and thereby undermines not only the lawyer's effectiveness, but also her ability to maintain a meaningful and rewarding practice. Indeed, because professionalism can be characterized, in part, as a collective effort on the part of lawyers to behave honestly, respectfully, and with integrity, the Oregon State Bar Statement of Professionalism provides:

Professionalism includes integrity, courtesy, honesty, and willing compliance with the highest ethical standards. Professionalism goes beyond observing the legal profession's ethical rules: professionalism sensitively and fairly serves the best interests of clients and the public. Professionalism fosters respect and trust among lawyers and between lawyers and the public, promotes the efficient resolution of disputes, simplifies transactions, and makes the practice of law more enjoyable and satisfying.

Chapter 7

COMPLAINTS

In the heat of litigation, it's so easy to lose perspective. When does a lawyer's conduct cross the line between crafty strategy and unethical behavior? When in doubt, use the "sunshine test." Imagine that all the facts you know eventually come to light. How would the situation look to others — to a judge or to a well-respected senior lawyer? If you're not sure of the answer, don't do it.

— Linda Edwards, Professor of Law and Coordinator of Legal Writing,
Mercer University School of Law

A complaint is a pleading that advances a claim for relief. Federal Rule of Civil Procedure 8(a) notes that a claim for relief may be set forth in an original complaint or in a counterclaim, cross-claim, or third-party claim. Therefore, the ethical and professional responsibilities associated with the claims made in pleadings apply not only to claims made in complaints and petitions, but also to claims for relief set forth in responsive or third-party pleadings.

The Federal Rules of Civil Procedure require that a complaint set forth a short and plain statement of the basis for jurisdiction, a short and plain statement of the claim showing that the pleader is entitled to relief, and a demand for judgment for the relief the pleader seeks. Fed. R. Civ. P. 8(a). Further, under Fed. R. Civ. P. 8(e)(1), all assertions set forth in pleadings should be set forth simply, concisely, and directly. Additional considerations found in the Model Rules require that a lawyer have a good faith belief in the facts and legal theory advanced in the claim, that the presentation of material in the claim be candid and truthful, and that lawyers behave fairly and responsibly toward opposing counsel. Rule 11 of the Federal Rules of Civil Procedure reveals that a lawyer's signature on any pleading attests to his good faith belief in the sufficiency of the pleading from a factual and legal perspective.

The considerations discussed in this chapter pertain to both the content and style of the document. Note that this text is not designed to illustrate what would be sufficient in terms of substantive content for pleading a valid claim, but what deficiencies in content or form rise to the level of an ethical or professional concern.

I. CONTENT-BASED CONSIDERATIONS

A. Overview

i. Competence

As an initial matter, when a lawyer drafts a claim on behalf of a client in a complaint, there is an ethical obligation of competence under Model Rule 1.1 and Canon 6 of the Model Code. In order to satisfy the obligation of competence in complaint drafting, the lawyer must have completed sufficient research and analysis to determine whether there is a viable claim based upon the law and the facts. The lawyer must also assess whether she has sufficient expertise to advance the claim on behalf of the client. As the comments to Model Rule 1.1 explain,

> Perhaps the most fundamental legal skill consists of determining what kinds of legal problems a situation may involve, a skill that necessarily transcends any particular specialized knowledge. A lawyer can provide adequate representation in a wholly novel field through necessary study. Competent representation can also be provided through the association of a lawyer of established competence in the field in question.

Model Rules of Prof'l Conduct R. 1.1 cmt. 2 (2008).

ii. Truthfulness and Meritorious Claims

In writing the claim, Federal Rule of Civil Procedure 8(a), as noted, requires that the complaint set forth a short and plain statement of the claim showing that the pleader is entitled to relief. Because the federal rules require only notice pleading, courts have allowed claims, even where no facts are alleged, when the complaint is sufficient to put the opposing party on notice of the claim. However, the lawyer does have an ethical responsibility under Model Rule 3.1 to have a good faith basis in the law and fact supporting the claim. Comment 2 provides:

> The filing of an action or defense or similar action taken for a client is not frivolous merely because the facts have not first been fully substantiated or because the lawyer expects to develop vital evidence only by discovery. What is required of lawyers, however, is that they inform themselves about the facts of their clients' cases and the applicable law and determine that they can make good faith arguments in support of their clients' positions. Such action is not frivolous even though the lawyer believes that the client's position ultimately will not prevail. The action is frivolous, however, if the lawyer is unable either to make a good faith argument on the merits of the action taken or to support the action taken by a good faith argument for an extension, modification or reversal of existing law.

Model Rules of Prof'l Conduct R. 3.1 cmt. 2 (2008).

Related to this obligation is the requirement under Fed. R. Civ. P. 11 that an attorney sign all pleadings and in so doing attest to the attorney's belief that "the claims, defenses, and other legal contentions therein are warranted by existing law or by a nonfrivolous argument for the extension, modification, or reversal of existing law or the establishment of new law . . ." With respect to the facts in the claim, Fed. R. Civ. P. Rule 11 requires that the lawyer have evidentiary support for all allegations or "if specifically so identified, [note that the allegations] are likely to have evidentiary support after a reasonable opportunity for further investigation or discovery." Rule 11 sanctions may be imposed for frivolous claims that are meritless because the attorney failed to investigate either the law or the facts, or for claims filed for an improper purpose. Sanctions are typically limited to "what is sufficient to deter repetition of such conduct or comparable conduct" and may include serious fines and public admonishment. Consequently, lawyers must take their signatures on pleadings very seriously.

In addition, lawyers have an obligation to be truthful and candid toward the court and opposing counsel. In this regard Model Rule 3.3 forbids a lawyer from knowingly making false statements of fact or offering false evidence. Comment 3 to the rule notes:

> An advocate is responsible for pleadings and other documents prepared for litigation, but is usually not required to have personal knowledge of matters asserted therein, for litigation documents ordinarily present assertions by the client, or by someone on the client's behalf, and not assertions by the lawyer . . . However, an assertion purporting to be on the lawyer's own knowledge, as in an affidavit by the lawyer or in a statement in open court, may properly be made only when the lawyer knows the assertion is true or believes it to be true on the basis of a reasonably diligent inquiry.

Finally, under Model Rule 3.4, a lawyer is forbidden from concealing, altering, or destroying documents with potential evidentiary value or falsifying evidence. Therefore, in determining the content of the complaint, the lawyer has an obligation to perform sufficient investigation to determine the truthfulness of the facts and to do sufficient research to determine the viability of the claim.

B.   Insufficient Research to Support Legal Claim

Ethical rules regarding competence require that a lawyer perform sufficient legal research to support her client's claim. As the comments to Model Rule 1.1 explain,

> Competent handing of a particular matter includes inquiry into and analysis of the factual and legal elements of the problems, and use of methods and procedures meeting the standards of competent practicioners. It also includes adequate preparation. The required attention and preparation are determined in part by what is at stake . . .

Model Rules of Prof'l Conduct R. 1.1 cmt. 5 (2008). Thus, the rules require that a lawyer have sufficient legal support to advance a claim. While novel claims and new interpretations of law are tolerated by the court, the following case demonstrates how a lawyer can run afoul of the ethical rules when the legal precedent does not genuinely support a claim for relief.

IN RE RICHARDS
986 P.2d 1117 (N.M. 1999)

Pursuant to the Rules Governing Discipline, 17-101 to -316 NMRA 1999, this matter came before this Court for consideration of the disciplinary board's findings, conclusions, and recommendations for discipline. The disciplinary proceeding which is the subject of this appeal involves two frivolous claims that Robert Richards ("Respondent") filed. The disciplinary board found that Respondent's conduct resulted in the violation of Rule 16-301, which prohibits the assertion of frivolous claims, and several other provisions of the Rules of Professional Conduct Rules, Rule 16-101 to -805 NMRA 1999. For the reasons set forth below, the Court adopts the Board's findings, conclusions and recommendations for discipline, as modified.

In October 1996, GE Capital Mortgage Services, Inc. ("GE") filed a foreclosure action against Diane Peterson, ("Peterson") after the note it secured had become delinquent. Respondent filed an answer for Peterson that admitted the delinquency, but asserted a counterclaim based upon a federal claim of common law lien. Peterson, as the owner of the property, claimed an attachment under a federal common law lien writ of attachment on real and personal property in the amount of $59,000. The counterclaim Respondent filed in the foreclosure action asserted that the common-law lien was paramount and superior to GE's mortgage.

Count I of the disciplinary charges brought against Respondent alleged that the filing of the counterclaim violated Rule 16-101 (requiring that attorneys are competent), 16-301 (requiring that attorneys only present meritorious claims and contentions), Rule 16-804(D) (prohibiting attorneys from engaging in conduct prejudicial to the administration of justice), and Rule 16-804(H) (prohibiting attorneys from engaging in conduct that reflects adversely on their fitness to practice law). The hearing committee and the board found that the evidence supported Count I. We agree.

A common-law lien is the right of one person to retain possession of something *belonging to another* until certain demands of the person in possession are satisfied. The corollary of this rule is that a property owner generally cannot have a lien on his or her own property. Although there are narrow exceptions to this general rule, they are inapplicable here. The "common law lien" advanced by Respondent does not come within the ambit of Rule 16-301 that a legal position is not frivolous if it states a good faith basis for the extension, modification, or reversal of existing law.

Respondent first misplaces his reliance on *Gould v. Day*, 94 U.S. 405 (1876), a United States Supreme Court case which involved a land fraud scheme . . .

* * *

[In *Gould*] [t]he Court stated: One cannot have a lien upon his own property, except where equity interposes, and, to prevent a failure of justice, keeps the lien outstanding; and here there was no interference of equity, and no occasion for its interference.

Respondent argued this language provided a good faith basis for his claim that Peterson could assert a lien on her own property for the amount of her equity. He argued that the purpose of the lien was to insure that the property was sold for fair market value to allow Peterson to receive her equity in the property. Respondent contended that the recognition of her lien would prevent a failure of justice by insuring that both his client and GE would receive all monies to which they were entitled. Thus, he contended that this was a good faith argument for an exception to the general rule that one cannot have a lien on his or her own property. We disagree.

The "common law lien" noted in *Gould* applies when a person attempts to preserve title to his [or her] property by acquiring another person's lien against the property. In that situation, the owner's intention for the lien to merge or not merge in his title will be honored. The owner simply will not be placed in a worse position for having acquired an outstanding lien for the purpose of protecting his title. Thus, the "common law lien" as discussed in *Gould* does not actually create a "lien", nor does *Gould* stand for the proposition that an owner's equity can be a lien, let alone a lien superior to the rights of a record mortgage holder.

Respondent would have been aware of the extremely limited parameters of the exception to the general rule that a property owner cannot have a lien on his own property had he further researched the *Gould* case and read the cases distinguishing it. Indeed, had he done so, he would have found cases very similar to the Peterson foreclosure where the exception had been found inapplicable . . .

Respondent's reliance on another United States Supreme Court case also is misplaced. While testifying before the hearing committee, Respondent proclaimed his reliance on *Rich v. Braxton*, 158 U.S. 375 (1895), stating that Peterson's equity was a federal lien because it was based upon *Rich*. He stated that *Rich* stood for the proposition that federal law, not state law, controlled if a federal lien is involved, and that federal liens, once filed, can only be removed by a federal court of equity upon a showing of facial invalidity of the lien. We are unpersuaded by Respondent's argument.

Rich did not involve a federal lien or claim but rather the interpretation of a West Virginia tax deed and redemption statute. It did not hold nor suggest that state law did not apply. On the contrary, the court looked first for a West Virginia decision construing the statutes in question. Addressing the issue of whether the bill in equity that the plaintiffs filed could provide the relief requested, the Court reiterated the general rule that equity will not interfere to remove a cloud on title where the instrument is void on its face because the remedy in that circumstance is at law.

Not only do these cases fail to provide a legal basis for the counterclaim Respondent filed, but they provide no basis for a "good faith argument for an extension, modification or reversal of existing law." Although Rule 16-301 recognizes that the law is not static, and that "account must be taken of the law's ambiguities and potential for change" a case upon which a lawyer relies to argue for the extension, modification, or reversal of existing law, must say what the lawyer says it says. Moreover, when relying upon an exception to a general rule of law, the position the lawyer asserts must either come within the exception, or provide a cogent argument for broadening the exception. We agree with the Board's conclusion that respondent has not provided a "good faith argument for an extension, modification or reversal of existing law" and thus has violated Rule 16-301.

*   *   *

NOTES

1.   The ethical and professional rules require that a lawyer perform research necessary to support her client's claim. What is the basis for such an obligation? What is the arguable limit of such an obligation? For example, if an attorney has performed research within her jurisdiction, to what extent should she be required to perform additional research outside the applicable jurisdiction?

2.   In *Richards*, the court concluded that the attorney's research was insufficient and his arguments to the contrary were unpersuasive. What if an attorney files a lawsuit without performing sufficient research but the claim is found viable and survives a motion to dismiss? Should the lawyer be sanctioned? What type of deterrent effect would a sanction have in this context?

3. Note that discovery occurs *after* the filing of a complaint. Further, notice pleading, which is applicable in federal and many state courts, requires only that a lawyer plead sufficient facts to put the opposing party on notice of the claim. Given these considerations, what level of investigation is necessary prior to filing a complaint on behalf of a client? Must the lawyer perform an independent inquiry to confirm the facts provided by the client? Recall the comment to Model Rule 3.1: "What is required of lawyers, however, is that they inform themselves about the facts of their clients' cases and the applicable law and determine that they can make good faith arguments in support of their clients' positions. Such action is not frivolous even though the lawyer believes that the client's position ultimately will not prevail." Model Rules of Prof'l Conduct R. 3.1 cmt. 2 (2008). If a lawyer does spend time and resources verifying facts that have been supplied by the client, can the lawyer bill the client for the time spent on verification?

4. Consider the relationship between the lawyer's responsibility to represent the client zealously and the limitations on frivolous lawsuits. In *In re Disciplinary Action Against Nora*, 450 N.W.2d 328 (Minn. 1990), a lawyer was sanctioned when her zealous representation of clients crossed the line to frivolity. The lawyer, Nora, filed a lawsuit against a bank on behalf of her clients who had mortgaged property to the bank. Nora advanced her own novel "money theory," and argued that the bank had extended credit rather than loaned money to the clients. *Id.* at 330. The court rejected the argument, concluding that it went

> well beyond the imaginative into the depths of absurdity . . . Although Nora acted upon her subjective beliefs and her personally held theories as to what the law should be, she stated at oral argument she now can distinguish political arguments that are improperly made from legal theories that are appropriately brought.

Id. The court explained the delicate relationship between zealous advocacy and frivolous claims, concluding, "While an attorney is properly a zealous advocate for his or her client, the perspective of an objective and detached judgment nevertheless must remain. This important objectivity is lost when an attorney becomes too personally involved in client matters and oversteps the bounds of ardent representation. . . ." *Id.* For additional reading on the distinction between novel, meritorious claims and those considered frivolous, see Jerold S. Solovy, Norman M. Hirsch, Margaret J. Simpson, & Christina T. Tomaras, *Sanctions under Rule 11: A Cross-Circuit Comparison*, 37 Loy. L.A. L. Rev. 727 (2004).

C. Viability of Legal Claim and Sufficiency of Facts to Support the Claim

Because the rules prohibit lawyers from filing frivolous claims, the research done in preparation of a claim made in a complaint must actually support that claim. This requires a lawyer to consider carefully the relevant precedent and its impact on the legal claim. There are many instances in which the state of the law is unclear, and therefore the ability to advise the client as to the viability of a claim is uncertain. The following case sets forth the court's analysis of the lawyer's options in filing a lawsuit where the viability of the claim is questionable based upon unsettled law.

MARY ANN PENSIERO, INC. v. LINGLE
847 F.2d 90 (3d Cir. 1988)

Counsel for plaintiffs appeal the imposition of sanctions under Federal Rule of Civil Procedure 11 for failure to reasonably investigate the facts and research the law before filing the complaint in this antitrust suit. We conclude that the record reveals adequate compliance with the pre-filing requirements of Rule 11, and we will therefore vacate the award of sanctions.. . .

[The plaintiffs owned a local retail beer outlet. The defendants operated a distributorship licensed by the state as the exclusive wholesaler of beer manufactured by certain out-of-state breweries. The plaintiffs wanted to sell two popular brands of beverages which were distributed exclusively by the defendants. The defendants initially refused to sell to the plaintiffs. The plaintiffs attempted to deal directly with other wholesalers of the beverages. The plaintiffs also hired a lawyer, Betz, who prepared and sent a letter to the defendants indicating that the defendants' actions violated federal antitrust laws. The defendants did not respond to Betz's letter but, in response to the plaintiffs' efforts to deal directly with other wholesalers, the defendants filed a state court action to enjoin the plaintiffs' purchase of disputed brands from other wholesalers. The plaintiffs brought an action in federal court asserting three claims: a conspiracy to restrain trade in violation of the Robinson-Patman Act; an attempt to monopolize interstate commerce in violation of section 2 of the Sherman Act; and price discrimination in violation of section 1 of the Robinson-Patman Act. The defendants filed a motion for summary judgment. In response, the plaintiffs asserted only the monopoly claim, voluntarily dismissing the other claims. The district court entered summary judgment against the plaintiffs and the defendants filed a motion for sanctions under Rule 11.]

In the context of preparing the federal complaint, [attorney] Betz conferred with both the Chief Counsel to the Pennsylvania Liquor Control Board and the Deputy Attorney General of the Antitrust Section of the Pennsylvania Attorney General's Office. The Chief Counsel concluded that the defendants' refusal to sell to Bargain Beer was a "citable offense" under the Pennsylvania Liquor Code, yet the Board elected not to take formal remedial action. The Deputy Attorney General opined that the defendants' conduct gave rise to a valid antitrust claim, citing legal authority in support of this view.

According to his unchallenged affidavit, Betz conducted further review of the applicable facts and additional legal research. Deciding that a federal antitrust action was warranted, Betz filed the complaint in this case on January 30, 1986.

Defendants moved for summary judgment in April 1986. In their legal memorandum submitted the following month, defendants asserted that they "should be awarded the attorneys' fees and costs incurred in defending this suit." They also noted their intention, after deposing Mrs. Pensiero, to file a separate motion "pursuant to Rules 11 and 56(g), Fed.R.Civ.P., and 28 U.S.C. § 1927" for costs and fees.

* * *

In analyzing the section 1 Sherman Act claim — which plaintiffs withdrew at the summary judgment stage — the court decided that the facts were "insufficient to establish grounds for a conspiracy," and that the plaintiffs' allegations were conclusory. With respect to the Robinson-Patman price discrimination claim, also voluntarily dismissed, the court noted the absence of a purchase and sale element, which caselaw establishes is necessary to "state a valid claim under this section."

As to the section 2 Sherman Act claim, the court initially commented that plaintiffs had not presented "specific facts to buttress [their] contention that particular brands of beer could constitute a product market. . . . Plaintiff[s] could have requested additional time for discovery but did not do so. . . ." The court rejected the plaintiffs' assertion that the section 2 claim was grounded in a good faith argument for the extension, modification, or reversal of existing law. On this point, the court faulted plaintiffs for not so characterizing the claim. The court commented that "the section 2 claim was presented in a cursory fashion and, under the circumstances of this case, sanctions are justified for its pursuit."

In a later memorandum after reconsideration, the court conceded that its holding on the relevant product market "may or may not have been correct." However, deeming the possibly erroneous ruling as harmless in light of the plaintiffs' failure to set forth facts relevant to that issue, the court reaffirmed the imposition of sanctions.

Finding that the plaintiffs' counsel had proceeded in good faith, the court concluded that a $5,000 sanction, rather than the larger sum requested by defendants, was appropriate. Furthermore, because "plaintiff had no part in the decision to pursue this case, other than to abide by the advice of counsel," the court imposed sanctions on counsel only. Plaintiffs' counsel appeals, denying a Rule 11 violation, but conceding the district court's jurisdiction.

We agree with the district court that it had jurisdiction to entertain the Rule 11 motion, but we turn first to the propriety of the imposition of sanctions.

Since Federal Rule of Civil Procedure 11 was amended in 1983, litigation under it has increased substantially as have the number of reported decisions defining the Rule's dimensions. We have explained that the intended goal of Rule 11 is accountability. It "imposes on counsel a duty to look before leaping and may be seen as a litigation version of the familiar railroad crossing admonition to 'stop, look, and listen.' " The Rule states:

> Every pleading, motion, and other paper . . . shall be signed. . . . The signature of an attorney or party constitutes a certificate by the signer that the signer has read the pleading, motion, or other paper; that to the best of the signer's knowledge, information, and belief formed after reasonable inquiry it is well grounded in fact and is warranted by existing law or a good faith argument for the extension, modification, or reversal of existing law, and that it is not interposed for any improper purpose, such as to harass or to cause unnecessary delay or needless increase in the cost of litigation.

To comply with these requirements, counsel must conduct "a reasonable investigation of the facts and a normally competent level of legal research to support the presentation."

In scrutinizing a filed paper against these requirements, courts must apply an objective standard of reasonableness under the circumstances. The wisdom of hindsight should be avoided; the attorney's conduct must be judged by "what was reasonable to believe at the time the pleading, motion, or other paper was submitted." At the time the district judge decided the issues in this case, he lacked the benefit of two opinions of this court, issued afterward, which guide us here.

In *Gaiardo v. Ethyl Corp.*, 835 F.2d 479, 482 (3d Cir. 1987), we emphasized that Rule 11 targets "abuse — the Rule must not be used as an automatic penalty against an attorney or a party advocating the losing side of a dispute." We cautioned that the Rule should not be applied to adventuresome, though responsible, lawyering which advocates creative legal theories. Rule 11 must not "be interpreted to inhibit imaginative legal or factual approaches to applicable law or to unduly harness good faith calls for reconsideration of settled doctrine."

We further stressed that proper Rule 11 analysis should focus on the circumstances that existed at the time counsel filed the challenged paper. Imposing a continuing duty on counsel to amend or correct a filing based on after-acquired knowledge is inconsistent with the Rule.

In *Teamsters Local Union No. 430 v. Cement Express, Inc.*, 841 F.2d 66, 68 (3d Cir. 1988), we reiterated that Rule 11 sanctions are appropriate "only if the filing of the complaint constituted abusive litigation or misuse of the court's process." In that case we added that "Rule 11 may not be invoked because an attorney, after time for discovery, is unable to produce adequate evidence to withstand a motion for summary judgment." We held that the theory of the plaintiff's complaint, "while novel and unsuccessful, was not plainly unreasonable."

Application of our precedents to the circumstances here requires that we reverse the sanctions order. As the recited facts establish, at the time the Pensieros' counsel filed this complaint his investigation revealed the exclusive dealership of the disputed product brands, the defendants' deliberate refusal to deal with Bargain Beer and Soda, support for the defendants' conduct by a trade association which included the plaintiffs' competitors, the apparent approval by the product manufacturers, and the opinion of a Pennsylvania Deputy Attorney General that the defendants' actions violated federal antitrust principles.

In gauging the reasonableness of an attorney's pre-filing inquiry, the Advisory Committee Notes to Rule 11 suggest consideration of four factors: the amount of time available to the signer for conducting the factual and legal investigation; the necessity for reliance on a client for the underlying factual information; the plausibility of the legal position advocated; and whether the case was referred to the signer by another member of the Bar. One court has proposed a fifth factor: the complexity of the legal and factual issues implicated. In light of these factors, we are persuaded that the complaint filed here, while unsuccessful, was not sanctionable.

Section 2 Sherman Act Claim

Plaintiffs had alleged that defendants attempted to monopolize the trade in Anheuser-Busch and Genesee products in the Lewistown area in violation of section 2 of the Sherman Act. The district court justified the imposition of sanctions for the filing of this claim on two grounds. First, the court ruled that existing law did not support the plaintiffs' proposition that particular product brands could constitute a relevant product market and that plaintiffs failed to properly characterize this claim as an attempt to extend, modify, or reverse current law. Second, the court faulted plaintiffs for failing to present "specific facts" to support their attempted extension of existing law.

As the first ground indicates, the district court read Rule 11 to impose an obligation, a "duty of candor," directing counsel to label their arguments as either supported by existing law, or contrary to existing law but supported by a good faith attempt to extend or modify the jurisprudence.

However, in *Golden Eagle Distributing Corp. v. Burroughs Corp.*, 801 F.2d 1531 (9th Cir. 1986), *reh'g denied*, 809 F.2d 584 (9th Cir. 1987), the court of appeals found no support for requiring such "argument identification" in either the language or history of Rule 11. The court held that the obligation "makes the Rule more complex than it needs to be and creates costly obstacles for lawyers." It also observed that the distinction between an argument based on established law and an argument for the extension of existing law is often not distinctly perceived. "Whether the case being litigated is or is not materially the same as earlier precedent is frequently the very issue which prompted the litigation in the first place. Such questions can be close."

We agree with those observations and hold that counsel may not be found to have violated Rule 11 merely for failing to "label" the argument advanced. Counsel should not be sanctioned for choosing the wrong characterization for their theories.

If an attorney explains that after adequate preliminary research, in good faith, he determined to seek reversal of a particular precedent, it is difficult to see how the prefiling legal inquiry could be faulted. Nevertheless, while proper argument identification may be a defense to a Rule 11 sanction, errors in argument identification do not constitute a Rule 11 violation.

Of course, this is not to suggest that prudent attorneys should avoid alerting the court when the position they advocate clearly departs from settled and controlling legal precedent. Such argument identifications might illuminate the thoroughness of the pre-filing legal investigation. We decide here only that counsel's errors in identifying their approach do not infringe on Rule 11.

The district court's second basis for imposing sanctions — a failure to present "specific facts" — did not adequately credit the information plaintiffs' attorney had uncovered. Plaintiffs were not obliged to prove their case in order to escape Rule 11 sanctions. "[M]ere failure to prevail does not trigger a sanction award. . . ." The correct Rule 11 inquiry is "whether, at the time he filed the complaint, counsel . . . *could* reasonably have argued in support" of his legal theory. The record here contains facts which justify the plaintiffs' decision to press this claim. We believe Mrs. Pensiero's affidavit describing the defendants' refusal to deal was adequate for this purpose.

Robinson-Patman Act Claim

Plaintiffs had alleged that defendants violated the Robinson-Patman Act, 15 U.S.C. § 13, by offering Anheuser-Busch and Genesee products to Bargain Beer at prices higher than those offered to other similarly situated distributors. Plaintiffs voluntarily dismissed this claim, explaining that the defendants' refusal to sell the disputed products to Bargain Beer made the claim "not ripe for adjudication." The district court believed that before filing the complaint, counsel should have discovered that an actual purchase was required to state a Robinson-Patman Act claim.

Although the plaintiffs' lack of an actual purchase makes this count quite weak, we cannot agree that presenting the claim in the circumstances here was unreasonable. That the state court suit prompted the Lingle's offer to sell at a discriminatory price was rather unusual. Creative counsel might well have urged this event as a distinguishing characteristic to excuse the ordinary Robinson-Patman purchase requirement. The fact that plaintiffs' counsel later decided against embarking upon such a novel course does not constitute an admission of the claim's unreasonableness at its inception.

Furthermore, we are not prepared to say that a doubtful count, such as this one, when included in the complaint with others of reasonable merit, so burdens the litigation process that it triggers Rule 11 penalties. Although we acknowledge that the practice of "throwing in the kitchen sink" at times may be so abusive as to merit Rule 11 condemnation, that threshold was not crossed in this case. In sum, we conclude that Rule 11 sanctions were not appropriate here.

* * *

NOTES

1.   The *Pensiero* court noted that courts should employ caution when considering Rule 11 sanctions, so as not to chill "adventuresome, though responsible, lawyering which advocates creative legal theories." How then should lawyers protect themselves when advancing causes of action that call for legal reform and are therefore unsupported by existing case law?

2.   The *Pensiero* court also noted that a Rule 11 inquiry requires an objective standard of reasonableness. The court then identified five factors to consider in evaluating the reasonableness of a claim:

- the amount of time available to the signer for conducting the factual and legal investigation;
- the necessity for reliance on a client for the underlying factual information;
- the plausibility of the legal position advocated;
- whether the case was referred to the signer by another member of the Bar;
- and the complexity of the legal and factual issues implicated.

Lawyers are paid to act as zealous advocates for their clients and to analyze the law in creative ways. Given the room for disagreement concerning the degree to which an argument can be characterized as implausible, how should a court evaluate that type of allegation?

3.   The *Pensiero* court rejected an argument that Rule 11 imposes upon attorneys a duty of candor to identify arguments in a complaint. The Model Rules, however, do impose a duty of candor upon attorneys. Should this duty require an attorney to identify, on the face of a complaint, whether the claim advanced departs from or is supported by existing law? What are the tactical advantages or disadvantages of employing or rejecting this format?

4.   In addressing Betz's first claim under the Sherman Act, the *Pensiero* court highlighted the difficulty of proving a conspiracy prior to completion of discovery. In connection with Rule 11's pre-filing investigation requirement, the court acknowledged that a

requirement that counsel, before filing a complaint, secure the type of proof necessary to withstand a motion for summary judgment would set a pre-filing standard beyond that contemplated by Rule 11. At the time plaintiffs' counsel filed the complaint here, he knew facts that supported a reasonable suspicion of cooperation between defendants and other parties who could have been expected to benefit from the defendants' intransigence. These factual circumstances and the rational inferences that may be drawn from them convince us that the allegations of the first count comported with Rule 11's pre-filing investigation requirement.

Pensiero, 847 F.2d at 95. Moreover, the court noted that the plaintiffs' later abandonment of the claim did not negate the reasonableness of the inferences that existed at the time the complaint was filed. Indeed, the court praised the plaintiffs' voluntary dismissal of the count, stating that the abandonment of

a claim that appears unlikely to succeed is responsible advocacy to be commended — not abuse of the court's process to be deterred. Courts benefit when counsel reduce the issues in dispute by objectively reappraising the evolving strengths of their positions throughout the course of litigation. Rule 11 was not intended to inhibit such activity by permitting it to be characterized by an adversary as an admission of liability.

Id. at 95–96.

5. In the previous chapter, there is a discussion of the protection afforded to lawyers with respect to factual assertions made prior to discovery in demand letters. This litigation privilege similarly protects statements made by lawyers in complaints and petitions.

The absolute privilege that an attorney has for statements made in connection with a judicial proceeding is based upon the ground that there are certain relations of life in which it is so important that the persons engaged in them should be able to speak freely that the law takes the risk of their abusing the occasion and speaking maliciously as well as untruly, in order that their duties may be carried on freely and without fear of any action being brought against them. However, a statement must have some reference to the subject matter of the pending litigation, and it must be made in connection with a judicial proceeding, in order to provide immunity to an attorney for defamatory statements.

50 Am. Jur. 2d *Libel & Slander* § 290.

II. FORMAT AND PRACTICE CONSIDERATIONS

A. Format of Allegations

Because the Federal Rules of Civil Procedure specifically require that the allegations in a complaint be concise and a "short and plain statement," a lawyer has a professional responsibility to write the complaint in a particular fashion. While complaints are construed liberally in favor of the plaintiff, sanctions may be imposed for failure to prepare the document properly, including dismissal or public reprimand. As the court explained in *Leuallen v. Borough of Paulsboro*, 180 F. Supp. 2d 615 (D.N.J. 2002), the rules that require a short and plain statement preserve the efficiency of the judicial system and conserve judicial resources. In *Leuallen*, a lawyer, Malat, filed a complaint on behalf of eleven plaintiffs but only raised claims in the complaint on behalf of one of the plaintiffs. *Id.* at 617. The court ordered Malat to file an amended complaint that conformed to the requirements of Fed. R. Civ. P. 11. *Id.* Malat filed an amended complaint that repeated the claims made in the initial complaint on behalf of the remaining plaintiffs, "thus increasing the length of the complaint from 34 to **160** pages." *Id.* (emphasis in original). Relating the excessive length of the complaint to Rule 11's requirement that the complaint be "short [and] plain," the court concluded

> the 160 pages of largely meritless allegations offended the concept that a complaint must be "a short, plain statement of the claim showing that the pleader is entitled to relief," Rule 8(a)(2), Fed.R.Civ.P., greatly multiplying the time and expense necessary to even understand plaintiffs' claims. That the Second Amended Complaint was filed soon after the Court had pointed out these deficiencies in its cautionary letter of September 21, 1999, further compounds these defects. Again, Rule 11(b)(1) was not a noticed basis for the sanction imposed herein. A discussion of this conduct, however, is useful in further illustrating the judicial resources that are wasted interpreting and clarifying the submissions made by Mr. Malat.

Id. at 618, n.5.

Sanctions under Rule 11 may be imposed on the attorney, the client, or both. Sanctions may include attorneys' fees and court costs or more public forms of reprimand. Indeed, "[a]ppropriate sanctions other than a monetary award may include reference to a bar association grievance committee, compulsory legal education, an oral or written reprimand, an order barring the attorney from appearing for a period of time, or even ordering the attorney who violated the rule to circulate in his or her firm a copy of the opinion in which the pleadings, motion, or other paper were criticized." *Total Television Entertainment Corp. v. Chestnut Hill Village Associates*, 145 F.R.D. 375 (E.D.Pa. 1992). In *Total Television*, the court considered a Rule 11 allegation against attorney Jackson and ruled that a written admonishment was an appropriate sanction. The court performed research into Jackson's other matters filed within the court's jurisdiction and admonished that Jackson had "developed a generally weak reputation for legal research." *Id.* at 385. Based upon the court's public condemnation of Jackson's catalog of practice in the jurisdiction, tempered by his lack of willfulness, the court concluded that "the sting of [the] opinion should be punishment enough." *Id.* Clearly, this published opinion was far from a ringing endorsement of Jackson's competence or credibility as a lawyer for prospective clients.

B.　　Prohibition against Abusive Tactics

Rule 11 also forbids an attorney from filing a claim for an improper purpose, notably to harass, cause unnecessary delay, or increase the cost of litigation. Similarly, the Preamble to the Model Rules cautions that "[a] lawyer should use the law's procedures only for legitimate purposes and not to harass or intimidate others." While courts are typically reluctant to sanction lawyers under the antiharassment rules, lawyers must still be cognizant of their obligations and the impact of inappropriate conduct on the reputation of the bar.

LAWYER DISCIPLINARY BD. v. NEELY
528 S.E.2d 468 (W. Va. 1998)

This disciplinary proceeding was instituted by the complainant, Office of Disciplinary Counsel [hereinafter "ODC"] of the West Virginia State Bar against Roger D. Hunter and Richard F. Neely, members of the Bar. Mr. Hunter and Mr. Neely were charged with violating Rule 3.1 of the West Virginia Rules of Professional Conduct. Mr. Neely was also charged with violating Rule 4.4. However, the Lawyer Disciplinary Board [hereinafter "Board"] found that the ODC only proved that Mr. Hunter and Mr. Neely violated Rule 3.1. The Board recommends admonishment. Based upon our review of the recommendation, all matters of record, and the briefs and argument of counsel, we disagree with the Board's recommendation, and we find that the complaint against Mr. Hunter and Mr. Neely should be dismissed.

The proceeding against Mr. Hunter and Mr. Neely involved their representation of Linda and Quewanncoii Stephens. Mr. and Mrs. Stephens have a son, Quinton, who is autistic. In September 1990, when Quinton was approximately nine months old, he was enrolled in the Fort Hill Child Development Center [hereinafter Center].

On December 2, 1994, Mrs. Stephens received a phone call from a staff member at the Center asking her to pick up Quinton because the day care employee who was responsible for his supervision was not at work, and Quinton was disrupting the other children during nap time. When Mrs. Stephens arrived at the Center, she found Quinton alone in the director's office strapped to a posture correcting chair, which she had provided, with his hands and face covered with partly-dried fecal material. According to Mrs. Stephens, the room was dark and the blinds were drawn. The employee who had been watching Quinton claimed that she left him alone for about ninety seconds to get a change of diaper for him. Mrs. Stephens immediately removed Quinton from the Center, and shortly thereafter, she and her husband consulted with [a lawyer by the name of] Mr. Hunter. . . .

After meeting with the Stephenses, Mr. Hunter wrote a letter to Jean Hawks, the Center's director and owner, and asked that she have her liability carrier contact him promptly. Mr. Hunter also sent letters of complaint to the state Child Protective Services and the federal Office of Civil Rights. Child Protective Services investigated the matter and concluded that Quinton had not been maltreated because he had been watched by an employee of the Center during the forty-five minutes it took Mrs. Stephens to arrive at the Center. The employee had only left Quinton alone for ninety seconds when she went to get a diaper.

Subsequently, Mr. Hunter [became associated with the law firm] Neely & Hunter. Mr. Hunter took the Stephens' case with him, and Mr. Neely took the lead in preparing the pleadings and handling of the case. On June 12, 1995, Mr. Neely filed a civil action in the name of Linda, Quewanncoii, and Quinton Stephens against the Center and Ms. Hawks.

The complaint alleged that Mr. and Mrs. Stephens and Quinton had suffered intentional infliction of emotional distress based upon the outrageous conduct of the defendants and that Quinton had suffered damages from an intentional battery on December 2, 1994. The complaint further alleged that as a result of interviews with persons associated with the Center, the plaintiffs believed that the December 2, 1994 incident was but one of many instances in which an autistic child, known to have special needs, in direct contravention of the expressed direction of his parents and of his health care providers, knowingly and willfully and intentionally was strapped to a chair in a dark room for many hours and left alone as a result of his mental and physical handicap.

The damages clause asked for $1,500,000.00 in compensatory damages and $1,500,000.00 in punitive damages.

Thereafter, Mr. Hunter submitted answers to interrogatories on behalf of the plaintiffs listing the names of several individuals who served as the basis for the allegation that Quinton had in many instances been left alone in a dark room for many hours. However, none of the individuals testified to such incidents during discovery.

On December 11, 1995, the defendants moved for summary judgment. The court dismissed Mr. and Mrs. Stephens causes of action for intentional infliction of emotional distress. The court also dismissed Quinton's claim for intentional infliction of emotional distress for the "many instances" in which he was allegedly strapped in a chair in a dark room for many hours. This claim was dismissed because the only evidence plaintiffs produced during discovery was the testimony of Mary Ellen Davis, Quinton's special education teacher, that one day she found Quinton in the chair in his classroom when all the other children were up and about in the same room. Finally, the claim for punitive damages was dismissed for being duplicative of the claim for damages from intentional infliction of emotional distress. Only Quinton's claim for intentional infliction of emotional distress was permitted to go forward.

Subsequently, the plaintiffs requested a voluntary dismissal of the remaining claim in order to appeal the summary judgment order. The defendants then filed a motion for sanctions under Rule 11 of the West Virginia Rules of Civil Procedure. Thereafter, the parties reached an agreement whereby the plaintiffs agreed to dismiss the appeal and all claims with prejudice in return for the defendants dismissing the Rule 11 motion and agreeing not to seek attorney sanctions against either Mr. Hunter or Mr. Neely.

On March 17, 1997, the Investigative Panel of the Board filed a Statement of Charges in this matter. Mr. Neely was charged with violating Rule 4.4 of the West Virginia Rules of Professional Conduct [5] based on the settlement demand letters he sent to the Center's insurance company. [6] Mr. Neely and Mr. Hunter were both

---

[5] Rule 4.4 of the West Virginia Rules of Professional Conduct provides: In representing a client, a lawyer shall not use means that have no substantial purpose other than to embarrass, delay, or burden a third person, or use methods of obtaining evidence that violate the legal rights of such a person.

[6] On May 26, 1995, Mr. Neely wrote a letter to Karen M. Meyd, senior claims representative for The Maryland Insurance Group, informing her that Mr. Hunter had entered law practice with him. The letter stated that he intended to file a civil action asking for "substantial damages, both compensatory and punitive." The letter further stated:

> I understand from my clients that effective next year, your clients are going to be doing a large amount of special care for the handicapped, particularly wheelchair bound special needs students. Since this law firm tends to be extraordinarily high-profile, and since the mere filing of a complaint may cause your clients unnecessary embarrassment, if you would like to discuss the settlement of this claim before the filing of the suit, I shall be more than pleased to do so.

In a subsequent letter which included a copy of the proposed complaint and first set of interrogatories

charged with violating Rule 3.1 [7] in that the complaint filed by Mr. Neely asserted emotional distress counts on behalf of Linda and Quewanncoii Stephens, a count of intentional battery on behalf of Quinton Stephens, and a count of emotional distress based on many alleged instances where Quinton had been left alone in a dark room for many hours.

On October 10, 1997, the Hearing Panel Subcommittee issued a report which dismissed the Rule 4.4 charge and by majority vote, found a violation of Rule 3.1 by both Mr. Hunter and Mr. Neely. The Board recommended admonishment. Thereafter, pursuant to Rules 3.11 and 3.13 of the West Virginia Rules of Lawyer Disciplinary Procedure, Mr. Hunter and Mr. Neely filed a notice of objection to the Hearing Panel Subcommittee Report with this Court.[8]

*   *   *

In this proceeding, the Board found a violation of Rule 3.1 based solely on the allegations set forth in paragraph VII of the complaint.[9] The Board concluded that a reasonable attorney should have known that the allegations set forth in paragraph

---

and requests for production of documents, Mr. Neely made a settlement demand of $151,516.00 and further stated:

> Although (as you can see from my immediate preparation of the included paperwork) I have little true expectation that this case will settle until right before trial, if at all, I nonetheless believe that it is in everyone's interest to devote the roughly $40,000 that you would need to spend to defend this lawsuit through a nasty trial to the settlement fund. In addition, of course, your client will be spared substantial embarrassment, as this is obviously a case that will attract substantial press attention because of the profile of my clients.

> Both of the parents involved in this case are prominent in the Charleston Community. Quewanncoii Stephens is a retired lieutenant colonel in the United States Army; he was a Ranger, Airborne troop who commanded special forces in Vietnam. LTC Stephens has been awarded two bronze stars and one army commendation medal (valor). LTC Stephens is currently a member of the West Virginia Board of Probation and Parole, and he formerly served as executive director of the West Virginia Human Rights Commission.

[7] Rule 3.1 of the West Virginia Rules of Professional Conduct provides, in pertinent part: A lawyer shall not bring or defend a proceeding, or assert or controvert an issue therein, unless there is a basis for doing so that is not frivolous, which includes a good faith argument for an extension, modification or reversal of existing law.

[8] The ODC did not object to the Board's dismissal of the Rule 4.4 charge against Mr. Neely. Therefore, that issue is not before this Court. However, we are troubled by the threatening content of the letters Mr. Neely sent to the insurance company. While Mr. Neely claims he only intended to facilitate a settlement, his predictions of adverse publicity and a nasty trial were inappropriate and overreaching. The claim that "this law firm tends to be extraordinarily high-profile" and the threat to cause "substantial embarrassment" and "unnecessary embarrassment," along with irrelevant character assertions and claims of high public position (i.e. that one is a member of the West Virginia Board of Probation and Parole and an executive director of the West Virginia Human Rights Commission) are all practices that play no legitimate role in settlement negotiations. We have a large body of law which compels insurance companies to negotiate fairly, and that requirement is a two-edged sword. Simply put, what the lawyer did in this case was unfair and inappropriate.

[9] Paragraph VII of the complaint stated:

> Plaintiffs Linda Stephens and Quewanncoii Stephens have diligently investigated the facts and circumstances surrounding this incident. As a result of interviews with persons associated with Fort Hill Child Development Center, Inc., plaintiffs verily believe that the incident described in paragraph III through VI is but one of *many instances* in which Plaintiff Quinton Stephens, an autistic child, who was known to have special needs, in direct contravention of the express directions of Quinton's parents of his health care providers, was knowingly, willfully and intentionally strapped to a chair in a dark room for many hours and left alone directly as a result of his mental and physical handicap.

VII were unwarranted and that Mr. Hunter and Mr. Neely knew they were without basis. In reaching this decision, the Board recognized that the entire lawsuit was not baseless or frivolous because Quinton Stephens' intentional tort claim survived the motion for summary judgment. In effect, the Board seeks to admonish Mr. Hunter and Mr. Neely for factual assertions set forth in a single paragraph of a complaint that later proved to be false.

This case illustrates the difficulties in determining what is a frivolous lawsuit. In *Committee on Legal Ethics of the West Virginia State Bar v. Douglas*, 370 S.E.2d 325 (1988), this Court set forth a test to determine whether a lawyer had advanced a frivolous claim. However, the Code of Professional Responsibility was in effect at that time. DR 7-102(A)(2) provided that a lawyer shall not "[k]nowingly advance a claim or defense that is unwarranted under existing law, except that he may advance such claim or defense if it can be supported by good faith argument for an extension, modification, or reversal of existing law." Recognizing that DR 7-102(A)(2) was aimed at frivolousness, this Court set forth a twofold inquiry under the rule. The test first required an objective determination of whether the claim or defense was "'unwarranted' under the law." A more subjective determination of whether the lawyer asserted the claim or defense with knowledge that it was unwarranted completed the inquiry.

With the adoption of the Rules of Professional Conduct, and more specifically Rule 3.1, an objective standard was established to determine the propriety of pleadings and other court papers. Nonetheless, the term "frivolous," now a part of the rule, remains undefined. However, the Comment to the rule is instructive regarding what conduct is permissible and what constitutes frivolousness. The Comment provides, in pertinent part:

> The filing of an action or defense or similar action taken for a client is not frivolous merely because the facts have not first been fully substantiated or because the lawyer expects to develop vital evidence only by discovery. Such action is not frivolous even though the lawyer believes that the client's position ultimately will not prevail. The action is frivolous, however, if the client desires to have the action taken primarily for the purpose of harassing or maliciously injuring a person or if the lawyer is unable either to make a good faith argument on the merits of the action taken or to support the action taken by a good faith argument for an extension, modification or reversal of existing law.

It is obvious that the drafters of the rules acknowledged that when lawyers prepare and file pleadings in civil actions, they routinely make factual allegations in support of their theories of liability and assert defenses in response thereto, some of which ultimately prove to be unsubstantiated. The Comment suggests that these practices do not warrant discipline under Rule 3.1. In fact, federal courts have been reluctant to impose sanctions for such practices under Rule 11.[12]

While we remain concerned about the increasing number of cases that clog our court dockets, we recognize that there are instances where an attorney has exhausted all avenues of pre-suit investigation and needs the tools of discovery to

---

[12] In *Douglas*, this Court also recognized the interrelationship between DR 7-102(A)(2) and Rule 11 of the West Virginia Rules of Civil Procedure. While Rule 11 provides a private remedy, Rule 3.1 is aimed at preventing repeat offenders escaping notice and building confidence in the legal system as a whole.

complete factual development of the case. An action or claim is not frivolous if after a reasonable investigation, all the facts have not been first substantiated. A complaint may be filed if evidence is expected to be developed by discovery. A lawyer may not normally be sanctioned for alleging facts in a complaint that are later determined to be untrue.

As previously discussed, the specific allegations in paragraph VII of the Stephens' complaint were not ultimately supported by the facts developed during discovery. Nonetheless, the record indicates that Mr. Hunter and Mr. Neely conducted a reasonable investigation of the case. Because of his autism, Quinton was unable to provide any information about his care at the Center. However, Mrs. Stephens provided the details of what happened on December 2, 1994. In addition, she related at least three other incidents which suggested that the Center may not have been rendering adequate supervision of Quinton. Mrs. Stephens also told Mr. Neely about conversations she had with some of the employees at the Center which caused her to believe that Quinton's posture correcting chair had been used for discipline or management purposes against her specific directions. The record indicates that Mr. Hunter and Mr. Neely received no cooperation from the defendants during their investigation. In the end, they were left with the choice of advising the Stephenses to give up or file the complaint and proceed with discovery. Given these circumstances, we find that Mr. Hunter and Mr. Neely did not violate Rule 3.1.

Accordingly, based on all of the above, the complaint filed against Mr. Hunter and Mr. Neely is dismissed.

Charges dismissed.

WORKMAN, JUSTICE, concurring:

I initially put down for a concurring opinion to say only that although the Lawyer Disciplinary Board dropped the charge involving the letter written to the complainant herein, it should be made clear that the tone and tenor of that letter was threatening and it was wrong. Indeed, it is the kind of thing that can give lawyers a very bad reputation.

The record shows that Mrs. Hawks runs a reputable business that provides a real service to children whose parents must leave them in day care in order to go to work. The letter sent to her by the lawyer here was intimidating and basically threatened to ruin her business and her reputation if she did not meet its demands. This is not a legitimate effort at settlement, but more in the manner of intimidation. As the majority opinion points out, had the charge involving the letter not been dropped by the Lawyer Disciplinary Board, Neely may well have been sanctioned.

After reading the local Charleston newspapers on July 16 and 17, however, I feel it necessary to expand this concurring opinion to say more. If quoted correctly in the newspapers, Mr. Neely and Mr. Hunter had the audacity to once again claim the lawsuit they brought against Mrs. Hawks and the Fort Hill Day Care Center had merit.[1] This is fairly incredible in view of the fact that the lower court dismissed

---

[1] The *Charleston Daily Mail* on July 16, 1998, and the *Charleston Gazette* on July 17, 1998, quoted Richard Neely as saying that the charges against him were "silly," and characterized the ethics complaint as an allegation "that I too vigorously went to bat for a black autistic child allegedly *abused* in a day care center." (emphasis added) Roger Hunter is quoted as saying that the lawsuit (against the center) was "meritorious."

part of the lawsuit as being without merit and in view of the fact that lawyers Neely and Hunter sought a voluntary dismissal of their remaining claims (and agreed not to appeal the lower court's dismissal)[2] in exchange for the defendants agreeing to dismiss a Rule 11 motion seeking monetary sanctions against them.

It is amazing that after getting off by the skin of their teeth for filing a spurious lawsuit and writing a threatening letter, Neely and Hunter would actually again attempt to cast aspersions against this individual and this day care center. These lawyers may never learn their lesson until the time comes when a real sanction is imposed, either through ethical proceedings or in the form of a lawsuit. If they were misquoted, they should immediately demand that a correction be printed. But if they were not misquoted, then shame on them for conducting themselves in this manner. It does not bring respect to the profession.

*   *   *

NOTES

1.   There is often a relationship between lack of merit in a claim and a finding that the claim was made for abusive or harassing purpose. In *Committee on Legal Ethics of the West Virginia State Bar v. Douglas*, 370 S.E.2d 325 (W. Va. 1988), a lawyer was charged with a violation of state rules prohibiting the filing of frivolous or harassing claims. The lawyer, Douglas, represented an individual in a paternity action. *Id.* at 333. Following the preparation of an answer to the paternity claim in which the client denied paternity, the lawyer filed a countersuit against the mother. *Id.* In the countersuit the client alleged that the defendant/mother had contracted with the client to impregnate her and that, in the event she gave birth to a normal child, the client was entitled to a "stud fee." *Id.* The claim was later dismissed. *Id.* In addressing the behavior of the lawyer in filing the countersuit, the court described the claim as factually unsupported, contrary to the defenses raised in the related paternity suit, and "strongly suggestive" of improper motive. *Id.* at 336.

2.   Sanctions for harassing or vexatious claims can be severe in egregious circumstances. In *In re Jafree*, 444 N.E.2d 143 (Ill. 1982), the court ordered disbarment of a lawyer in a disciplinary proceeding. The court concluded that the lawyer, during his 10-year career, had instituted more than 40 frivolous lawsuits and appeals. *Id.* at 148. The court noted some of the more objectionable suits, including a claim on behalf of all the trees in the United States to have the in forma

---

[2] According to the majority opinion: On December 11, 1995, the defendants moved for summary judgment. The court dismissed Mr. and Mrs. Stephens causes of action for intentional infliction of emotional distress. The court also dismissed Quinton's claim for intentional infliction of emotional distress for the "many instances" in which he was allegedly strapped in a chair in a dark room for many hours. This claim was dismissed because the only evidence plaintiffs produced during discovery was the testimony of Mary Ellen Davis, Quinton's special education teacher, that one day she found Quinton in the chair in his classroom when all the other children were up and about in the same room. Finally, the claim for punitive damages was dismissed for being duplicative of the claim for damages from intentional infliction of emotional distress. Only Quinton's claim for intentional infliction of emotional distress was permitted to go forward.

Subsequently, the plaintiffs requested a voluntary dismissal of the remaining claim in order to appeal the summary judgment order. Defendants then filed a motion for sanctions under Rule 11 of the West Virginia Rules of Civil Procedure. Thereafter, the parties reached an agreement whereby plaintiffs agreed to dismiss the appeal and all claims with prejudice in return for the defendants dismissing the Rule 11 motion and agreeing not to seek attorney sanctions against either Mr. Hunter or Mr. Neely.

pauperis forms used in the Federal District Court declared unconstitutional. *Id.* Jafree had also filed a complaint with the Pollution Control Board charging an individual with pollution of the mind and contamination of the air in the context of a character assassination. *Id.* In assessing what degree of discipline was warranted, the court concluded:

> Since admittance to the bar of this State, respondent's legal career has been characterized by the filing of frivolous lawsuits and scurrilous charges. He continuously repeats irrelevant and unfounded charges against everyone whom he feels has wronged him. . . . We cannot help but conclude that respondent is incapable of conforming his conduct to an acceptable standard. His unprofessionalism is an abuse of the privilege to practice law and clearly tends to bring the judicial system and legal profession into disrepute. Accordingly, we adopt the recommendations of the hearing panel and Review Board and order that respondent be disbarred.

Id. at 149–150.

3. Note that the rule on meritorious claims, like many ethics rules, seeks to protect the public confidence in the legal system and maintain the reputation of the legal profession. Thus, where a lawyer filed numerous frivolous suits against judges, other lawyers, and laymen, the court upheld disciplinary action against the lawyer, noting that while he did not forfeit his personal access to the courts by reason of becoming a lawyer, he became an officer of court and was required to "accept the imposition of certain standards of conduct, which, hopefully, are conducive to maintaining faith in the integrity of the legal profession and the judiciary." *In re Sarelas*, 277 N.E.2d 313, 318 (Ill. 1971). Noting that a review of the lawyer's prior lawsuits was a "a tribute to the patience and tolerance of those conducting the proceeding that they were able to maintain any semblance of an orderly procedure," the court concluded that the lawyer's conduct warranted disbarment, but that a lack of evidence relating to other professional persuaded the court to suspend the lawyer for two years. *Id.* How do frivolous claims — particularly those initiated on behalf of lawyers themselves — impact the reputation of the legal profession and the public confidence in the legal system?

Chapter 8

APPELLATE BRIEFS

One of the greatest things that can cause a court to favorably view a brief's argument is the hard-won, long-term reputation of the authoring lawyer as an ethical, candid, and honest writer.

— Coleen Barger, Professor of Law, UALR Bowen School of Law

The Model Rules of Professional Conduct set forth ethical rules relating to competence and candor that should influence lawyers as they prepare appellate briefs. In addition, appellate court rules govern the format and content of appellate briefs and therefore impose standards of competence and professionalism. For example, the Federal Rules of Appellate Procedure indicate the required components of federal appellate briefs and, for many components, proscribe certain minimum content requirements. Fed. R. App. P. 28. Under Federal Rule of Appellate Procedure 38, a lawyer many be sanctioned for filing a frivolous appeal. The Federal Rules of Civil Procedure also impose ethical obligations on attorneys. For example, Rule 11 requires an attorney to attest to the truthfulness of material contained in pleadings and motions. Fed. R. Civ. P. 11.

The portion of this chapter devoted to content-based considerations is designed to highlight the ethical and professional considerations associated primarily with the argument section of an appellate brief. These obligations arise primarily in the context of the lawyer's ethical duties involving competence and candor to the court. The portion of this chapter devoted to format considerations addresses lapses in professionalism attributable to failure to conform to local rules.

I. CONTENT-BASED CONSIDERATIONS

A. Overview

i. Competence

With regard to the filing of an appellate brief, the lawyer's initial ethical obligation involves selecting the appropriate issues for appeal. Comment 5 to Model Rule 1.1 requires that the competent lawyer inquire into and analyze "the factual and legal elements of the problem, and use methods and procedures meeting the standards of competent practitioners. [The lawyer's duty] also includes adequate preparation." Model Rules of Prof'l Conduct R. 1.1 cmt. 5 (2008). Similarly, DR 6-101(A)(1) provides that a lawyer shall not "handle a matter which he knows or should know that he is not competent to handle, without associating himself with a lawyer who is competent to handle [the matter.]" DR 6-101(A)(2) requires "preparation adequate in the circumstances." Consequently, thorough research into the legal issues to be appealed is critical. Related to this is the obligation of the lawyer to properly analyze the law and present that analysis in a thorough, reasoned manner. Finally, competence requires familiarity with local rules applicable to the appeal.

ii.   Candor

Lawyers also have an obligation of candor under the Model Rules. Model Rule 3.3 prohibits an attorney from submitting false material to a tribunal and requires the lawyer to disclose adverse authority. Chapter 8 of the Model Rules contains various prohibitions against engaging in conduct that involves dishonesty or deceit. The disciplinary rules under Canon 7 of the Model Code contain similar requirements. Therefore, in connection with the preparation of an appellate brief, the lawyer's obligation of candor requires that she properly present the facts of the appeal as well as the applicable law, including authority that is adverse to her appeal.

B.   Competence and Candor in Appellate Briefs

i.   Proper Identification of an Appealable Issue

Model Rule 3.1 introduces the lawyer's obligation as an advocate and includes the following ethical prohibition: "A lawyer shall not bring or defend a proceeding, or assert or controvert an issue therein, unless there is a basis in law and fact for so doing so that it is not frivolous, which includes a good faith argument for an extension, modification or reversal of existing law." In assessing whether an action is frivolous, the comments explain that "[t]he action is frivolous . . . if the lawyer is either unable to make a good faith argument on the merits of the action taken or to support the action taken by a good faith argument for an extension, modification or reversal of existing law." Model Rules of Prof'l Conduct R. 3.1 cmt. 2 (2008). A lawyer can be sanctioned under Federal Rule of Appellate Procedure for filing a frivolous appeal. Fed. R. App. P. 38. In addition, Rule 11 of the Federal Rules of Civil Procedure requires that the lawyer have a good faith belief in the viability of claims made in pleadings. So, as an initial matter, the lawyer must assess whether a good faith argument does exist to support the client's claim. The following case provides a detailed discussion of the justifications behind Rule 11 and the court's requisite analysis of an allegedly frivolous claim. Bear in mind that the underlying dispute in *Eastway* involved fairly complex antitrust issues. Your focus should not be on the underlying dispute, but on the court's analysis of the lawyer's behavior in advancing the claims.

EASTWAY CONST. CORP. v. CITY OF NEW YORK
637 F. Supp. 558 (E.D.N.Y. 1986)

This matter was remanded for the awarding of attorney's fees under Rule 11 of the Federal Rules of Civil Procedure and 42 U.S.C. § 1988. *Eastway Construction Corp. v. City of New York*, 762 F.2d 243 (2d Cir.1985) (*"Eastway I"*). For the reasons indicated below, a modest portion of defendant's attorney's fees is assessed against the plaintiffs, while no fees are assessed against plaintiffs' counsel.

I. FACTS AND PROCEDURAL HISTORY

[Plaintiff Eastway Construction Corporation (Eastway") is a general contractor. During the 1960s and 1970s Eastway engaged exclusively in construction work on publicly financed housing rehabilitation projects in New York City. Between 1966 and 1974, defendant City of New York ("City") loaned nearly twelve million dollars to certain limited partnerships of Eastway. However, the partnerships fell behind in their loan payments, so that by March 1983 all but three buildings had reverted to City ownership through default. The mortgages on the remaining three buildings were in arrears for a total of approximately three million dollars.

In the early 1970's, following a corruption scandal, the City revised its public housing finance laws. Under the new laws, the City refused to enter into rehabilitation contracts with entities that had defaulted on loans from the City.

Community Preservation Corporation ("CPC") was a private consortium of banks that did business with the City. CPC provided low interest loans to developers to facilitate rehabilitation projects.

Because Eastway was not eligible for City financing, one of its affiliates attempted to secure a loan from CPC. The loan was rejected.

Because Eastway was unable to secure work on either publicly or privately financed rehabilitation projects, it brought suit in federal court. The complaint raised two claims under federal law. The first claim was an antitrust claim in which Eastway claimed that the City and CPC conspired to prevent Eastway from doing business. The second claim was a due process claim in which Eastway claimed that the City had deprived Eastway of its rights without due process of law.

The City and CPC moved for summary judgment and each requested an award of attorneys' fees. The district court granted summary judgment but denied the requests for attorneys' fees, stating that Eastway's claims were not frivolous. Eastway appealed the grant of summary judgment and the City and CPC appealed the denial of attorneys' fess.

The Court of Appeals affirmed the grant of summary judgment, but characterized Eastway's claims as "groundless" for purposes of the attorneys' fees request. It remanded the attorneys' fees issue to the district court. Costs incurred in defending the due process claim were to be assessed under 42 U.S.C. § 1988, and costs incurred in defending the antitrust claim were to be assessed against plaintiffs or plaintiffs' counsel or both under Rule 11 of the Federal Rules of Civil Procedure.]

The case is therefore now before this court for a determination of 1) the proper amount of attorney's fees to be awarded to the municipal defendants, and 2) the person or persons who should pay those fees.

II. LAW

A. *Purpose and Relationship of Rule 11 and 42 U.S.C. § 1988*

The traditional American rule is that each party to litigation bears its own costs, including attorney's fees. This furthers our policy, demonstrated also by fee absorption and other devices such as contingency fees, of keeping the courts as open as possible. Congress has over the years enacted numerous statutory exceptions to the general rule against fee-shifting. The courts, through rules and interpretation, have gradually expanded these exceptions.

Courts have quite properly distinguished between two different purposes of the fee-shifting statutes and rules. One purpose is to compensate *plaintiffs* for the actual cost of vindicating legal rights, by partial analogy to the English system, in order to encourage private attorney general suits in enforcement of important public policies. The second is to deter unfounded claims and defenses by assessing fees as a punitive measure. The second purpose is usually applied in favor of *defendants*, with the secondary effect of compensating the aggrieved litigant for legal fees that he should never have been forced to incur.

Prominent among statutes providing an incentive for private enforcement of federal law is the Civil Rights Attorney's Fees Awards Act of 1976, which provides for grants of attorney's fees to successful parties in actions brought under 42 U.S.C. §§ 1981–1983 & 1985–1986 and other civil rights provisions. Similarly, the Civil Rights Act of 1964 contains a provision awarding attorney's fees to successful parties in actions brought under Title VII of the Act.

In applying these statutes to determine when to make awards of attorney's fees to plaintiffs, courts have been quite liberal, concluding that attorney's fees are routinely available to all prevailing plaintiffs. There are two reasons for such openness. "First, . . . the plaintiff is the chosen instrument of Congress to vindicate 'a policy that Congress considered of the highest priority.' Second, when a district court awards counsel fees to a prevailing plaintiff, it is awarding them against a violator of federal law." The plaintiff, in short, is acting as a private attorney general, and such behavior is to be encouraged by liberal compensation.

In addition to fee-shifting provisions that are intended to encourage the bringing of some lawsuits, there are provisions intended to deter the bringing of others. It is these provisions that are of primary interest in this case. Among them are the two provisions just discussed, 42 U.S.C. § 1988 and 42 U.S.C. § 2000a-3(b), as applied in determining whether to award fees to prevailing *defendants*, as well as Rule 11 of the Federal Rules of Civil Procedure. The purpose of these provisions is to discourage litigants from bringing frivolous cases or making frivolous motions.

Because such provisions 1) are in derogation of the general American policy of encouraging resort to the courts for peaceful resolution of disputes, 2) tend to breed time-consuming and expensive satellite litigation, and 3) increase tensions among the litigating bar and between bench and bar, the standard for imposition of sanctions is high. The provisions do not entitle all prevailing defendants to an award of fees; instead, fees are to be awarded only if the claim or motion was entirely unjustified, i.e., frivolous. Although they do contain a compensation element, the primary purpose of this group of provisions is deterrence. . . .

While none of the deterrence-oriented provisions actually uses the word "frivolous," courts nonetheless consistently employ a "frivolousness" standard in determining whether an award of fees is appropriate. To properly inform the bar, simplify administration, and maximize substantive impact, it is advisable that the degree of frivolousness needed to trigger sanctions under each of these provisions be the same.

"Frivolous" is of the same order of magnitude as "less than a scintilla." It is defined in Webster's Third New International Dictionary (1967) as "of little weight or importance: having no basis in law or fact: light, slight, sham, irrelevant, superficial." The Oxford English Dictionary (1971) defines it as "[o]f little or no weight, value or importance; paltry; trumpery; not worthy of serious attention; having no reasonable ground or purpose. . . . In pleading: Manifestly insufficient or futile."

*   *   *

(1) Objective and Subjective Standards.

Rule 11 read literally contains both subjective and objective components. In pertinent part, it states:

> Every pleading, motion, and other paper of a party represented by an attorney shall be signed by at least one attorney of record.. . . The signature of an attorney . . . constitutes a certificate by him that he has read the pleading, motion, or other paper; that *to the best of his knowledge, information, and belief* formed after *reasonable inquiry* it is well grounded in fact and is warranted by existing law or a good faith argument for the extension, modification, or reversal of existing law. . . . If a pleading, motion, or other paper is signed in violation of this rule, the court . . . shall impose upon the person who signed it, a represented party, or both, an appropriate sanction, which may include an order to pay to the other party or parties the amount of the reasonable expenses incurred because of the filing of the pleading, motion, or other paper, including a reasonable attorney's fee.

(Emphasis added). The text suggests that the obligation imposed by the Rule is partly objective, and partly subjective. The requirement that the attorney base his certification on a "reasonable inquiry" is objective, because what is "reasonable" is judged by objective norms of reasonable attorneys. But the certification itself need only state that the motion is well grounded "to the best of [the attorney's] knowledge, information, and belief." Since the certification relates to the attorney's own beliefs, it appears that it should be judged by a subjective standard. Even the subjective component has objective aspects since, as a matter of evidence, the judge will rely on what reasonable lawyers would have known or believed under the circumstances in deciding what this lawyer believed.

The objective "reasonable inquiry" element of Rule 11 serves to protect attorneys who reach reasonable, but erroneous, conclusions about the validity of their cases. Before a suit is filed, often only a limited investigation into the law and facts is possible. If an attorney makes a reasonable investigation under the circumstances and concludes based on that investigation that the pleading is well grounded in law and fact, he cannot be sanctioned for filing the pleading when time and discovery prove that the plaintiff does not in fact have a viable claim. *See Advisory Committee Notes to Rule 11* ("[W]hat constitutes a reasonable inquiry may depend on such factors as how much time for investigation was available to the signer . . . [and] whether he had to rely on a client for information as to the facts underlying the pleading. . . .").

A more difficult question is whether the apparently subjective element of Rule 11 can protect attorneys who honestly reach unreasonable conclusions about the factual or legal strength of their cases. What if an attorney conducts a reasonable inquiry into the facts and the law and concludes, honestly but mistakenly, that the law supports his pleading, even though the pleading would be recognized as plainly frivolous by a minimally competent member of the bar? A literal reading of the Rule would indicate that such conduct is not sanctionable because the attorney has clearly complied with the letter of the Rule: he has certified that to the best of his knowledge, information and belief, formed after a reasonable inquiry into the facts and the law, that the pleading is well grounded. This reading is also supported by the rationale behind the Rule, namely deterrence. While sanctioning an attorney's failure to make a reasonable inquiry might make him more diligent in the future, sanctioning honest errors is unlikely to prevent their recurrence. *Cf.* The American Law Institute, *Model Penal Code Tentative Draft No. 4*, at 140 (1955) ("In the absence of minimal culpability, the [criminal] law has neither a deterrent nor corrective nor an incapacitative function to perform.").

Eastway I holds that policy requires that Rule 11 not be read according to its literal terms. In a telling paraphrase of the language of Rule 11, the Second Circuit restated the requirement of the Rule as follows: "[S]anctions shall be imposed [if], after reasonable inquiry, a *competent* attorney could not form a *reasonable* belief that the pleading is well grounded in fact and is warranted by existing law. . . ." While the Rule requires certification only by the actual attorney of his actual beliefs, *Eastway I* requires the reasonable beliefs of a hypothetical competent attorney. The Second Circuit's restatement of the rule effectively eliminates the subjective element incorporated by the drafters of the Rule. As a result, an attorney's erroneous conclusion that a pleading is well grounded may lead to sanctions. *Eastway I*, in other words, holds attorneys strictly liable for mistakes in judgment that lead to the filing of papers later deemed frivolous. While application to lawyers of a penal rule from which mens rea has been eliminated is inconsistent with American penal and professional traditions, the courts of this circuit are bound by *Eastway I*.

* * *

Rule 11 authorizes the trial court to impose sanctions upon the attorney, his client, or both, but provides no standards to guide the court's decision as to how the allocation should be made. Both courts and commentators have suggested that the court should direct sanctions at whoever is responsible for the filing of the frivolous paper.

In practice, assessment of fault between attorney and client is rather difficult. There are some cases in which it is fairly clear who should be sanctioned. For example, the attorney alone is generally responsible for sharp practice, such as a frivolous motion to disqualify opposing counsel. And where the client misleads his attorney and thus causes him to file frivolous papers, it is apparent that the client, not the attorney, should be sanctioned. Most cases, however, will not fall into either extreme, leaving the court with a great deal of discretion and very little direction in allocating sanctions.

Even this analysis, modest as it is, is not quite accurate. In the case in which it was suggested that fees be assessed against the client alone, Rule 11 does not — technically speaking — even apply. Rule 11 does not, by its terms, provide for sanctions against the filing of frivolous papers. Rather, it provides for sanctions against an attorney's filing papers without making an adequate inquiry. In a case in which an attorney makes a reasonable inquiry into the facts but still ends up filing a frivolous pleading because his client deceived him, there has technically not been any violation of Rule 11. Consequently, there is technically no basis for the imposition of sanctions, even against the client who in bad faith induced the filing a frivolous suit. This conclusion, however, is completely at odds with the spirit of the Rule. It would also lead to bizarre consequences, because it would mean that clients could be sanctioned in cases where they were partially responsible for filing frivolous papers, but not in cases where their responsibility was total. The better conclusion is that sanctions may be imposed against the client under the circumstances described above despite the flaw in the Rule's language.

As the trial court attempts to determine fault and allocate fees on that basis, the risk of creating substantial satellite litigation at great cost to the parties increases. First, there is a problem because of conflict of interest. If attorney and client disagree about who is at fault and point their fingers at each other, the interests of the two are now clearly adverse. The client, therefore, will need new counsel to represent him against his former counsel in the proceedings to determine fault. Second, the question of who is at fault is likely to involve disputed issues of fact, making further evidentiary hearings necessary. The implications of such a hearing, turning attorney against client, and the effect on attorney-client privilege and trust, may be devastating.

The reverse scenario, in which attorney and client not only do not contest relative fault before the court, but have agreed between themselves to privately reallocate any sanction imposed against them, may also present problems. The attorney and his client do not stand as equals before the court. Sanctions are imposed against the client purely for their deterrent effect. But sanctions are imposed against the attorney also for disciplinary purposes, as a punishment for dereliction of duty by an officer of the court who should know better. Allowing the client to reimburse the attorney would interfere with the court's attempt to maintain discipline. Therefore, reimbursement by the client should be prohibited. An attorney's agreement to reimburse his client presents no analogous problems, and therefore need not under usual circumstances be interfered with. Unless, therefore, the court explicitly rules otherwise, the attorney may assume fees assessed against the client, but the client may not pay fees imposed on the attorney.

*   *   *

Determining the kinds of sanctions and the amount of fees, if any, to be imposed requires consideration of the following factors: a) the cost of the Rule 11 violation to the party seeking sanctions, and b) mitigating factors such as (i) whether the client and lawyer believed they were correct in taking the course they did; (ii) whether there was vindictiveness or a desire to punish an opponent; (iii) whether the lawyer is a neophyte who needs education, a repeat offender, or a person of standing at the bar whose actions have heretofore been ethical and in the high tradition of the bar; (iv) the ability to pay; (v) the need for compensation; (vi) the degree of frivolousness; and (vii) the dangers in chilling the particular kind of litigation involved. In addition, there are questions relating to compensation for time spent on Rule 11 sanction litigation and on appeals.

*   *   *

The logical starting point for a determination of attorney's fees is a calculation of the number of hours reasonably expended in responding to the frivolous paper, multiplied by a reasonable hourly attorney's fee based on the prevailing market rate. . . .

* * *

While agreeing on the propriety of starting the calculation of an award of attorney's fees by multiplying a reasonable number of hours by a reasonable hourly rate, courts have not ended their inquiries at that point. Without explaining why they are doing it — and often without even noting that they are doing it — courts have reduced their awards of fees to prevailing defendants in both Rule 11 and section 1988 cases. In many cases a nominal award results. This unbroken line of authority requires us to consider the factors apart from the lodestar figure that courts must take into account in determining monetary Rule 11 sanctions.

* * *

Degree of frivolousness. Court opinions on attorney's fees speak easily of cases being either frivolous or nonfrivolous, as if all cases fit easily into one or the other category. Reality is more complicated. In the legal world, claims span the entire continuum from overwhelmingly strong to outrageously weak. Somewhere between these two points, courts draw a line to separate the nonfrivolous from the frivolous, the former category providing safe shelter, the latter subjecting attorney and client to sanctions.

Attorneys are thus placed in a dilemma because they have the right — in fact, they have an ethical obligation (subject to tactical considerations) — to present to the court all the nonfrivolous arguments that might be made on their clients' behalf, even if only barely nonfrivolous. They are forced by their position as advocates in the legal profession to live close to the line, wherever the courts may draw it. Yet Rule 11 threatens them with severe sanctions if they miscalculate ever so slightly the location of that line. As a result many members of the bar are concerned that Rule 11 will discourage attorneys from pursuing novel yet meritorious legal theories. The necessity of avoiding such an effect has also been widely recognized. As the Court of Appeals so eloquently put the matter:

> [W]e do not intend to stifle the enthusiasm or chill the creativity that is the very lifeblood of the law. Vital changes have been wrought by those members of the bar who have dared to challenge the received wisdom, and a rule that penalized such innovation would run counter to our notion of the common law itself.

Unless Rule 11 is applied in a way that minimizes the tension between creativity and sanctions, a chilling effect seems inevitable.

In part, the solution seems to lie in frank recognition of the fact that rather than being adequately described by the frivolous-nonfrivolous dichotomy, cases really do lie along a continuum. Some are clearly frivolous, some clearly nonfrivolous, and some are difficult to call. Attorney fee awards of the full market value of services rendered should be reserved for extremely frivolous cases, while more moderate awards should be given for frivolous filings near the border. This approach harmonizes with the deterrent approach of the Rule. It penalizes more severely conduct that society seeks more strongly to deter. But it penalizes only lightly filings in that zone where the bar's imagination and creativity assert themselves most strongly, thus helping to insulate attorneys from the chill of the Rule.

The Importance of Not Discouraging Particular Types of Litigation. By providing that when the court finds the pleading or other papers to be frivolous, it "shall" impose sanctions, Rule 11 takes the decision whether to impose sanctions out of the trial judge's hands. The premise underlying the Rule's mandatory sanction is that frivolous pleadings are worthless and are to be always condemned. But such an interpretation takes too narrow a view of the purposes of litigation.

Some litigations should be, if not encouraged, at least not discouraged. Of particular importance are cases brought against government officials and government agencies. Such suits are often the only effective channel for keeping within bounds official arrogance and lawlessness. At the very least, they publicize grievances and thus permit the ventilation of private outrage that the First Amendment's right to petition protects. They serve the public policy of avoiding violence by providing a peaceful forum. They may provide the basis for legislative and executive ameliorative action even when the courts lack power to act. Many civil rights cases fall into this category. So, too, do many prisoner habeas corpus cases. And even in what appear to be purely commercial actions, the threat of suit may deter official abuses such as favoritism.

Sometimes there are reasons to sue even when one cannot win. Bad court decisions must be challenged if they are to be overruled, but the early challenges are certainly hopeless. The first attorney to challenge *Plessy v. Ferguson* was certainly bringing a frivolous action, but his efforts and the efforts of others eventually led to *Brown v. Board of Education.*

*   *   *

Award of attorney's fees for time spent on appeal.

Prevailing plaintiffs in section 1988 cases are routinely awarded attorney's fees for time spent on a successful appeal. This is the logically correct result because success is the criterion for an award of fees to a civil rights suit plaintiff, and plaintiff's efforts on appeal have, by hypothesis, been successful.

In the case of Rule 11, an award of attorney's fees for the costs of defending an appeal can be made only if the appeal was frivolous. Generally the appellate court is in the best position to pass on whether an appeal is frivolous, and the district court is without authority to award attorney's fees for an appeal in the absence of instructions from the appellate court to do so. In the absence of an explicit direction from the appellate court, trial courts should not grant attorney's fees under Rule 11 for legal fees incurred on appeal.

*   *   *

The Court of Appeals found plaintiffs' complaint legally, rather than factually, frivolous. Under *Eastway I*'s purely objective standard holding attorneys strictly liable for unreasonably filing frivolous papers, there was, the appellate court implicitly found, no need for a hearing to determine whether the Rule had been violated. Although the plaintiff was still entitled to an evidentiary hearing to provide proof of any factual circumstances supporting mitigation of the amount of attorney's fees, the plaintiff did not request a hearing and none was therefore held. The court did hear oral argument on the legal standards involved, and the legal issues were briefed.

* * *

Frivolousness of the Complaint: The severity of the sanction to be imposed depends in part on the degree of frivolousness of the underlying claim. While the law of the case is that Eastway's claims were frivolous, investigation of the underlying substantive law reveals considerable support for Eastway's position.

The antitrust claim.

The Court of Appeals' analysis of Eastway's antitrust claim was very brief; it did "not tarry over Eastway's appeal," no doubt because the appellate court thought the frivolousness of the claim obvious. Nonetheless, it is possible to discern three separate points in the Second Circuit's discussion of the antitrust claim. First, the court seems to suggest that Eastway did not have antitrust standing, because the injury alleged was not "of the type that the antitrust laws are designed to prevent." Second, the court found that Eastway's complaint did not allege a group boycott of a sort that would constitute a *per se* violation of the antitrust laws. Finally, the court found that Eastway could not prevail by proving the existence of a group boycott that violated the rule of reason, because 1) even if there had been a conspiracy between the City and the CPC, "such action could not possibly have injured competition. Indeed, Eastway does not even allege anti-competitive effect,"; and 2) "neither the City nor CPC stood to gain from inhibition of competition among general contractors."

On the antitrust standing issue, the Court of Appeals appears, by citing and quoting Supreme Court decisions on antitrust standing, to be suggesting that Eastway lacks such standing. But *Associated General Contractors of California v. California State Council of Carpenters*, 459 U.S. 519 (1983), one of the opinions quoted by *Eastway I*, lends some support to plaintiffs' assertion of standing. The Court in *Associated* noted that "[t]here is a similarity between the struggle of common-law judges to articulate a precise definition of the concept of 'proximate cause' and the struggle of federal judges to articulate a precise test to determine whether a party injured by an antitrust violation may recover treble damages," The Court further explained that one factor to consider in determining whether the plaintiff has standing "is the directness or indirectness of the asserted injury," Since Eastway would have been a direct victim of the alleged conspiracy between the City and the consortium of many banks constituting the CPC, the quoted language arguably could be read to support its claim to standing.

In addition, the very complexity of the law on antitrust standing makes it difficult to say with assurance that any plaintiff's claim to have standing is obviously frivolous. One district court complained: "We must confess at the outset that we find antitrust standing cases more than a little confusing and certainly beyond our powers of reconciliation." Under the circumstances, [this] court finds that Eastway's claim that it had standing to bring an antitrust claim was not obviously frivolous.

Regarding the question whether Eastway's complaint had made out a *per se* violation of the antitrust laws, the Court of Appeals listed the cases relied upon by the plaintiffs and then commented in a footnote: "In those and other *per se* unlawful group boycott cases, the excluded plaintiff was in competition with some or all of the defendants. The same certainly cannot be said here; neither the City nor CPC competes in any way with any [plaintiff]." The Second Circuit's characterization of the three cases it listed by name, is accurate, and the factual distinction between those cases and the instant one is quite real. It is not obvious, however, that the distinction should be dispositive. While the three Supreme Court cases listed did indeed involve situations in which the plaintiff was in competition with at least one of the alleged conspirators, in none of those cases was that fact stated to be a basis for the decision. Put another way, while the competition in those cases between the plaintiff and at least one defendant was a fact, it was not necessarily a material fact.

Legal scholars have long been troubled by the question of when a group boycott constitutes a *per se* violation of the antitrust laws as opposed to simply being subject to the "rule of reason." The Court of Appeals' analysis distinguishing between *per se* and non-*per se* group boycotts on the basis of the existence or nonexistence of competition between the plaintiff and the defendants represents a logical attempt to devise simple rules to determine whether claims state a *per se* cause of action. But it does not represent any fully settled law.

Several circuits have attempted to devise tests for determining the extent of the *per se* rule. . . . The Supreme Court has itself noted the attempts by various courts and commentators to provide a workable definition of a group boycott that constitutes a *per se* violation, and concluded: "We express no opinion, however, as to the merit of any of these definitions." For the reasons stated, it is not completely clear that plaintiff's being a competitor of at least one of the parties to a group boycott is a *sine qua non* of a *per se* violation.

One Supreme Court decision provides at least some support for the opposite proposition, namely, that a group boycott can constitute a *per se* violation even when the plaintiff competes with none of the defendants. . . .

*   *   *

Whether or not a concerted refusal to deal is an illegal *per se* group boycott is, in sum, often difficult to say. As one court recently put it, "A concerted refusal to deal is generally subject to a rule of *per se* illegality. . . . However, a confusing array of exceptions and qualifications to this rule have developed, and case law in this area is unsettled."

Even if the alleged conspiracy did not constitute an illegal boycott *per se*, it might still have been found illegal under the rule of reason. The Second Circuit found to be frivolous even Eastway's claim that the boycott was illegal under the rule of reason, because the "conspiracy could not possibly have injured competition. Indeed, Eastway does not even allege anti-competitive effect." The Second Circuit's statement that the conspiracy *could not* have affected competition might be subject to factual dispute; nothing in the record indicates that anticompetitive effect was inconceivable. Certainly, the defendants' actions decreased the number of persons who could bid on rehabilitation projects. Furthermore, that Eastway's complaint did not allege anti-competitive effect is immaterial. All a pleading need do, even in antitrust cases, is give notice of the nature of the claim to the opposing side.

*   *   *

The Court of Appeals also found the rule of reason claim to be frivolous for a second reason, that "neither the City nor CPC stood to gain from inhibition of competition among general contractors." The Court of Appeals' position appears to be that unless the conspirators intended to improve their position at the expense of the victim of the conspiracy, the victim cannot prevail. But as other courts dealing with similar situations have noted, whether the conspirators intended to improve their positions at the victim's expense is only one of many factors to be considered in a rule of reason analysis. As one court stated:

> The motive which underlies a challenged restraint is but one element in the examination for reasonableness. . . . Additionally, we should consider the relative positive and negative effects, the power of the parties in the markets they serve, and whether other less restrictive means could be employed to achieve the same desired ends. . . .

The City and CPC dominate the relevant rehabilitation market, the boycott had a devastating effect on Eastway, and less restrictive alternatives may have been feasible. These factors arguably support Eastway's position.

For all of the above reasons, even though we are bound by the Court of Appeals' characterization of frivolousness, we cannot say that Eastway's antitrust claim was more than marginally frivolous. Many competent attorneys might have believed the claim viable.

The due process claim.

The Court of Appeals found Eastway's due process claim frivolous for two reasons. First, the court found that Eastway had not made out a claim for deprivation of "property" without due process of law because Eastway's interest in bidding on contracts did not rise to the level of a constitutionally protected, state-created property interest. Second, the court found that even if Eastway had a property right, the state court Article 78 proceeding had provided Eastway with sufficient process to protect Eastway's rights.

The Second Circuit emphasized that because Eastway had no entitlement to receive future contracts with the City, it possessed no protectible property interest. But the fourteenth amendment protects liberty interests as well as property interests, and several cases have held that government contractors may have a liberty interest in being allowed to bid for new contracts. As one court put it:

> One who has been dealing with the government on an ongoing basis may not be blacklisted, whether by suspension or debarment, without being afforded procedural safeguards including notice of the charges, an opportunity to rebut those charges, and under most circumstances, a hearing. . . . While the deprivation of the right to bid on government contracts is not a property interest . . . the bidder's liberty interest is affected when that denial is based on charges of fraud and dishonesty.

In addition, a recent Third Circuit case has held that government contractors do have a property right to bid on state contracts. *Berlanti v. Bodman*, 780 F.2d 296 (3d Cir.1985), involved a fact pattern remarkably similar to the one in *Eastway-*.. . . Because there is caselaw supporting the proposition that government contractors have a liberty or property interest in the right to bid, we cannot say that Eastway's assertion of constitutionally protected interests was more than marginally frivolous.

*   *   *

One final point in the Court of Appeals' *Eastway I* opinion deserves mention. In explaining its decision to award attorney's fees under section 1988, the court relied upon Eastway's prior unsuccessful state litigation, commenting: [W]e find it particularly noteworthy that Eastway had already challenged the City's policy in the state courts, and had been unsuccessful. These proceedings should at least have put it on notice of the possibility that its adversary might be awarded counsel fees. *See Carrion v. Yeshiva University*, 535 F.2d 722, 728 (2d Cir.1976) (upholding an award of attorney's fees to successful defendant in Title VII action, where plaintiff had brought similar claims in a state proceeding and had lost). The question of what Eastway should have learned from its setback in the state court is an interesting one, reminiscent of the dispute about whether the glass is half full or half empty. Eastway's loss on its state law claim in the Appellate Division certainly put it on notice that its federal claim might fail as well. But its successful motion for summary judgment in the New York Supreme Court also gave Eastway reason to believe that its case had some merit. This, in turn, gave Eastway some grounds to believe that it would not be sanctioned, especially considering *Eastway I*'s definition of "frivolousness" as a case where "it is patently clear that a claim has absolutely no chance of success." The *Carrion* case relied upon in *Eastway I* is arguably distinguishable, because plaintiff's state court action in *Carrion* had failed at *both* trial and appellate levels.

For all the above reasons, even though it is bound by the Second Circuit's characterization of frivolousness, this court cannot say that Eastway's due process claim was extremely frivolous. Many competent lawyers might have believed this claim to be viable.

*   *   *

Chilling This Type of Litigation.

Suits of this kind should not be kept out of court by threats of sanctions except in the clearest case of frivolousness. What lies below the surface in real estate litigation of this type against the City is the suspicion of widespread cronyism, favoritism and corruption. Contributions of real estate people to political campaigns are of major importance in New York City and State. Political connections are worth many millions of dollars in city contracts and other favors. There is no continuing method by which the criminal law, political processes or even the press can police this dangerously explosive combination of politics, money and power.

This litigation, had it been permitted to go forward, might have revealed unseemly aspects of the City's real estate transactions, an area long shadowed by charges of favoritism and politicization. Lurking behind the allegations in this suit were implications of serious misconduct by the City in granting favored — and unfavored — treatment. Under such conditions it becomes dangerous to throttle any avenue to the courts for vindication of rights of private real estate developers.

*   *   *

In accord with the mandate of the Court of Appeals, attorney's fees must be awarded in this case. Heavy sanctions would be unfair because *Eastway I* is a case of first impression; there was no reason for plaintiffs or their counsel to have predicted the objective standard Rule 11 ruling of the Court of Appeals. In addition, because the case was brought in good faith, because of the otherwise exemplary conduct of plaintiffs' counsel, because the pleading was only marginally frivolous, and for other reasons set forth in this opinion, attorney's fees in the amount of $1,000, jointly and severally, against plaintiffs Eastway Construction Corporation, Jaffee, Kanarek, and Jacobs, are sufficiently punitive.

This award is considerable in light of the nominal $100 sanctions imposed by other courts under similar circumstances. Courts must take care not to use their almost unlimited Rule 11 powers to punish in a vindictive and excessively harsh manner.

So ordered.

NOTES

1. In *Eastway*, the court clarified that the test for frivolousness under Rule 11 is an objective one. Similarly in *Dries & Krump v. International Ass'n of Machinists and Aerospace Workers*, 802 F.2d 247 (7th Cir. 1986), the court noted that the test under Rule 11 was objective and that the attorneys in question had "flunked" it. *Id.* at 255. In stressing the importance of the rule, the court admonished:

> Mounting federal caseloads and growing public dissatisfaction with the costs and delays of litigation have made it imperative that the federal courts impose sanctions on persons and firms that abuse their right of access to these courts. The rules, whether statutory or judge-made, designed to discourage groundless litigation are being and will continue to be enforced in this circuit to the hilt — as a recital of opinions published by this court since the first of the year imposing sanctions for groundless litigation should make clear. . . . Lawyers practicing in the Seventh Circuit, take heed!

Id. at 255–6.

2. Under *Eastway*, can a lawyer bring an appeal that asks for a reversal of existing law? What does the court mean by the acknowledgement that lawyers "are forced by their position as advocates in the legal profession to live close to the line" with respect to frivolous claims?

3. Were the lawyers in *Eastway* sanctioned because they failed to research the law properly? Or was it because they failed to analyze the law properly?

4. The *Eastway* court acknowledged that Rule 11 can have the effect of chilling certain types of claims that should be brought forth notwithstanding a lack of authoritative support, such as the claims advanced by the lawyers who first challenged the Supreme Court's ruling in *Plessy v. Ferguson*. Are there other types of claims that might be undermined by the threat of Rule 11 sanctions?

5. Note the *Eastway* court's acknowledgment of the limited burden associated with notice pleading. In noting that the City and CPC's alleged conspiracy might have been illegal under a rule of reason, the district court stated:

> The Second Circuit's statement that the conspiracy *could not* have affected competition might be subject to factual dispute; nothing in the record indicates that anticompetitive effect was inconceivable.. . . Fur-

thermore, that Eastway's complaint did not allege anti-competitive effect is immaterial. All a pleading need do, even in antitrust cases, is give notice of the nature of the claim to the opposing side.

Eastway, 637 F. Supp. at 580.

ii.   Competence in the Research and Analysis of the Legal Issue

As noted in the comment to Model Rule 1.1, "[c]ompetent handling of a particular matter includes inquiry into and analysis of the factual and legal elements of a problem." Model Rules of Prof'l Conduct R. 1.1 cmt. 5 (8). Further, "the analysis of precedent [and] the evaluation of evidence" are minimal obligations of competence required in all legal problems. Model Rules of Prof'l Conduct R. 1.1 cmt. 2 (2008). Therefore, the lawyer has an affirmative obligation to research and analyze the law. As an advocate, the lawyer's obligation of analysis requires her to "recognize the existence of pertinent legal authorities." Model Rules of Prof'l Conduct R. 3.3 cmt. 4 (2008). Minimum standards for research and analysis are also imposed by the Federal Rules of Appellate Procedure. Federal Rule of Appellate Procedure 28 governs appellate briefs and requires that the argument section include "the contentions [on appeal] and the reasons for them, with citations to the authorities and parts of the record on which the appellant relies." Finally, as noted in the previous section, under Federal Rule of Civil Procedure 11, the lawyer must have a good faith belief in the arguable viability of a claim.

STATE v. THOMAS
961 P.2d 299 (Utah 1998)

[Criminal suspect Richard Dee Thomas ("Thomas") was charged with a robbery of a fast food restaurant. During the criminal investigation, the manager of the restaurant was shown a photo array of six men and he identified Thomas as the man who committed the robbery.

During the criminal trial, Thomas moved to suppress the eyewitness identification, arguing that the photo array of the six men was overly suggestive. The motion was denied. Thomas was convicted.]

On appeal to the Utah Court of Appeals, Thomas asserted, inter alia, that the trial court erred when it denied Thomas's motion to suppress evidence and his motion to suppress eyewitness identification. In an unpublished memorandum decision, the court of appeals affirmed the trial court's rulings. Thomas then petitioned this court for certiorari review, and we granted the petition.

*   *   *

The second issue we address is whether the court of appeals erred when it declined to address Thomas's claim that the trial court erred in denying his motion to suppress a positive eyewitness identification made from a suspect photo array because Thomas failed to adequately brief the issue. The court of appeals stated: Thomas ignores several decisions addressing proper challenges to photo array cases. Because Thomas fails to adequately brief this argument, it is without merit and we decline to address it. *See* Utah R.App. P. 24(a)(9) (requiring "citations to the authorities [and] statutes . . . relied on").

A review of the record reveals that Thomas devoted four pages of his brief before the court of appeals to his photo array argument. However, almost three of these pages consisted of direct quotes from the trial transcript. On the basis of the trial testimony, Thomas then asserted that the photo array was overly suggestive. His only reference to any legal authority is contained in the bald assertions that the identification also taints any other identification of Mr. Thomas in violation of due process under the Fifth and Fourteenth Amendments to the United States Constitution. The overly suggestive photo array also violates Art. I, § 7 of the Utah State Constitution (Due process). These statements concluded his argument.

It is well established that a reviewing court will not address arguments that are not adequately briefed. *State v. Herrera*, 895 P.2d 359, 368 n. 5 (Utah 1995) (refusing to address defendant's state due process argument where argument entailed only superficial statement concerning Utah's unique history and reference to another part of defendant's brief); *State v. Wareham*, 772 P.2d 960, 966 (Utah 1989) (declining to rule on issue where defendant's brief "wholly lack[ed] legal analysis and authority to support his argument"); *State v. Amicone*, 689 P.2d 1341, 1344 (Utah 1984) (declining to rule on separation of powers argument where argument was not supported by any legal analysis or authority).

In deciding whether an argument has been adequately briefed, we look to the standard set forth in rule 24(a)(9) of the Utah Rules of Appellate Procedure. This rule states that the argument in the appellant's brief "shall contain the contentions and reasons of the appellant with respect to the issues presented . . . with citations to the authorities, statutes and parts of the record relied on." Implicitly, rule 24(a)(9) requires not just bald citation to authority but development of that authority and reasoned analysis based on that authority. We have previously stated that this court is not "a depository in which the appealing party may dump the burden of argument and research."

In his brief to the court of appeals, Thomas did cite to the Fifth and Fourteenth Amendments of the United States Constitution, to article I, section 7 of the Utah Constitution, and to the case of *State v. Ramirez*. However, this is all he did. Analysis of what this authority requires and of how the facts of Thomas's case satisfy these requirements was wholly lacking. The court of appeals also noted, "Thomas ignores several decisions addressing proper challenges to photo array cases." While failure to cite to pertinent authority may not always render an issue inadequately briefed, it does so when the overall analysis of the issue is so lacking as to shift the burden of research and argument to the reviewing court. Because of Thomas's lack of analysis, the photo array issue was inadequately briefed and the court of appeals was justified in declining to address it.

* * *

NOTES

1. Was the lawyer in *Thomas* criticized for failing to include the proper authority or for failing to analyze the authority submitted?

2. A failure to adequately brief issues on appeal may result in the court's rejection of those issues entirely. In a Utah opinion, the court, citing *Thomas*, rejected the majority of claims raised in appeal because the claims were not adequately briefed:

Taking a shotgun approach to his appeal, Green's brief identifies thirty-nine separate issues for our review. The 'argument' for eight of these issues consists of nothing more than a heading and the statement 'this issue will not be briefed at this time.' For another three issues, the argument consists merely of a heading and a reference to another part of the brief. Many of Green's remaining issues receive only one paragraph of argument or argument that recites facts and states a desired outcome, but is devoid of authority to explain the legal basis for the desired outcome. In those rare instances where Green does cite authority, he fails to provide any pinpoint citations that would assist the court in locating the relevant statements or holdings claimed to be supportive of his position. 'It is well established that a reviewing court will not address arguments that are not adequately briefed.' Consequently, we will restrict our review of this case to those issues to which Green has devoted sufficient attention for us to conduct an informed, meaningful analysis. Only three of Green's arguments on appeal meet this standard.

State v. Green, 99 P.3d 820, 824 (2008).

3.   Judicial opinions are filled with admonitions to lawyers who fail to research and analyze the law properly. A failing in this regard can have serious consequences. For example, in *Smith v. Four Corners Mental Health Center, Inc.*, 70 P.3d 904 (Utah 2003), the court refused to consider an argument for which there was no analysis. In addition, in *In LINC Finance Corp. v. Onwuteaka*, 129 F.3d 917 (7th Cir. 1997), the court criticized an experienced attorney for failing to include authority for arguments advanced in an appellate brief. The court reminded counsel that the Federal Rule of Appellate Procedure 28(a)(6) "requires that arguments in briefs contain 'citations to the authorities, statutes, and parts of the record relied on.'" *Id.* at 921. Further, while a failure to include requisite authority may not result in the dismissal of the appeal, it can constitute waiver of the issue on appeal. *Id.*

4.   In *Pearce v. Sullivan*, 871 F.2d 61 (7th Cir. 1989), the court criticized a lawyer for insufficient research, noting that an inadequate brief can constitute grounds for dismissal of the appeal:

A brief observation, finally, on the brief submitted to this court by Pearce's counsel, Mr. Burt L. Dancey of Pekin, Illinois. The brief is execrable. The argument portion is a paltry six pages of extra-large type, with nary a citation. Mr. Dancey was heard to grumble that this court had allotted him a mere ten minutes to present his argument. He was lucky that we did not dismiss the appeal for failure to present issues properly. It is not enough for an appellant in his brief to raise issues; they must be pressed in a professionally responsible fashion.. . . That was not done here, and we warn that the penalty for a perfunctory appeal brief can be dismissal of the appeal.

Id. at 64.

iii.   Accurate Representation of Facts

Model Rule 3.3 prohibits a lawyer from making false statements of law or fact to the court or offering evidence to the court the lawyer knows to be false. Comment 5 clarifies that the lawyer cannot offer evidence the lawyer knows to be false, "regardless of the client's wishes. This duty is premised on the lawyer's obligation as an officer of the court to prevent the trier of fact from being misled by false evidence." Further, Federal Rule of Civil Procedure 11 imposes upon the lawyer the obligation to assure, "to the best of his knowledge, information, and belief, formed after a reasonable inquiry [that a claim] is well grounded in fact. . . ." Thus, as the lawyer prepares the statement of fact for the appellate brief, he must ensure that the facts presented are true and accurate and that they properly refer back to the record. The following cases showcase instances in which a failure to accurately set forth facts in an appellate brief can have severe consequences for both the client and the lawyer.

MITCHEL v. GENERAL ELEC. CO.
689 F.2d 877 (9th Cir. 1982)

Mitchel filed this Title VII action against his employer, General Electric, and his supervisor, Joe Morgan, alleging employment discrimination on the basis of race. The complaint contains numerous allegations; however, this appeal is based essentially on the claim that Mitchel, a black, was passed over for promotion in favor of white employees with less seniority.

After thirteen months of discovery, defendants filed a motion for summary judgment which rebutted Mitchel's allegations with specific facts and presented detailed evidence in support of their defense that other employees were better qualified than Mitchel for the promotions. Defendants also presented evidence that Mitchel had a substantial record of discipline, attitude, and attendance problems.

Mitchel's response to defendants' summary judgment motion contained more allegations, none of which referred for support to affidavits or discovery documents. The trial judge granted defendants' motion for summary judgment, ruling that Mitchel had failed to establish a prima facie case of employment discrimination under the [applicable] standard[ ]. Mitchel appeals, contending that triable facts were present which, if proven, would have established a prima facie case.

Mitchel's brief on appeal follows the same pattern as his memoranda to the court below. It contains allegation after allegation, all of which are unsubstantiated by sworn affidavits or references to discovery documents. In a fourteen-page brief, Mitchel refers to the record below a single time, and that reference is to notify us of the facts upon which he is not relying. Rather than specific references to the record, Mitchel informs us that "(t)he depositions of (all witnesses deposed) . . . are filled with instances in which Mr. Mitchel was treated differently than non-minorities." Brief for Appellant at 10. We are left to ferret out of ten days of deposition testimony the facts upon which Mitchel relies. We decline to do so.

Rule 28(a)(3), Fed.R.App.P., requires that "(t)he brief of the appellant shall contain . . . a statement of the facts relevant to the issues presented for review, with appropriate references to the record." Mitchel has exhibited complete disregard for the requirements of Rule 28(a)(3). This is inexcusable in view of our instruction to Mitchel's counsel at oral argument concerning the requirements of our appellate rules and the accepted techniques of appellate practice. We deferred submission of the case to give Mitchel's counsel an opportunity to file a list of citations to the record in support of the numerous assertions of fact. What we received was exactly that — a list — of over 100 unannotated references to some

250 pages of deposition testimony, none of which referred back to any particular assertion of fact in Mitchel's brief. It is impossible to discern which of the citations are meant to support Mitchel's various assertions; many appear to have no relevance to anything at all.

The brief and list of citations are of little use to us. The basis of Mitchel's appeal is that he raised genuine issues of fact in the district court as to defendants' discrimination, yet he fails to reveal at what points in the record those alleged facts appear. Mitchel's failure to refer to the record works a hardship not only on this court, but also on the opposing litigants. We should not expect a party to expend large amounts of time and money sifting through the trial record in search of support for an opposing party's allegations.

This appeal is dismissed for failure to comply with Fed.R.App.P. 28(a)(3) and (e), Ninth Circuit Rule 13(b), and the order of this court entered August 13, 1982. We acknowledge the apparent harshness to Mitchel of our refusal to consider the merits of this appeal because his counsel failed to comply with the rules. On the merits, however, we note that Mitchel's unsubstantiated and conclusory allegations would be insufficient to oppose defendants' evidentiary showing under Fed.R.Civ.P. 56(e). See Mas Marques v. Digital Equipment Corp., 637 F.2d 24, 27 (1st Cir. 1980) (conclusory allegations in opposition to summary judgment which are "unsworn and unsupported by affidavits" failed to comply with the Rule 56(e) requirement that plaintiff "set forth specific facts;" summary judgment affirmed); Downes v. Beach, 587 F.2d 469, 472 (10th Cir. 1978) (summary judgment affirmed in employment action where plaintiff claimed disputed issues of fact were contained in previous trial record but "did not draw the court's attention to the particular testimony or portions of the record that support her contention."); British Airways Board v. Boeing Co., 585 F.2d 946, 951–52 (9th Cir. 1978) ("legal memoranda and oral argument are not evidence, and they cannot by themselves create a factual dispute sufficient to defeat a summary judgment motion where no dispute otherwise exists."), cert. denied, 440 U.S. 981, 99 S.Ct. 1790, 60 L.Ed.2d 241 (1979).

Appeal DISMISSED.

MOSER v. BRET HARTE UNION HIGH SCHOOL DIST.
366 F. Supp. 2d 944 (E.D. Cal. 2005)

[Plaintiff Robert Moser ("Plaintiff") was a student at Defendant Bret Harte Union High School District. Plaintiff alleged that Defendant denied him a free and appropriate public education under the Individuals With Disabilities Education Act ("IDEA"). Following a lengthy series of administrative hearings, Plaintiff appealed to the United States District Court.

In the district court proceedings, both parties filed numerous motions. The district court noted that "The evaluation of the matter was significantly delayed due to both parties' repeated incorrect, irrelevant or unsupported citations to the Administrative Record in their Chronological Statements of Facts and Defendant's repeated misstatement of the facts contained in the Administrative Record."

Following a hearing, the court granted the plaintiff's motion for summary judgment and denied the defendant's motion for summary judgment. The court also, on its own initiative, filed an Order to Show Cause, ordering Ms. Yama, Lozano, Smith and their client, Bret Harte Unified School District, to show cause why they should not be sanctioned for misrepresenting facts and law, violating their duty of candor, and willfully and vexatiously multiplying the proceedings.]

* * *

Federal Rule of Civil Procedure 11 ("Rule 11") gives the court authority to issue sanctions against a party whose attorney of record signs a "pleading, written motion, or other paper" is not well grounded in fact, is not warranted by existing law, is not made in good faith, or is brought for any improper purpose. . . .

The Ninth Circuit has stated:

> Under the provisions of Rule 11, when an attorney signs a pleading, he [or she] is certifying that he [or she] has read it and that to the best of his [or her] knowledge, information and belief, formed after a reasonable inquiry, it is well grounded in fact and is warranted by existing law or a good faith argument for the extension, modification, or reversal of existing law, and that it is not interposed for an improper purpose. Rule 11 further provides that if the pleading is signed by the attorney in violation of the rule, the court shall impose . . . an appropriate sanction.

Rule 11 creates and imposes on a party or counsel an affirmative duty to investigate the law and facts before filing. . . .

* * *

Under ABA Model Rules of Professional Conduct, "[a] lawyer shall not knowingly: (1) make a false statement of fact or law to a tribunal or fail to correct a false statement of material fact or law previously made to a tribunal by the lawyer; (2) fail to disclose to the tribunal legal authority in the controlling jurisdiction known to the lawyer to be directly adverse to the position of the client and not disclosed by opposing counsel; or (3) offer evidence that the lawyer knows to be false." The consequences of violating these rules depend upon whether the violation was intentional and/or systematic:

> 6.11 Disbarment is generally appropriate when a lawyer, with the intent to deceive the court, makes a false statement, submits a false document, or improperly withholds material information, and causes serious or potentially serious injury to a party, or causes a significant or potentially significant adverse effect on the legal proceeding.

> 6.12 Suspension is generally appropriate when a lawyer knows that false statements or documents are being submitted to the court or that material information is improperly being withheld, and takes no remedial action, and causes injury or potential injury to a party to the legal proceeding, or causes an adverse or potentially adverse effect on the legal proceeding.

> 6.13 Reprimand is generally appropriate when a lawyer is negligent either in determining whether statements or documents are false or in taking remedial action when material information is being withheld, and causes injury or potential injury to a party to the legal proceeding, or causes an adverse or potentially adverse effect on the legal proceeding.

> 6.14 Admonition is generally appropriate when a lawyer engages in an isolated instance of neglect in determining whether submitted statements or documents are false or in failing to disclose material information upon

learning of its falsity, and causes little or no actual or potential injury to a party, or causes little or no adverse or potentially adverse effect on the legal proceeding.

*   *   *

Misstatement and Mischaracterization of Facts Contained in the Administrative Record

(1) Defendant contends "Mrs. Moser only wanted transportation, tracking of progress and some counseling." Defendant contends that "At no time did Mrs. Moser indicate to Mr. Smith that she wanted more accommodations." Mr. Smith's testimony contradicts Defendant's claim. Mr. Smith testified he believed the accommodations were sufficient, but, in answer to a question, acknowledged that he knew Mrs. Moser would not "feel that [Robert] was getting . . . enough accommodations."

(2) Defendant alleges Ms. Pape-Reynoso, Plaintiff's sophomore learning director, "communicated with Plaintiff's teachers about his special physical health needs and the accommodations required as to assignments."

Ms. Pape-Reynoso's testimony contradicts Defendant's claim:

Q: About how often would you say you . . . spent working with him [Robert] through the course of the year?

A: I didn't see Robert very often. Typically, it was a phone call from home requesting work because he was out and it was coordinating with teachers.

Q: Do you recall being . . . given anything to read about Chronic Fatigue Syndrome?

A: At the . . . student study team meeting, Sheila Silcox did- . . . share information . . . and there was certainly a long discussion . . . in terms of how that would play out. And, and what kind of support he would need.

Q: . . . And, was anyone going to come out of that meeting and share this information with Robert's regular education teachers to your knowledge?

A: Someone probably was, I can't tell you who that person was. It wasn't me.

Q: Did teachers talk to you about the Chronic Fatigue Syndrome diagnosis during Robert's sophomore year?

A: Usually the contact had more to do with, 'where is he?' 'Here's the work for him.' 'Mom said she was coming to get the work.' 'She didn't come.' 'Where is it?' and those kinds of things.

*   *   *

[The court then meticulously addresses an additional 24 statements (for a total of 26 misrepresentations) presented by the Defendants that were contradicted by the record. Approximately 12 pages of the opinion are devoted to a detailed discrediting of factual statements made by the Defendants.]

* * *

Ms. Yama has submitted a separate brief and declaration which attempts to explain that the misstatements and frivolous objections were due to either mistake, misunderstanding, or carelessness. Ms. Yama contends she misunderstood the nature of the proceedings and did not realize they were to be conducted as a "standard summary judgment motion," with separate statements of undisputed facts. Ms. Yama contends she believed she was merely submitting a statement of chronological facts, and that in this statement she could state "any fact which had a scintilla of evidence in support of it," regardless of credibility issues or the strength of evidence to the contrary.

* * *

By this letter, Ms. Yama sought to create an unorthodox procedure which she claims partially excuses two areas of improper conduct. Ms. Yama points to her suggestion that all facts had to be cited to the administrative record, as justification for her patently frivolous objections to Plaintiff's statement of simple, indisputable background facts. Ms. Yama also explains her misstatements and mischaracterizations of the administrative record and law were based on her "belief" that the existence of some faintly colorable evidence was sufficient to substantiate a "fact" for inclusion in the Chronological Statement of Material and Relevant Facts in the face of much stronger evidence contradicting that "fact." As she has stated, "I understood that the parties were not submitting *undisputed* facts, as would normally be the case with a summary judgment motion. Accordingly, I never referred to my statement of facts as 'undisputed' facts."

* * *

While isolated errors or misstatements might be excused given the size of the record, the sheer volume of misstatements coupled with the fact that they universally favor the Defendant suggests a concerted attempt to distort the record to make it say what it does not. For example, in addressing the sample of issues listed in the Order to Show Cause, Ms. Yama admits she overstated or incorrectly stated the evidence at least seven times and made a mistake in her interpretation, reading, or note taking with regard to the administrative record approximately *seventeen times*. Ms. Yama admits her objections to Plaintiff's facts were "hyper technical," i.e., *frivolous*, improper or unclear at least six times. She acknowledges that on at least four occasions she objected to obviously indisputable facts simply because Plaintiff did not cite to the record, based on her self-suggested assumption that the proceedings would not be subject to the federal rules of civil procedure governing a summary judgment motion (an assumption which has since been disproved by Ms. Yama's July 26, 2002, letter acknowledging she understood the nature of the proceedings).

Taken as a whole, Ms. Yama admits she made mistakes, misinterpreted the evidence, overstated the facts or made hyper-technical or improper objections approximately *thirty-four* times. These examples are limited to the instances of problems listed in the Order to Show Cause. The only reasonable inference that can be drawn is that Ms. Yama and her law firm intended to obstruct at every step and stand education law on its head. . . .

A negligent or too attenuated examination of the record would not result in the extremely skewed view of the record Ms. Yama presented. Her presentation was carefully constructed to omit or minimize adverse facts, *e.g.*, portions of transcripts were cited out of context to support made-up facts, that, when viewed in their entirety, contradict the true record. It is obvious Ms. Yama clearly scrutinized the record to explicitly cite only portions of it, or to refer to testimony favorable to the District, but was only "mistaken" when she misrepresented the remainder of the record, her explanations are not credible. . . .

Counsel found ways to ostensibly conform record references to support Defendant's case by misreading context, omitting critical facts, and sometimes by simply stating the opposite of what was in the record. This kind of disinformation is insidious because it was provided by an officer of the court. It created a greater burden on plaintiff and the court. Defendant's counsel treated the law with the same contempt for accuracy. Attorneys have a duty to actively advocate on behalf of their clients but they have no duty to misrepresent facts or misstate law.

*   *   *

Ms. Yama's declaration and brief in response to the Order to Show Cause give the impression she is a neophyte lawyer who was unable to grasp the complexity of the case or record and made a few errors due to her misunderstanding of the specialized nature of the law, the proceedings and the record. This portrayal is belied by the history of the case and Ms. Yama's experience. Ms. Yama is not a first year attorney, she is a *seventh* year attorney — in some firms she would already be a principal. She has been practicing in the area of education law for over three years, for a law firm which holds itself out as a leading specialist in California in this area of law.

Assuming, *arguendo*, that a seventh year attorney is somehow not experienced enough to understand the nature of a summary judgment proceeding or to verify the record facts or the law underlying her legal arguments, as an attorney licensed to practice law in the State of California, Ms. Yama had an ethical obligation to ask for help and get instructions from her superiors if she truly could not deal with the "complexities" of the case. Rule 11 creates and imposes on a party or counsel an affirmative duty to investigate the law and facts before filing.

What is hard to understand is Ms. Yama's alleged inability to understand the background of the case before submitting briefs, verifying statements of fact against the record, and asking for help, if she needed it. All of these actions, Ms. Yama now contends she will take in the future, are actions that should be second nature to a seventh year associate. It should not require an Order to Show Cause proceeding and prospect of sanctions to actuate professional responsibilities.

Ms. Yama's contention that this is not a situation where she "knowingly concealed material facts or knowingly asserted a frivolous position," is simply untrue given the evidence discussed in this order. Ms. Yama still does not candidly accept responsibility for her actions, instead she repeatedly states only that "mistakes were made." *See* Doc. 134. Her assertions that the "pressure of private practice" requires that mistakes will inevitably be made, demonstrate her complete lack of understanding of her ethical responsibilities as an officer of the court or the serious nature of this proceeding and the allegations against her. Ms. Yama's contention that while the "mistakes" she made "may be the result of a certain degree of carelessness, they do not involve the type of recklessness required to warrant [Sect.] 1927 sanctions," is contradicted by the evidence. Ms. Yama made more than a few "mistakes" and was much more than simply "careless." She was reckless. She systematically distorted the record and repeatedly ignored Plaintiff's objections and warnings that she was doing so.

* * *

The totality of the sanctioned conduct visits an unendurable burden on the justice system in the name of misguided advocacy. It is appropriate that a public record be made of this conduct for the purpose of deterrence, particularly as it implicates unacceptable written advocacy and obstruction which violates rules of court and professional conduct, forcing an opposing party and the court to spend inordinate time addressing such issues.

For the reasons above stated, IT IS ORDERED:

1. Ms. Elaine Yama, Lozano Smith and Bret Harte Unified School District, as a party, engaged in bad faith litigation tactics through their systematic and repeated misstatements of the record, frivolous objections to Plaintiff's statement of facts, and repeated mischaracterizations of the law.

2. Under Fed. R. Civ. P. Rule 11, 28 U.S.C. § 1927, *and* the Court's inherent powers, Ms. Yama is ordered to personally pay Plaintiff and his counsel $5,000 for the increased costs and expenses related to causing Plaintiff's need to repeatedly respond to Defendant's blatant misrepresentations, throughout the four year history of this litigation; Ms. Yama is PUBLICALLY REPROVED and ordered to attend 20 hours of CLE ethics training in programs approved by the California State Bar Association by December 31, 2005, and must submit proof of such training to the Court by December 31, 2005; training received by Ms. Yama while this decision was pending will count towards this requirement. Proof of training must be submitted when the training is complete, not piecemeal.

3. Under Rule 11, 28 U.S.C. § 1927, *and* its inherent powers, Lozano Smith is ordered to pay Plaintiff and his counsel $5,000 for the increased costs and expenses related to Plaintiff's need to repeatedly respond to Ms. Yama's misrepresentations, and briefs on which partners of the firm were appearing counsel, throughout the four year history of this litigation. Lozano Smith is PUBLICALLY REPROVED. Lozano Smith is further ordered to provide a minimum of 6 hours of CLE ethics training for all its associates and shareholders, in programs approved by the California State Bar Association, by December 31, 2005, and must submit proof of such training to the Court by January 30, 2006; training received while this opinion was pending will count towards this requirement. Proof of training must be submitted when the training is completed, and not piecemeal.

4. Under Rule 11 and the Court's inherent power, Bret Harte Unified School District, a party, is ordered to pay to plaintiff Robert Moser the sum of $5,000 for his expense, inconvenience, and delay for its role in obstruction, delay in relief, and unnecessarily multiplying the proceedings in this case.

The payment of such sanctions shall be made within forty (40) days following the date of service of this decision by the clerk of court.

A copy of this decision shall be served on the California State Bar Association by the Clerk of Court.

NOTES

1.   In *Mitchel*, the lawyer's violation related to a failure to provide references to the record for facts cited in the brief. Why was this particularly troubling? The court notes that such a failure on behalf of one party shifts the burden to the opposing party and/or the court to discern the facts. This then results in a waste of judicial resources. The lawyer's conduct in *Moser* appeared to be more reprehensible and clearly resulted in an enormous expenditure of judicial resources as evidenced by the lengthy, meticulous opinion. Compare this with *Bush v. Dictaphone Corp.*, 161 F.3d 363 (6th Cir. 1998), a case in which the appellant, relying on *Moser*, argued that opposing counsel's brief should be dismissed for failure to cite to the record. The court disagreed, noting that "dismissal is appropriate only when a brief is so inadequate that a court cannot interpret it at all." *Id.* at 366. The court further emphasized that the cases cited in support of dismissal included instances in which lawyers submitted deficient briefs, were given an opportunity to correct the errors, and failed to do so. *Id.*

2.   In both *Mitchel* and *Moser* the factual inaccuracies were related to the primary issue(s) before the court. Lawyers have also been sanctioned for misrepresentations that do not involve the primary issue before the court. In *In re Chovanec*, 640 N.E.2d 1052 (Ind. 1994), a lawyer was disciplined for lying to the court in order to gain a continuance for trial. The lawyer told the court that he was too ill to proceed with the trial, but later admitted that he was merely unprepared. *Id.* at 1053. The court's admonition illustrates how such a misrepresentation, even though not related to the matter before the court, undermines the judicial system: "Clearly, Respondent's act of intentionally making a false statement to a court of law in order to secure a continuance demonstrates a lack of respect for the court's interests in fostering orderly administration of justice, and as a practical matter wasted valuable judicial time and resources." *Id.*

3.   Note the imposition of significant monetary sanctions on all lawyers involved in *Moser*. In addition, note the court's requirement that all lawyers within the Lozano Smith law firm complete continuing legal education in the area of ethics.

4.   In connection with the failure to accurately and honestly portray the facts in an appellate brief, courts have explicitly called attention to the impact on the credibility and reputation of a lawyer who engages in such dishonesty. In *Howells v. Com., Unemployment Compensation Bd. of Review*, 442 A.2d 389 (1982), the court considered a brief in which the lawyer misstated certain facts critical to the legal issue. Upon reciting the accurate facts in contrast with the lawyer's inaccurate portrayal, the court noted "In the face of this evidence, counsel for the claimant has seriously undermined his professional credibility with this court by submitting" an inaccurate, misleading brief. *Id.* at 299 n. 1. Similarly, in *Hickman v. Fraternal Order of Eagles, Boise No. 115*, 758 P.2d 704 (Id. 1988), the court, upon learning facts relevant to the legal issue which were omitted from one lawyer's brief, noted

> Counsel for appellant Hickman failed to include these facts in his brief, contrary to Idaho Appellate Rule 35, which requires that appellant give an accurate statement of the facts. Counsel for appellant further failed to provide an adequate transcript of the trial proceeding. Counsel for appellant damages both his credibility and his client's position when he fails to state the facts to this Court with the utmost candor.

Id. at 705 n.1.

iv. Accurate Representation of Authority

In *Thomas* the court made clear that the brief filed by Thomas's attorney lacked the requisite analysis for the court to properly consider the issue raised by Thomas in his brief. The court also alluded to a minimum level of authority required for the court to consider the issue. *Thomas*, 961 P.2d at 305 (noting that a brief "requires not just bald citation to authority but development of that authority and reasoned analysis based on that authority.") Rules relating to competence require advocates to include sufficient authority to enable appellate courts to render judgments consistent with applicable law. This responsibility is also imposed on the advocate in relation to his obligation of candor to the court. Under Model Rule 3.3, "[a] lawyer is not required to make a disinterested exposition of the law, but must recognize the existence of pertinent legal authorities. . . . [A]n advocate has a duty to disclose directly adverse authority in the controlling jurisdiction that has not been disclosed by the opposing party. The underlying concept is that legal argument is a discussion seeking to determine the legal premises properly applicable to the case." Model Rules of Prof'l Conduct R. 3.3 cmt. 4 (2008). The duty of candor imposed by Model Rule 3.3 prohibits the lawyer from offering false statements of law or fact to the tribunal and requires the lawyer to disclose adverse authority. "Legal argument based on a knowingly false representation of law constitutes dishonesty toward the tribunal." Model Rules of Prof'l Conduct R. 3.3 cmt. 4 (2008).

These considerations then place an obligation on the lawyer to present the law accurately and thoroughly. This obligation can be subtle, requiring not only that the lawyer accurately quote material from sources cited in appellate briefs, but also that the lawyer make explicit note of added or omitted language and points of emphasis in cited material. In the following case, the court dismissed several claims as not supported by the relevant authority. While the underlying claims involve relatively complex trademark infringement issues, you should focus your attention on the court's consideration of the law underlying the claims and the extent to which it supports those claims.

PORTER v. FARMERS SUPPLY SERVICE, INC.
790 F.2d 882 (Fed. Cir. 1986)

Florence Porter, as executrix of Wellington W. Porter's estate, and Porterway Harvester Manufacturing Co., Inc. (collectively, "Porterway"), appeal from a final judgment of the United States District Court for the District of Delaware (Wright, Senior Judge) granting summary judgment of non-infringement to Farmers Supply Service, Inc. (Farmers). We affirm.

Background

Porterway, owner of U.S. Patent No. 3,999,613 ('613 patent) issued to Wellington W. Porter, sued Farmers for patent infringement, trademark infringement, and unfair competition under federal and state law.

The '613 patent relates to a "Tomato Harvester Header." The header includes two counter-rotating notched disks with overlapping edges, two power-driven shafts to rotate the disks, and a supporting structure to position the disks and permit adjustment. The notches on the disks facilitate the uprooting of plant stems.

Farmers sells disks exclusively to owners of Porterway harvesters, and solely to replace worn out disks. For each replacement disk, Farmers charges $79.50 and Porterway charges $112.70. Porterway sells the harvester for $42,400, and does not sell headers separately from harvesters. The useful life of a disk is measured in weeks, that of a harvester is five or six years. The district court found, and it is undisputed, that a purchaser can expect to wear out many disks during the useful life of the header.

Porterway contended before the district court that Farmers directly and contributorily infringed claims 9 and 10 of the '613 patent. . . .

*   *   *

Porterway based its trademark and unfair competition counts on the assertion that Farmers used the "Porterway" trademark, Reg. No. 583,362, to cause purchaser confusion, citing as the sole evidence of that use two Farmers invoices indicating that the disks were sold to fit a Porterway Harvester.

The District Court's Decision

The district court granted Farmers' motion for summary judgment on all counts. Respecting the patent counts, the court: (1) construed the claims as including more than the disks; (2) found that sale of disks could not directly infringe the claims; (3) held that replacement of the disks is permissible repair, not direct infringement; and (4) held that, because of (3) and because direct infringement is absent, sale of the disk could not constitute contributory infringement.

The district court dismissed the trademark and unfair competition counts because Porterway failed to set forth specific facts supporting their allegations of purchasers deception and failed to point to any non-functional aspect of the disk's design. The court noted that the invoices support an inference that customers would not have been deceived.

Lastly, the district court denied Farmers' request for attorney fees, stating that:

> The Court is not of the opinion that this action was of such an exceptional nature which would justify the imposition of sanctions in the form of attorneys' fees pursuant to Fed.R.Civ.P. 11. While certain of [Porterway's] claims were weak, especially those concerning trademark infringement and unfair competition, the Court believes the action was neither frivolous, nor brought in bad faith.

The Appeals

In Appeal No. 85-2748, Porterway appeals only from the portion of the judgment holding Farmers not liable for contributory infringement, arguing that if the district court had properly construed claim 9 it would have found direct infringement by owners of Porterway Harvesters because they reconstructed the harvester when they replaced worn disks. That finding, Porterway argues, would make Farmers a contributory infringer.

In Appeal No. 85-2802, Farmers cross-appeals the denial of its motion for attorney fees, arguing that the suit was frivolous. Farmers also requests an award of its costs and attorney fees expended in this court, on the ground that this appeal is frivolous.

Issues

(1)   Whether the district court erred in granting summary judgment of non-infringement.

(2)   Whether the district court abused its discretion in denying Farmers' motion for attorney fees.

(3)   Whether this appeal is frivolous.

OPINION

* * *

It is well settled that, absent direct infringement, there can be no contributory infringement. However, as above indicated, Porterway argues that owners of Porterway Harvesters are direct infringers because they impermissibly reconstruct the header when they replace a disk. Porterway says to conclude otherwise "is to ignore all prior law on the subject."

Citing *Paper Converting Machine Co. v. Magna-Graphics Corp.*, 745 F.2d 11, 223 USPQ 591 (Fed.Cir.1984), Porterway argues that the district court must have thought there could be no infringement unless the entire combination of claim 9 left the *seller* fully assembled. Porterway misunderstands or distorts the district court's analysis, citing nothing of record to support its conjecture. Moreover, the focus of the direct infringement inquiry is, as it was in the district court, on *owners* of Porterway Harvesters. The argument is frivolous.

* * *

Porterway's contentions on repair v. reconstruction are contrary to the law pronounced by the Supreme Court. The Court has "eschewed the suggestion that the legal distinction between 'reconstruction' and 'repair' should be affected by whether the element of the combination that has been replaced is an 'essential' or 'distinguishing' part of the invention." The district court cited *Dawson* and correctly explicated the reasons for that rule.[3] We need not repeat that explication here. Despite its reduction of the charge against Farmers to one of contributory infringement, Porterway effectively seeks to extend its patent rights to cover its unpatented disks. Farmers asserts that Porterway's view would require every owner of one of its harvesters to purchase disks (at least two sets each year) from Porterway. The assertion that Porterway is attempting in this suit to extend its patent rights is simply ignored in Porterway's briefs.

The district court noted that it was undisputed that the relatively inexpensive harvester disks must be repeatedly replaced due to wear, and that Porterway sells replacement disks. This case thus fits squarely within, and is governed by, the Supreme Court holding [in *Aro I*] that a license to use the patented combination (which license is held by each owner of a Porterway Harvester) includes the right "to preserve its fitness for use so far as it may be affected by wear or breakage" and that a licensed user may replace any element no matter "how essential it may be to

---

[3] Porterway's briefs ignore *Dawson*.

the patented combination," as long as the replaced element is not itself, i.e., separately, claimed.[5]

Courts have decided a number of cases, before and after *Aro I*, that involve tools having parts subject to wear, and, as Judge Wright noted, those courts "have held almost uniformly that replacement of a worn part in a patented combination is repair rather than reconstruction." Porterway's briefs address not one of the foregoing authorities.[6]

* * *

Accordingly, we affirm the grant of summary judgment of non-infringement.

Attorney Fees in the District Court

We are unable to conclude that the district court clearly erred in refusing to find Porterway's suit an "exceptional" case. Farmers says the district court's "findings were clearly erroneous". However, we are not persuaded that the court incorrectly found Porterway's charges "weak" but not frivolous or made in bad faith. Thus, we do not reach the issue of whether the denial of attorney fees was an abuse of its discretion. That this court, were it sitting at trial, might have differently appraised the suit is not a basis for holding that the district court's appraisal was error. Accordingly, we affirm the district court's denial of attorney fees.

Costs and Attorney Fees on Appeal

Our affirmance of a district court's denial of attorney fees does not preclude us from awarding appellees the costs and attorney fees which they have been forced to incur in opposing frivolous appeals. This court has made such awards repeatedly. "An appeal clearly hopeless and unquestionably without any possible basis in fact or law, as here, wastes the time of the court and of opposing counsel, and imposes unnecessary costs on the parties and on fellow citizens whose taxes support this court and its staff." This is such a case. In quoting from *Monroe Auto Equipment Co. v. Precision Rebuilders, Inc.*, 229 F.Supp. 347, 351, 141 USPQ 626, 629 (D.C. Kan.1964), Porterway distorted the quote by omitting language devastating to its position on appeal. In its reply brief, Porterway ignores the distortion pointed to by Farmers. The necessity of distortion should have alerted Porterway to the frivolity of this appeal.

As above indicated, each of Porterway's arguments is frivolous. None is based on "sound common sense and an intelligent judgment". The district court adequately treated Porterway's arguments in its thorough opinion, and Porterway has presented no plausible premise for possible reversal. Further, Porterway makes no true effort to distinguish authorities cited by the district court and by appellee which squarely reject the "heart of the invention" argument to which all of

---

[5] Porterway cites two cases in support of its argument that repair v. reconstruction must be decided on a comparison of elements replaced with those remaining of the patented combination. Both cases predated Aro I and are therefore of at least doubtful viability.

[6] Porterway mentions the district court decision affirmed in National-Standard Co., but inexcusably disregards the appellate court's decision, though it was cited below by appellee and in Judge Wright's opinion. That appellate decision contains language directly applicable here and destructive of Porterway's arguments before us.

Porterway's arguments on contributory infringement and reconstruction resolve. The inability to distinguish those authorities should also have alerted Porterway's counsel to the frivolity of this appeal. Simply stated, there was not even a colorable basis for this appeal.

Farmers is entitled to its costs and attorney fees expended in connection with this appeal, under the exceptional case standard of 35 U.S.C. § 285 and the frivolous appeal standard of Fed.R.App.P. 38.

The judgment of the district court is affirmed in all respects. Porterway and its counsel on appeal are jointly and severally liable to Farmers for the latter's costs and attorney fees expended in connection with this appeal.

NOTES

1. In *Porter* the lawyers were sanctioned not only for distorting relevant language from the briefs on appeal, but for failing to respond to arguments that were based on the relevant but omitted and ultimately fatal language. The case is noteworthy because the appellate court refused to reconsider the decision not to impose sanctions in the form of attorneys' fees at the district court level, but affirmatively imposed such fees at the appellate level, largely because of the disingenuous omission of relevant language on appeal. What was the legal basis for the fines on appeal?

2. Note that in *Porter* the omitted language went to the "heart of the [] argument." Lawyers can be sanctioned for more subtle distortions. In *Sobol v. Capital Management Consultants, Inc.*, 726 P.2d 335 (Nev. 1986), the court held that a party to an action could be monetarily sanctioned for misrepresenting stipulated facts and for quoting of language from the dissent of a case as though it were the case's majority holding. The court noted that "[w]hile vigorous advocacy of a client's cause is expected and encouraged, these representations transcend the outer limits of zeal and become statements of guile and delusion." *Id.* at 337.

PRECISION SPECIALTY METALS, INC. v. UNITED STATES
315 F.3d 1346 (Fed. Cir. 2003)

In an unpublished opinion, the Court of International Trade formally reprimanded the appellant Mikki Graves Walser, a Department of Justice attorney, for misquoting and failing to quote fully from two judicial opinions in a motion for reconsideration she signed and filed. We hold that we have jurisdiction to review that action, and affirm the reprimand.

In the underlying case, Precision Specialty Metals, Inc. ("Precision") contested the decision of the United States Customs Service denying it drawback (the refund of duties paid on imported products upon their subsequent export.) Walser represented the United States in that case. Precision filed a motion for summary judgment. Under the court's scheduling order, the government's response and any cross-motion were required to be filed by May 5, 2000. At 5:51 p.m. on May 4, the government moved for a 30-day extension of time for such filing. Walser stated during a subsequent court hearing that when she filed the extension motion, she had not started preparing the government's cross-motion for summary judgment.

On May 10, the court denied the extension motion and ordered that the government's response to Precision's motion be filed "forthwith." Twelve days later, on May 22, the government filed its opposition to and its cross-motion for summary judgment. Two days later, the court struck from the record as untimely the government's response and granted Precision's motion for summary judgment as unopposed.

The government then filed a motion for reconsideration, which contained the miscitations that resulted in Walser's reprimand. The document listed three names as the submitters, only two of whom signed it: Walser and the Attorney in Charge of the Department of Justice's International Trade Field Office in New York City. (The third name on the motion was that of the Acting Assistant Attorney General.) Walser stated that she "wrote" the motion.

A major argument the government made in support of reconsideration was that it had filed its motion for summary judgment in compliance with the order that it do so "forthwith." The government relied on and quoted the following definition of "forthwith" in BLACK'S LAW DICTIONARY 654 (6th ed.1990):

> Immediately; without delay; directly; within a reasonable time under the circumstances of the case; promptly and with reasonable dispatch. Within such time as to permit that which is to be done, to be done lawfully and according to the practical and ordinary course of things to be performed or accomplished. The first opportunity offered.

The motion stated that "[a] review of several court decisions which construed the term 'forthwith' revealed that there is no uniform definition of the term" and that "several courts" have relied on the *Black's Law Dictionary* definition. It stated that "[t]he term is clearly ambiguous and has subjective application." To support this contention, Walser quoted from several judicial opinions.

The following table sets forth in the left column two of the quotations in the motion (one in the text and the other in a footnote), and the right column contains the complete language of the pertinent portion of the opinion:

Motion	Opinion
See City of New York v. McAllister Brothers, Inc., 278 F.2d 708, 710 (1960) (" 'Forthwith' means immediately, without delay, or as soon as the object may be accomplished by reasonable exertion." Emphasis added.)	"Forthwith" means immediately, without delay, or as soon as the object may be accomplished by reasonable exertion. The Supreme Court has said of the word that "in matters of practice and pleading it is usually construed, and sometimes defined by rule of court, as within twenty-four hours." Dickerman v. Northern Trust Co., 1900 176 U.S. 181, 193, 20 S.Ct. 311, 315, 44 L.Ed. 423. McAllister, 278 F.2d at 710.

Motion

While we did not review the Supreme Court's decision in Henderson v. United States, 517 U.S. 654, 680, 116 S.Ct. 1638, 134 L.Ed.2d 880 (1996), in interpreting the meaning of "forthwith," it is noteworthy that in his dissenting opinion, Justice Thomas, with whom The Chief Justice and Justice O'Connor joined, citing Amella v. United States, 732 F.2d 711, 713 (C.A.1984), stated that "[a]lthough we have never undertaken to define 'forthwith'. . ., it is clear that the term 'connotes action which is immediate, without delay, prompt and with reasonable dispatch.' "

Opinion

Although we have never undertaken to define "forthwith" as it is used in the SAA, it is clear that the term "connotes action which is immediate, without delay, prompt, and with reasonable dispatch." Amella v. United States, 732 F.2d 711, 713 (C.A.9 1984) (citing Black's Law Dictionary 588 (5th ed.1979)). See also Dickerman v. Northern Trust Co., 176 U.S. 181, 192–193, 20 S.Ct. 311, 315, 44 L.Ed. 423 (1900). Henderson, 517 U.S. at 680, 116 S.Ct. 1638 (Thomas, J., dissenting).

In *Dickerman*, the Supreme Court stated:

> But "forthwith" is defined by Bouvier as indicating that "as soon as by reasonable exertion, confined to the object, it may be accomplished. This is the import of the term; it varies, of course, with every particular case." In matters of practice and pleading it is usually construed, and sometimes defined by rule of court, as within twenty-four hours.

The omissions from the judicial opinions that Walser quoted thus were as follows:

> 1. She omitted the sentence in *McAllister* that follows the sentence she quoted, referring to and quoting from the Supreme Court's *Dickerman* opinion.

> 2. The quotation in the footnote from Justice Thomas' dissent left out, after "forthwith," the limiting words "as it is used in the SAA [Suits in Admiralty Act]," thereby making Justice Thomas' statement seem broader than it actually was. She also left out his citation to *Dickerman*. Finally, she failed to state "emphasis added" for the quoted material in bold face, although she had so stated about the bold face portions of the quotation from *McAllister* in the text. This difference would lead a reader to assume that the emphasis in Justice Thomas' dissent was provided by him, not by her.

At the oral argument on the government's motion for reconsideration, the court questioned Walser extensively about the foregoing omissions from the judicial opinions she cited and indicated its concern about her conduct. The court said it would issue an order to show cause to give Walser "an opportunity to discuss" what it "consider[ed] to be an egregious problem."

The court subsequently issued an order to Walser to show cause why she should not be held in contempt "by reason of misrepresentations" in the government's motion for reconsideration. It issued a second order to show cause why she should not be held in contempt "by reason of the specific misrepresentations discussed by the court during oral argument on June 29, 2000," "those misrepresentations including the omission of language in quotations from *Henderson v. United States*, 517 U.S. 654, 116 S.Ct. 1638, 134 L.Ed.2d 880 (1996) and *City of New York v.*

McAllister Brothers, Inc., 278 F.2d 708 (2nd Cir.1960); the failure to cite the court to *Dickerman v. Northern Trust Company*, 176 U.S. 181, 20 S.Ct. 311, 44 L.Ed. 423 (1900), and false implication resulting therefrom that a Justice of the United States Supreme Court had stated the Court had 'never undertaken' to define the term 'forthwith,' that according to that Justice, its definition was limited to the terminology cited by Defendant, and that the Supreme Court had not further defined the term, adversely to Defendant's position, in *Dickerman v. Northern Trust Company.*"

At the hearing on the order to show cause, the court first indicated that it believed that "the omissions from *McAllister* and *Henderson* were . . . an intentional attempt by competent counsel to mislead the Court" and that it would find that "the representation to the Court was in bad faith, and that as a result it was contemptuous." After a lengthy statement by and colloquy with Walser, however, the court stated that it would not find her "in bad faith" and that she was "purged of the contempt," but that it would take under advisement "whether to find a Rule 11 violation or not."

In an unpublished opinion, the court held that Walser had violated Rule 11 of the Rules of the Court of International Trade, and formally reprimanded her. The court stated:

> As counsel for the United States, Ms[.] Walser signed a brief before this court which omitted directly relevant language from what was represented as precedential authority, which effectively changed the meaning of at least one quotation, and which intentionally or negligently misled the court. That conduct is a direct violation of USCIT Rule 11. Accordingly, a sanction under that Rule is appropriate in this case[.]

In the concluding paragraph of its opinion, the court stated: "[A]n attorney before this court violated USCIT Rule 11 in signing motion papers which contained omissions/misquotations. Accordingly, the court hereby formally reprimands her."

The court determined not to impose monetary sanctions, because it concluded that the unpublished reprimand would be a sufficient deterrent sanction.

In the present appeal Walser is proceeding pro se. She challenges the Court of International Trade's determination that she violated Rule 11 and reprimanding her for that conduct. The Department of Justice, which had represented her before the Court of International Trade in responding to the order to show cause, has filed a brief amicus curiae "in support of" her, in which it argues that her conduct did not violate Rule 11 and was not sanctionable.

*   *   *

On the merits, Walser contends her conduct did not violate Rule 11. As noted above, that rule provides in pertinent part that "[b]y presenting to the court (whether by signing, filing, submitting, or later advocating) a pleading, written motion, or other paper, an attorney . . . is certifying that to the best of the person's knowledge, information, and belief, formed after any inquiry reasonable under the circumstances, (2) the claims, defenses, and other legal contentions therein are warranted by existing law or by a non-frivolous argument for the extension, modification, or reversal of existing law or the establishment of new law."

Although "the central purpose of Rule 11 is to deter baseless filings in district court," the scope of the rule is not that limited. As noted, it provides that by presenting legal documents to the court, an attorney is certifying her belief, formed after reasonable inquiry, that the "claims, defenses and other legal contentions therein are warranted by existing law or a non-frivolous argument" to change the law.

The Court of international trade stated that Walser either willfully or through an unacceptable level of negligence, and the use of selective quotations and direct misquotation, concealed a Supreme Court case of which she was or should have been aware. Counsel's argument that the case was inapposite or dicta is simply irrelevant to this analysis; her misconduct lies not in deciding the case was irrelevant but in attempting to **conceal** it from the court and opposing counsel. That, simply put, is a violation of any attorney's fundamental duty to be candid and scrupulously accurate.

The court concluded that Walser violated Rule 11 because she "signed a brief before this court which omitted directly relevant language from what was represented as precedential authority, which effectively changed the meaning of at least one quotation, and which intentionally or negligently misled the court."

We conclude that the Court of International Trade properly described and characterized Walser's actions and properly concluded that those actions violated Rule 11.

In the motion for reconsideration, Walser argued that the government's filing of its cross-motion for summary judgment twelve days after it was told to file "forthwith" satisfied that requirement. She began her argument with a quotation from *Black's Law Dictionary's* definition of "forthwith" as including "within a reasonable time under the circumstances of the case; promptly and with reasonable dispatch." She then stated that "the term has been defined by several courts based upon all, or portions of, the definition contained in prior editions of" that dictionary, followed by quotations from two judicial opinions that included the dictionary definition. She also cited in a footnote the dissenting opinion of Justice Thomas in *Henderson*, which stated the various dictionary definitions of the term.

Walser did not cite or mention the 1900 Supreme Court *Dickerman* decision, which stated regarding "forthwith": "In matters of practice and pleading it is usually construed, and sometimes defined by rule of court, as within twenty-four hours." The *McAllister* opinion included that quotation, and Justice Thomas' dissent cited *Dickerman*.

In his dissent, Justice Thomas also stated that "[a]lthough we have never undertaken to define 'forthwith' as it is used in the SAA [Suits in Admiralty Act]." In her brief Walser eliminated the words "as it is used in the SAA," substituting ". . ." for that language. This omission, as the Court of International Trade pointed out, "effectively changed the meaning" of Justice Thomas' language, and gave it a broader meaning than it had.

The effect of Walser's editing of this material and ignoring the Supreme Court decision that dealt with the issue — a decision that seriously weakened her argument — was to give the Court of International Trade a misleading impression of the state of the law on the point. She eliminated material that indicated that her delay in filing the motion for reconsideration had not met the court's requirement that she file "forthwith," and presented the remaining material in a way that overstated the basis for her claim that a "forthwith" filing requirement meant she could take whatever time would be reasonable in the circumstances. This distortion of the law was inconsistent with and violated the standards of Rule 11.

By signing the motion for reconsideration, Walser certified that the "claims, defenses, and other legal contentions therein are warranted by existing law." Inherent in that representation was that she stated therein the "existing law" accurately and correctly. She did not do so, however, because her omissions from and excisions of judicial authority mischaracterized what those courts had stated. The effect of her doctored quotations was to make it appear that the weight of judicial authority was that "forthwith" means "a time reasonable under the circumstances." This was quite different from the Supreme Court's statement in *Dickerman* that "[i]n matters of pleading and practice," forthwith "is usually construed, and sometimes defined by rule of court, as within twenty-four hours." By suppressing any reference to *Dickerman*, which both the Second Circuit in *McAllister* and Justice Thomas in his dissent in *Henderson* cited and which the Second Circuit quoted, Walser gave a false and misleading impression of "existing law" on the meaning of "forthwith."

This court has dealt with lawyers' miscitations in sanctioning lawyers under Federal Rule of [Appellate] Procedure 38 for frivolous appeals. In *Abbs v. Principi*, 237 F.3d 1342 (Fed.Cir.2001), we recently gave these examples of appeals that are "frivolous as argued": "distorting cited authority by omitting language from quotations"; "misrepresenting facts or law to the court"; "failing to reference or discuss controlling precedents." In one of the cases there cited, *Porter v. Farmers Supply Service*, 790 F.2d 882 (Fed.Cir.1986), this court held an appeal frivolous and sanctioned the appellant by requiring payment of costs and attorneys fees because the appellant failed to distinguish relevant authorities and cropped a quote. We noted that the appellant was culpable for "distort[ing] the quote by omitting language devastating to its position on appeal."

Those cases did not involve Rule 11, but Rule 38 dealing with frivolous appeals. They are relevant, however, because they reflect the judicial view of concealment and miscitation of relevant precedent and cropping of quotations to alter their meaning. There is no reason why misconduct condemned under Rule 38 also should not violate Rule 11.

It is no answer to say, as the Department of Justice argues, that because the Supreme Court's statement in *Dickerman* was dictum, Walser was not obligated to refer to it. The Second Circuit and Justice Thomas believed that the statement was sufficiently important to quote it (*McAllister*) and to cite it (*Henderson*). The failure to include the reference to *Dickerman* in both of those citations made Walser's citations themselves misleading. Walser, of course, could have distinguished *Dickerman* as she saw fit or urged the Court of International Trade not to follow it. Consistent with her obligations as an officer of the court, however, she could not simply ignore it by deleting it from the material she quoted.

Other courts of appeals that have considered the application of Rule 11 to attorney-case-citation issues have reached differing results. In some of the cases that have rejected sanctions, the attorney's alleged violation was failure to discover precedents that negated his position. Understandably, courts have been reluctant to punish a lawyer for inadequate or unsound research. That may constitute negligence, but not conduct sanctionable under Rule 11. Similarly, a mere failure to cite contrary authority, without regard to the facts of the particular case, is not necessarily enough to show a violation of Rule 11. As the court stated in so ruling in *Golden Eagle*: "neither Rule 11 nor any other rule imposes a requirement that the lawyer, in addition to advocating the cause of his client, step first into the shoes of opposing counsel to find all potentially contrary authority, and finally into the robes of the judge to decide whether the authority is indeed contrary or whether it is distinguishable. It is not in the nature of our adversary system to require lawyers to demonstrate to the court that they have exhausted every theory, both for and against their client. Nor does that requirement further the interests of the court."

In the present case, however, Walser was sanctioned not for failure to discover pertinent precedents or to cite adverse decisions. She violated Rule 11 because, in quoting from and citing published opinions, she distorted what the opinions stated by leaving out significant portions of the citations or cropping one of them, and failed to show that she and not the court has supplied the emphasis in one of them. We know of no appellate decision holding that Rule 11 does not cover such misstatements of legal authority. *Cf. Teamsters Local No. 579 v. B & M Transit, Inc.*, 882 F.2d 274, 280 (7th Cir.1989) (upholding Rule 11 sanction for "misstating the law"); *Borowski v. DePuy, Inc.*, 850 F.2d 297, 304–05 (7th Cir.1988) (Counsel's "ostrich-like tactic of pretending that potentially dispositive authority against [his] contention does not exist[ ][is] precisely the type of behavior that would justify imposing Rule 11 sanctions." (internal citation omitted)).

In *Jewelpak Corp. v. United States*, 297 F.3d 1326 (Fed.Cir.2002), this court stated, in a footnote about a lawyer's failure to cite a case that he admitted at oral argument "would doom his appeal":

> [W]e note our significant dismay at counsel's failure to cite *Heraeus-Amersil* as controlling (or at the very least, persuasive) authority in his opening brief. Although counsel subjectively may have believed that another case was more persuasive, officers of our court have an unfailing duty to bring to our attention the most relevant precedent that bears on the case at hand — both good and bad — of which they are aware.

Similarly, if the Court of International Trade had followed the Supreme Court's statement in *Dickerman* that "[i]n matters of practice and pleading," "forthwith" "is usually construed . . . as twenty-four hours," that case would have "doom[ed]" Walser's contention that her filing after 12 days was "forthwith."

* * *

The ultimate responsibility for the completeness and accuracy of papers that are filed by Department of Justice lawyers rests with the Department itself. We find it troubling that the Department's Amicus Brief seeks to defend Walser's actions on the grounds that the Supreme Court decision in *Dickerman* was not controlling authority; that the motion supposedly did not misrepresent the law; that "the issue of whether or not the Supreme Court had addressed the meaning of 'forthwith' is not important;" and that the court was not misled. While the court did not err in formally reprimanding Walser, that reprimand should not be seen as in any way detracting from the Department's own responsibility to establish high standards for its lawyers and to provide adequate training and supervision, so that episodes such as this are not repeated.

The Court of International Trade's reprimand of Walser under Rule 11 is
AFFIRMED.

NOTES

1. Note the *Precision Specialty* court's emphasis on what might be considered subtle citation infractions, including failure to identify added emphasis and the failure to explicitly note omitted language. Recognize how even these subtle errors change the meaning of quoted material and therefore mislead the court.

2. Was Walser, the lawyer, sanctioned for failing to locate applicable authority? Does Rule 11 impose a penalty upon a lawyer who is unable to locate an applicable authority? Can a lawyer be sanctioned under Rule 11 when he chooses not to cite an authority he deems is distinguishable or of limited value to the appeal?

THORNTON v. WAHL
787 F.2d 1151 (7th Cir. 1986)

Elizabeth Thornton expelled her husband in 1975 from Thornwood, the family home, and he took up residence in one of the estate's coachhouses. In 1978 the state court with jurisdiction of the Thorntons' divorce proceedings ruled that Thornwood is Mr. Thornton's property. After the two were divorced, Mrs. Thornton refused to leave Thornwood. On November 10, 1983, the state court entered a supplemental judgment requiring Mrs. Thornton to depart no later than December 1. She filed an appeal (on November 29) and an application for a stay; although the court did not issue a stay by December 1, Mrs. Thornton did not leave.

Mr. Thornton asked Robert Wahl, the sheriff of LaSalle County (where Thornwood is located) to help him regain the main house of the estate. On December 7 Mr. Thornton, Wahl, and three deputy sheriffs arrived at Thornwood. Mrs. Thornton refused to let them in. While the sheriff awaited the arrival of a locksmith, Mrs. Thornton called her attorney, who (according to the complaint) told her that she was entitled to stay. After the locksmith opened the front door, Mrs. Thornton locked herself in her bedroom. When she emerged, she refused to leave the house without a box of personal possessions, a box too large to fit in her car. It looked like her departure would be indefinitely postponed. The sheriff then arrested her for criminal trespass, in violation of Ill.Rev.Stat. ch. 38 § 21-3(a). This statute provides that anyone who "remains upon the land of another after receiving [oral or written] notice from the owner or occupant to depart, commits a class C misdemeanor." Mrs. Thornton was jailed for 2 1/2 hours and released on bond. The State's Attorney later dropped the criminal charge against her. On December 9 the court finally denied Mrs. Thornton's motion for a stay, so Mr. Thornton retained possession of Thornwood.

This suit is Mrs. Thornton's revenge. She charged the sheriff, three deputy sheriffs, and her former husband with violating her rights under five amendments to the constitution. She also invoked the court's pendent jurisdiction and charged the defendants with five torts. Her theory is that Mr. Thornton should have filed still another state action — for ejectment, forcible entry and detainer, or contempt of court — to procure her departure from the house. The district court granted summary judgment for the defendants, concluding that although forcible entry and detainer rather than criminal trespass is the right way to settle disputes between tenants and landlords, Mrs. Thornton had had her day (rather her eight years) in court, and Mr. Thornton was entitled to enforce the judicial order that Mrs. Thornton leave. Because Mr. Thornton had one judicial order, he did not need another. Mrs. Thornton cited to the district court (and to us) several state cases saying that trespass is the wrong way to try disputed claims of right to interests in land. The district court properly replied that Mr. Thornton had tried his claim to judgment and was not using the criminal law to settle the dispute. He was using it only to enforce the court's order. He was entitled to enter the house; once there, he as owner was entitled to instruct Mrs. Thornton to leave; when she refused to leave except on conditions satisfactory to herself, the sheriff was entitled to take her away.

Mrs. Thornton replies that Mr. Thornton was not authorized to enter or tell her to leave. This is so, her brief says, because "[a]ccording to Illinois Supreme Court rules, a Motion for Stay automatically stays judgement [sic] until such time as a ruling is made on the Motion for Stay." A motion for a stay was pending on the morning of December 7 when the sheriff arrived, and Mrs. Thornton therefore concludes that her ex-husband had to bide his time. Her brief does not cite any rule for this proposition, but it cites Ill.Rev.Stat. ch. 110 § 2-1305 for the statement that "once a Motion for Stay was filed, all proceedings were stayed pending a decision on the Motion for Stay."

We publish this opinion to remind counsel that they may not make assertions of law for which there is no support. Fed.R.Civ.P. 11 provides that every pleading or "other paper" — a term that includes notices of appeal and appellate briefs — shall be signed, and that the signature "constitutes a certificate . . . that the [person signing] has read the . . . paper; that to the best of his knowledge, information, and belief formed after reasonable inquiry it is well grounded in fact and is warranted by existing law or a good faith argument for the extension, modification, or reversal of existing law, and that it is not interposed for any improper purpose, such as to harass or to cause unnecessary delay or needless increase in the cost of litigation." If a paper violates this rule, "the court, upon motion or upon its own initiative, shall impose upon the person who signed it, a represented party, or both, an appropriate sanction, which may include" attorneys' fees. The appellate proceedings in this case are unsupported by any colorable legal argument. They must have been pursued to vex Mr. Thornton and the sheriff. We therefore award attorneys' fees to the appellees on our own initiative.

The argument that a motion for a stay automatically stays a judgment pending the appellate court's decision is preposterous. It would deprive courts of the power to set enforceable deadlines. Mrs. Thornton cites Ill.Rev.Stat. ch. 110 § 2-1305 and "Illinois Supreme Court rules." Section 2-1305 authorizes the filing of a motion to stay "proceedings" in court pending resolution of other issues. It does not deal with stays of outstanding orders, let alone say that an application for a stay has the same effect as the issuance of a stay. It allows a judge to issue a "certificate" staying "further proceedings," and this certificate acts as a stay, but this is a far cry from an automatic stay. Mrs. Thornton does not cite any rule of the Supreme Court of Illinois, and we cannot find one with the effect she describes. Rule 305(b)(1), the only one close to the point, states that a reviewing court "may stay pending appeal . . . the enforcement, force and effect of any . . . final or interlocutory judgment or judicial or administrative order." The Rule does not hint that the filing of a motion has the same effect as the issuance of a stay. Mrs. Thornton does not cite any case construing § 2-1305 or Rule 305 in this way; we have not found one.

In sum, this appeal rests on a serious misstatement of state law. It is hard to imagine that a lawyer could advise a client to defy an outstanding judgment on the ground that an application for a stay had been filed but had not been granted, or that a lawyer could inform us — without a shred of authority — that in Illinois an application for a stay has the effect of a stay itself. We do not want to discourage vigorous advocacy, but an advocate must represent his client within the existing structure of the law, and not some imagined version of it. Mrs. Thornton's presentation also cannot be described as a reasoned request for a change in the law. Her brief misrepresents existing law; she does not accurately describe the law and then call for change. (It would not matter if she had. A federal court hearing an action under 42 U.S.C. § 1983 is not the right forum in which to request a change in the appellate procedures of Illinois, if the existing procedures comply with the constitution.)

Rule 11 requires counsel to study the law before representing its contents to a federal court. An empty head but a pure heart is no defense. The Rule requires counsel to read and consider before litigating. Counsel who puts the burden of study and illumination on the defendants or the court must expect to pay attorneys' fees under the Rule. We do not say that Mrs. Thornton and her lawyers acted with the subjective purpose to misstate the law and harass the defendants. The test under Rule 11 is objective. The point, rather, is that every lawyer must do the necessary work to find the law *before* filing the brief. It is not acceptable to make an assertion of law and hope that it will turn out to be true.

This assertion turned out not to be true, turned out indeed to be wildly untrue. Ordinarily we impose attorneys' fees on the party, leaving party and lawyer to settle accounts. But we do not suppose that the representations about state law were approved by Mrs. Thornton personally; although she is responsible for pursuing this litigation, she has received bad legal advice. We therefore impose part of the award on counsel personally. Mrs. Thornton and her counsel must pay double costs and the reasonable attorneys' fees incurred by the defendants. Counsel must pay half of the bill personally, and Mrs. Thornton must pay the other half. Counsel for appellees have 15 days to file appropriate statements with the clerk.

AFFIRMED.

NOTES

1. Did the lawyers in *Walser* and *Thornton* argue that the law they relied upon in the briefs was accurate? Do these opinions preclude a novel interpretation of existing law where the meaning of an opinion is ambiguous?

2. In *Golden Eagle Distributing Corp. v. Burroughs Corp.*, 801 F.2d 1531 (9th Cir. 1986), the court addressed the relationship between Rule 11 and the arguable limit of the lawyer's responsibility to locate and cite applicable cases. In rejecting an opinion of the district court that assessed sanctions against a lawyer for failing to cite adverse authority, the court concluded:

Were the scope of the rule to be expanded as the district court suggests, mandatory sanctions would ride on close decisions concerning whether or not one case is or is not the same as another. We think Rule 11 should not impose the risk of sanctions in the event that the court later decides that the lawyer was wrong. The burdens of research and briefing by a diligent lawyer anxious to avoid any possible rebuke would be great. And the burdens would not be merely on the lawyer. If the mandatory provisions of the Rule are to be interpreted literally, the court would have a duty to research authority beyond that provided by the parties to make sure that they have not omitted something . . . It is not in the nature of our adversary system to require lawyers to demonstrate to the court that they have exhausted every theory, both for and against their client. Nor does that requirement further the interests of the court. It blurs the role of judge and advocate. The role of judges is not merely to match the colors of the case at hand against the colors of many sample cases spread out upon their desk. . . . It is when the colors do not match, when the references in the index fail, when there is no decisive precedent, that the serious business of the judge begins. In conducting this "serious business," the judge relies on each party to present his side of the dispute as forcefully as possible. The lawyers cannot adequately perform their role if they are required to make predeterminations of the kind the district court's approach to Rule 11 would necessitate.

Id. at 1541–42.

3. What are justifications for assessing costs under Rule 11 to both the lawyer and the client?

v. Citation to Adverse Authority

Model Rule 3.3 imposes on the lawyer a duty of candor toward the tribunal, which requires the lawyer to disclose adverse authority and prohibits the lawyer from misleading the court with false statements or misrepresentations of law. The comments explain that the

lawyer acting as an advocate in an adjudicative proceeding has an obligation to present the client's case with persuasive force. . . . Consequently, although a lawyer in an adversary proceeding is not required to present an impartial exposition of the law or to vouch for the evidence submitted in a cause, the lawyer must not allow the tribunal to be misled by false statements of law or fact or evidence the lawyer knows to be false.

Model Rules of Prof'l Conduct R. 3.3 cmt. 2 (2008).

IN RE THONERT
733 N.E.2d 932 (Ind. 2000)

The respondent in this attorney disciplinary matter is charged with failing to disclose to an appellate tribunal controlling authority known to him, not disclosed by opposing counsel, that was directly adverse to his client's position. He also failed to advise his client of the adverse authority when his client was contemplating his legal options.

This matter is presented to this Court upon the Disciplinary Commission's and the respondent's *Statement of Circumstances and Conditional Agreement for Discipline*, entered pursuant to Ind. Admission and Discipline Rule 23(11)(c), in resolution of this matter. That agreement is before us now for approval. We note that our jurisdiction of this matter derives from the respondent's admission to the practice of law in this state in 1974.

The parties agree that the respondent represented a client charged with operating a motor vehicle while intoxicated. Prior to the client's initial hearing and before the client met with or hired the respondent, the client was advised by videotape of his rights. He pleaded guilty to the charge, and the matter was set for sentencing hearing. Prior to that hearing, the client met with the respondent to discuss the possibility of withdrawing his guilty plea. During their meeting, the respondent told the client of another criminal case, *Snowe v. State*, 533 N.E.2d 613 (Ind.Ct.App.1989), in which the respondent had prevailed on appeal for the defendant. He provided a copy of the Indiana Court of Appeals decision to his new client. The respondent agreed to represent the client for $5,000, which the client paid.

Snowe also involved a prerecorded videotaped televised advisement of rights, but the record in that case failed to indicate whether the defendant had ever viewed the tape advising him of his rights. Further, the opinion held that a trial court judge cannot rely solely on displaying a videotape advisement of rights, but instead must also determine whether the defendant knows of and understands his rights, the nature of the charge or charges against him, the full import of the rights waiver in his guilty plea, and the sentencing possibilities for the charges against him.

At the client's initial hearing, it was established that he had viewed the videotape, that the videotape advised him of his rights and the sentencing possibilities under the charges filed against him, that he understood the charge against him and his rights as explained in the videotape, and that he voluntarily waived those rights and pleaded guilty.

On May 30, 1996, the respondent entered an appearance on behalf of the client and filed a motion to withdraw the guilty plea. The trial court denied the motion without hearing. The respondent appealed that ruling, alleging that his client had a right to withdraw the plea because, due to the absence of counsel at the time he entered it and the fact that the record did not reflect that the trial court properly examined the client as to waiver of his rights, the client had not made it knowingly, intelligently, or voluntarily. The respondent further argued that the client had a right to a hearing on his motion to withdraw the plea.

The respondent represented the defendant in *Fletcher v. State*, 649 N.E.2d 1022 (Ind.1995). In that case, this Court addressed the questions that the respondent raised in his client's case. The ruling in *Fletcher* was adverse to the arguments that the respondent offered on appeal of his client's case.1 The respondent had served as counsel of record for defendant Fletcher in the appeal before this Court. This Court's ruling in *Fletcher* was issued on May 1, 1995, over one year before the respondent filed his appeal on behalf of the client. In his appellate brief filed on behalf of the client, the respondent failed to cite to *Fletcher* or argue that its holding was not controlling authority in the client's case. The respondent also failed to argue that the holding in *Fletcher* should be changed or extended.

Although he advised his client of the *Snowe* case, he failed to advise him of *Fletcher* or explain any impact *Fletcher* might have on his case. Opposing counsel had not previously disclosed *Fletcher* to the Court of Appeals.

Indiana Professional Conduct Rule 3.3(a)(3) provides that a lawyer shall not knowingly fail to disclose to a tribunal legal authority in the controlling jurisdiction known to the lawyer to be directly adverse to the position of the client and not disclosed by opposing counsel. The concept underlying this requirement of disclosure is that legal argument is a discussion seeking to determine the legal premises properly applicable to the case. The respondent's intimate familiarity with *Fletcher* is established by his having served as counsel to the defendant. Accordingly, we find that the respondent violated the rule by failing to disclose *Fletcher* to the Court of Appeals in his legal arguments on behalf of the client.

Professional Conduct Rule 1.4(b) provides that a lawyer shall explain a matter to the extent reasonably necessary to permit a client to make informed decisions regarding a representation. A client should have sufficient information to participate intelligently in decisions concerning the objectives of the representation. By failing to advise his client of a ruling in the controlling jurisdiction that was adverse to the legal arguments contemplated for his client's case on appeal, and instead choosing only to advise the client of an earlier appellate decision favorable to his position, the respondent effectively divested his client of the opportunity to assess intelligently the legal environment in which his case would be argued and to make informed decisions regarding whether to go forward with it. Accordingly, we find that the respondent violated Prof.Cond.R. 1.4(b).

The parties agree that the respondent should be publicly reprimanded for his misconduct. We agree that a public admonishment is appropriate in this case, given the negative impact on the efficient resolution of the client's appeal occasioned by the respondent's lack of disclosure and its attendant deception of the client as to the viability of any efforts to withdraw the guilty plea. Accordingly, we accept the parties' agreement and the discipline called for therein.

It is, therefore, ordered that the respondent, Richard J. Thonert, is hereby reprimanded and admonished for his violations of Prof.Cond.R. 3.3(a)(3) and 1.4(b).

The Clerk of this Court is directed to provide notice of this order in accordance with Admis.Disc.R. 23(3)(d) and to provide the clerk of the United States Court of Appeals for the Seventh Circuit, the clerk of each of the United States District Courts in this state, and the clerks of the United States Bankruptcy Courts in this state with the last known address of respondent as reflected in the records of the Clerk.

Costs are assessed against respondent.

NOTES

1.   In *Thonert*, the court criticized the lawyer not only for his failure to disclose adverse authority to the court, but also to the client. As an advisor, the lawyer has the obligation to communicate with his client and to render candid advice. Model Rules of Prof'l Conduct R. 2.1 (2008). Where a client seeks to pursue an appeal that is not supported by relevant law, the lawyer must so advise the client. In fact,

> [l]egal advice often involves unpleasant facts and alternatives that a client may be disinclined to confront. In presenting advice, a lawyer endeavors to sustain the client's morale and may put advice in as acceptable a form as honesty permits. However, a lawyer should not be deterred from giving candid advice by the prospect that the advice will be unpalatable to the client.

Model Rules of Prof'l Conduct R. 2.1 cmt. 1 (2008).

2. A lawyer's duty of candor toward the court clearly requires the lawyer to consider and disclose adverse authority. However, the lawyer's claim on appeal, made in the face of adverse authority, is not frivolous simply because of the existence of adverse authority. Indeed, an action "is not frivolous even though the lawyer believes the client's position ultimately will not prevail." Model Rules of Prof'l Conduct R. 3.1 cmt. 2 (2008). So, how does the lawyer, faced with adverse authority that may undermine the client's claim, proceed with an action? Indeed, to the extent that a lawyer can argue that a case is distinguishable and therefore not controlling of an issue, how can a court evaluate whether the attorney has violated her duty of disclosure? Refer to the following case for an explanation.

TYLER v. STATE
47 P.3d 1095 (Ala. App. 2001)

On May 18, 2001, this court ordered attorney Eugene B. Cyrus to show cause why sanctions should not be imposed on him under Appellate Rule 510(c) for his conduct in this appeal. Having considered Mr. Cyrus's response, we conclude that Mr. Cyrus should be fined under Appellate Rule 510(c). In his opening brief, Mr. Cyrus misstated the facts of the case in a way that masked this court's potential lack of jurisdiction to entertain the appeal. Then, after the true facts were revealed and the jurisdictional problem became known, Mr. Cyrus knowingly failed to cite a decision of the Alaska Supreme Court that was directly adverse to his contention that this court had jurisdiction to decide the appeal.

Procedural history of Tyler v. State

To explain our decision, we need to describe the procedural history of the underlying appeal: *Tyler v. State*, File No. A-7779.

David A. Tyler was convicted of felony DWI — driving while intoxicated after having been twice previously convicted of DWI within the preceding five years. Tyler, represented by Mr. Cyrus, appealed his conviction to this court.

In his brief to this court, Mr. Cyrus conceded that Tyler was guilty of driving while intoxicated on the date alleged in the indictment, but he asserted that Tyler's two prior DWI convictions were invalid because, in both prior cases, Tyler had not knowingly waived his right to counsel before he pleaded no contest to the charges. Mr. Cyrus therefore argued that Tyler's prior convictions should be set aside and that Tyler's current DWI offense should be reduced to a misdemeanor.

Mr. Cyrus stated in his brief that Tyler was entitled to litigate this issue because he had gone to trial and had been convicted. But when the State's attorney reviewed the record in preparation for writing the appellee's brief, he discovered that Tyler had not gone to trial. Rather, Tyler had been convicted of felony DWI after convincing the superior court to let him enter a *Cooksey* plea over the objection of the prosecutor. Under the terms of this *Cooksey* plea, Tyler purportedly reserved the right to litigate the validity of his pleas to the two prior DWI charges.2

Based on this discovery, the State moved to dismiss Tyler's appeal. The State argued that Tyler's *Cooksey* plea was invalid because the issue that Tyler had preserved for appeal — the validity of his two prior DWI pleas — was not dispositive of Tyler's case.

The State pointed out that even if we ultimately concluded that Tyler had not knowingly waived his right to counsel before he pleaded no contest to the two prior charges, this would not mean that Tyler was entitled to an acquittal of the prior charges. Rather, Tyler would be entitled to withdraw his no contest pleas — but the charges would still stand, and Tyler would face trial on those charges. The State argued that if Tyler was again convicted of these charges (either following trial or after entering counseled pleas of no contest), then Tyler would still be a third offender for purposes of his current offense, and thus Tyler's felony DWI conviction would remain valid.

In his response, Mr. Cyrus conceded that he had incorrectly stated the facts in his brief: Tyler had not gone to trial, but rather had entered a *Cooksey* plea. Mr. Cyrus further conceded that Tyler's *Cooksey* plea would be invalid *if* the State's legal argument was correct — *i.e.*, if the State was correct in arguing that Tyler would remain a third offender if he was ultimately re-convicted on the two prior DWI charges. But Mr. Cyrus contended "that the present state of the law does not permit such a relation back." He argued that even if Tyler was again convicted of the two prior DWIs, those convictions would be new — that is, they would no longer be "prior" to his current DWI conviction, and thus Tyler's current offense would be a misdemeanor, not a felony: [I]f there [sh]ould be . . . new conviction[s] . . . on the [two prior] misdemeanor DWI cases, [these convictions] would be after the offense date in the instant case . . ., and thus, [Tyler's] priors would not [support] enhanced punishment [for his current offense].

In support of his argument, Mr. Cyrus cited three prior decisions of the Alaska Supreme Court. . . .

But the supreme court's holdings in these three cases are, at best, tangentially related to the proposition of law advanced by Mr. Cyrus. None of these cases addresses the particular question posed by Tyler's appeal: Would Tyler remain a third offender for purposes of the felony DWI statute if he were allowed to withdraw his pleas in his two prior DWI cases, but then were re-convicted of these same offenses?

Although the three cases cited by Mr. Cyrus do not involve or address this legal issue, the Alaska Supreme Court has in fact addressed this very issue in a slightly different setting. The case is *McGhee v. State*, 951 P.2d 1215 (Alaska 1998).

In *McGhee*, the Division of Motor Vehicles revoked McGhee's driver's license after he was arrested for DWI. McGhee's period of revocation was increased because he had two prior DWI convictions.

After his license was revoked, McGhee filed a motion in district court attacking one of his prior DWI convictions. McGhee argued that he should be allowed to withdraw his plea because the judge failed to expressly advise him of his right to a jury trial. McGhee was successful; the court allowed him to withdraw his plea. But after obtaining this favorable ruling, McGhee immediately re-entered a no contest plea, and he was again convicted of the charge.

Following this series of events, McGhee returned to the Division of Motor Vehicles and challenged the length of his license revocation. McGhee argued that he should no longer be subjected to the same enhanced revocation period because, now, one of his prior convictions was no longer "prior." McGhee contended that even though he had been re-convicted of the same DWI offense, his conviction should be considered "new" because it was entered *after* his current DWI arrest. Thus, McGhee argued, his re-conviction of the old DWI offense could not be used to trigger the enhanced suspension period.

But the supreme court rejected this argument. The court declared: "Because McGhee remains convicted of the same DWIs that subjected him to an enhanced revocation [in the first place], the temporary set-aside of the prior DWI requires no alteration of the original [license] revocation."

Neither Mr. Cyrus nor the State's attorney cited *McGhee* in their pleadings. We found the case ourselves. And, having found it, we concluded that it provided the answer to Tyler's appeal.

Based on *McGhee*, we concluded that even if Tyler were allowed to withdraw his pleas to the two prior offenses, this would not necessarily mean that he should be acquitted of felony DWI in his current case. Rather, if Tyler were later re-convicted of the two prior offenses, he would continue to be a third offender (*i.e.*, a felony DWI offender) for purposes of his current case. We therefore agreed with the State that the issue Tyler preserved for appeal (the validity of his pleas to the two prior DWI charges) was not dispositive of his case, and that Tyler's *Cooksey* plea was therefore not valid. Accordingly, we dismissed Tyler's appeal.

*   *   *

Mr. Cyrus's failure to cite McGhee v. State, legal authority that was directly adverse to the proposition of law he was advancing

Once the State discovered that Tyler had entered a *Cooksey* plea instead of going to trial, the State moved to dismiss Tyler's appeal. The State argued that Tyler's *Cooksey* plea was invalid because the issue that Tyler had preserved for appeal — the validity of his pleas to the two prior DWI charges — was not dispositive of Tyler's case.

As we explained above, the State's motion to dismiss Tyler's appeal presented the following legal issue: If Tyler were allowed to withdraw his no contest pleas to the two prior DWI charges, but if the State then succeeded in re-convicting Tyler of these same charges, would those two DWI convictions still be "prior convictions", so that Tyler could properly be charged with felony DWI in the current case? Or would the re-convictions be "new" convictions, so that Tyler would technically be a "first offender" for purposes of his current case (and thus guilty of only misdemeanor DWI)?

The State argued that if Tyler was convicted again of the two earlier charges (either following trial or after entering counseled pleas of no contest), Tyler would continue to be a third offender for purposes of his current offense, and therefore his current felony DWI conviction would remain valid. Mr. Cyrus argued the opposite. He contended that even if Tyler was re-convicted of the two previous DWIs, those convictions would be new — that is, they would no longer be "prior" to Tyler's current DWI offense. According to Mr. Cyrus's argument, even if the State re-convicted Tyler of the two earlier DWIs, Tyler would still be a "first offender" for purposes of his current offense, and thus his current offense would be a misdemeanor, not a felony.

When the parties submitted their pleadings on this issue, neither Mr. Cyrus nor the State's attorney alerted us to *McGhee v. State*, the Alaska Supreme Court decision that addresses this re-conviction issue in the context of an administrative revocation of a driver's license for a third-offense DWI. The State's attorney apparently did not find the *McGhee* case when he researched the State's motion to dismiss Tyler's appeal-for if the State's attorney had found *McGhee*, he doubtless would have cited it. But Mr. Cyrus plainly knew of the supreme court's decision in *McGhee*: he was the attorney who represented McGhee in the supreme court.

Alaska Professional Conduct Rule 3.3(a)(3) declares that a lawyer shall not knowingly "fail to disclose . . . legal authority in the controlling jurisdiction" if the lawyer knows that this legal authority is "directly adverse to the position of the [lawyer's] client" and if this authority has "not [been] disclosed by opposing counsel". *McGhee* was decided by our supreme court, so it is "legal authority in the controlling jurisdiction". Mr. Cyrus knew about the *McGhee* decision, and he knew that the State's attorney had not brought *McGhee* to our attention. The remaining question is whether Mr. Cyrus knew that *McGhee* was "directly adverse" to his legal position — directly adverse to his contention that Tyler would have to be treated as a "first offender" even if he was re-convicted of the two prior DWIs.

Our decision in *Tyler v. State* — *i.e.*, our dismissal of Tyler's appeal — is clearly premised on our conclusion that *McGhee* is, in fact, directly adverse to Mr. Cyrus's legal position. However, it would be unfair to judge Mr. Cyrus's ethical duties in hindsight. Obviously, Mr. Cyrus had not read our decision when he wrote his brief. The question is whether, at the time Mr. Cyrus wrote his brief, he knew that *McGhee* was directly adverse to his position.

Mr. Cyrus's response to our order to show cause

In his response to our order to show cause, Mr. Cyrus asserts that he did not tell us about the *McGhee* decision because he believed that *McGhee* did not control the outcome of Tyler's case. Mr. Cyrus contends that "*McGhee* is unique because of its fact pattern" and, because of this, he did not believe (and still does not believe) that *McGhee* was "controlling authority" in Tyler's case. To back up his argument, Mr. Cyrus points out that at least one superior court judge shared his views concerning *McGhee*:

> [J]ust four months previous to my writing [Tyler's] brief . . . , a detached neutral judicial officer of the Anchorage Superior Court in a litigated case *of mine* . . . ruled that *McGhee* was not controlling authority on a similar issue regarding the propriety of an attack on a prior conviction. . . . [I]f an attorney [knows of] a written judicial opinion verifying his belief that a case is not applicable, . . . it is not possible to [condemn the] attorney [for] intentionally withholding controlling authority. Simply [put], if attorneys could disagree as to [whether a case is] controlling authority, there should not be a violation [of Professional Conduct Rule 3.3(a)(3)].

The superior court case that Mr. Cyrus refers to is *Sjoblom v. State*. Susan Sjoblom was Mr. Cyrus's client. After Sjoblom was convicted of felony DWI (*i.e.*, third-offense DWI), Mr. Cyrus filed a motion in district court on her behalf, seeking to set aside one of her prior misdemeanor DWI convictions. Mr. Cyrus claimed that Sjoblom had received ineffective assistance of counsel in that prior case. Ultimately, Mr. Cyrus negotiated a deal with the Municipality of Anchorage that embodied the same strategy he pursued in *McGhee*: the Municipality agreed to concede the ineffective assistance of counsel issue (so that Sjoblom's prior conviction would be set aside), and Sjoblom agreed to immediately plead no contest to that same charge (so that she would again be convicted of the prior DWI).

Having accomplished this, Mr. Cyrus returned to superior court (the court having jurisdiction over Sjoblom's felony DWI conviction) and asked the court to reduce her felony conviction to a misdemeanor. His argument was the same one he presented in *McGhee*: Mr. Cyrus argued that Sjoblom should no longer be considered a third offender because, now, one of her prior DWI convictions was no longer "prior". That is, even though Sjoblom had been re-convicted of the same DWI offense, her conviction should be considered "new" because it was entered *after* her arrest in the felony case.

Mr. Cyrus did not tell the superior court about the *McGhee* decision, and the State's attorney did not find it. Superior Court Judge Dan A. Hensley discovered *McGhee* on his own, but he concluded that it was factually distinguishable:

> *McGee v. State* [sic], not cited by either party, addresses a similar issue, but is distinguishable on its facts. McG[h]ee negotiated a deal manipulating the date of a DWI conviction and then moved to modify the terms of an administrative license revocation based on that prior conviction. The [supreme] court held that a license revocation could be set aside only for manifest injustice, and found that McG[h]ee's manipulation did not qualify.

> But [the portion of the post-conviction relief statute], . . . on which Ms. Sjoblom relies here, does not employ a manifest injustice test. Under its terms Ms. Sjoblom need only prove that her prior conviction was set aside — nothing more. Statutes imposing criminal liability must be construed narrowly. I find that the statute provides no basis for this court to make an independent evaluation of the merits of Ms. Sjoblom's motion in the 1996 case or the validity of the deal setting aside her conviction.

To summarize: Mr. Cyrus offers two defenses to our order to show cause. First, he argues that even though we relied on *McGhee* when we dismissed Tyler's appeal, we were wrong to do so. Mr. Cyrus contends that because of *McGhee's* procedural context (an attack on the ruling of an administrative agency), the case had little or no relevance to the proper decision of Tyler's criminal appeal. Second, Mr. Cyrus argues that even if this court was right when we concluded that *McGhee* was dispositive of Tyler's appeal, this conclusion was reasonably debatable. Based on Judge Hensley's analysis in *Sjoblom*, Mr. Cyrus points out that competent attorneys and judges might reasonably conclude that *McGhee* was factually distinguishable from Tyler's case — and that, therefore, *McGhee* did not control the outcome of Tyler's appeal. Mr. Cyrus argues that if reasonable attorneys could conclude that *McGhee* was not controlling authority in Tyler's appeal, he was under no obligation to cite the case in his brief.

Of the two defenses advanced by Mr. Cyrus, this second one is clearly the stronger. Judge Hensley's decision in the *Sjoblom* case shows that Mr. Cyrus was not alone in thinking that *McGhee* should be limited to an administrative context and should not be viewed as controlling authority in criminal cases that raise the same re-conviction issue. And if reasonable attorneys and judges could disagree on the question of whether *McGhee* was controlling authority in Tyler's case, then regardless of whether this court correctly interpreted *McGhee* when we decided Tyler's appeal, it would be improper to fault Mr. Cyrus for taking another reasonable view of the matter.

We agree with Mr. Cyrus that, for present purposes, it does not matter whether our decision in *Tyler* was correct, or whether our decision in *Tyler* is arguably inconsistent with Judge Hensley's decision in *Sjoblom*, or whether Judge Hensley was right or wrong when he concluded that *McGhee* did not control Sjoblom's case. Instead, as Mr. Cyrus correctly points out, Judge Hensley's decision shows that reasonable judges might differ as to whether *McGhee* precludes the type of post-conviction claim presented by Sjoblom or the appellate claim made by Tyler — the claim that if a defendant is convicted of felony DWI but later wins a plea withdrawal in one of the prior DWI cases, then even if the defendant is re-convicted of that prior offense, the superior court must set aside the felony DWI conviction. Thus, Mr. Cyrus might reasonably have concluded that the *McGhee* decision did not control the outcome of Tyler's appeal.

But Mr. Cyrus's defense to our order to show cause also hinges on his assertion that Professional Conduct Rule 3.3(a)(3) only requires attorneys to reveal "controlling" court decisions and statutes. This is not correct.

As used in Professional Conduct Rule 3.3(a)(3), "directly adverse" is not synonymous with "controlling" or "dispositive"

Fortified by Judge Hensley's decision in *Sjoblom*, Mr. Cyrus argues that "if attorneys could [reasonably] disagree as to [whether *McGhee* was] controlling authority", then his failure to cite *McGhee* can not constitute a violation of Professional Conduct Rule 3.3(a)(3). The problem with Mr. Cyrus's argument is that Rule 3.3(a)(3) does not speak of an attorney's failure to cite "controlling authority". Instead, it speaks of an attorney's failure to cite authority in the "controlling jurisdiction" if that authority is *directly adverse* to the [lawyer's] position".

McGhee was decided by our state supreme court, so it clearly constitutes "authority in the controlling jurisdiction". The next question is whether *McGhee* was "directly adverse" to Mr. Cyrus's position in Tyler's appeal. The legislative history of Professional Conduct Rule 3.3(a)(3) and the commentaries on the rule show that "directly adverse" does not mean "controlling". It refers to a broader range of cases and statutes.

The meaning of "directly adverse" is explained in Formal Opinion No. 280 issued by the American Bar Association's Committee on Professional Ethics and Grievances. The Committee had been asked to clarify the "duty of a lawyer . . . to advise the court of decisions adverse to his client's contentions that are known to him and unknown to his adversary". The Committee wrote:

> We would not confine the [lawyer's duty] to "controlling authorities" —
> *i.e.*, those decisive of the pending case — but, in accordance with the tests

hereafter suggested, would apply it to a decision directly adverse to any proposition of law on which the lawyer expressly relies, which would reasonably be considered important by the judge sitting on the case.

Canon 22 should be interpreted sensibly, to preclude the obvious impropriety at which the Canon is aimed. In a case involving a [settled question of law], there would seem to be no necessity whatever of citing even all the relevant decisions in the jurisdiction, much less those from other states or by inferior courts. [But w]here the question is a new or novel one, such as the constitutionality or construction of a statute, on which there is a dearth of authority, the lawyer's duty may be broader.

The Committee then defined the duty of disclosure:

The test in every case should be: Is the decision which opposing counsel has overlooked one which the court should clearly consider in deciding the case? Would a reasonable judge properly feel that a lawyer who advanced, as the law, a proposition adverse to the undisclosed decision, was lacking in candor and fairness to him? Might the judge consider himself misled by an implied representation that the lawyer knew of no adverse authority?

This ethics opinion was issued in June 1949. The Committee was not discussing current Professional Conduct Rule 3.3(a)(3), but rather a predecessor rule, Canon 22 of the Canons of Professional Ethics adopted by the American Bar Association in 1908. However, the Committee has since declared that the same test applies to Professional Conduct Rule 3.3(a)(3).

In March 1984, the American Bar Association's Committee on Ethics and Professional Responsibility issued Informal Opinion No. 84-1505, in which the Committee discussed a lawyer's duty under Rule 3.3(a)(3) to disclose a decision of a controlling court "which may be interpreted as adverse to his client's position". The Committee concluded that the lawyer was obligated to disclose the decision, although the lawyer could "[o]f course . . . challenge the soundness of the other decision, attempt to distinguish it from the case at bar, or present other reasons why the court should not follow or even be influenced by it." The Committee explained that this question was governed by the test the Committee had earlier announced in Formal Opinion 280:

Rule 3.3(a)(3) of the Model Rules of Professional Conduct provides, "A lawyer shall not knowingly fail to disclose to the tribunal legal authority in the controlling jurisdiction known to the lawyer to be directly adverse to the position of the client and not disclosed by opposing counsel." This provision is virtually identical to its predecessor, DR 7-106(B)(1) of the Model Code of Professional Responsibility. Both provisions continue essentially unchanged the theme of Canon 22 of the Canons of Professional Ethics adopted by the American Bar Association in 1908.

Under Canon 22, this Committee issued two opinions bearing on the question presented. In 1935 the Committee decided that a lawyer has a duty to tell the court in a pending case of decisions, unknown to his adversary, that are adverse to his client's contentions. We said, "He may, of course, after doing so, challenge the soundness of the decisions or present reasons which he believes would warrant the court in not following them in the pending case." In 1949, the Committee, in Formal Opinion 280, first interpreted Opinion 146 to limit the duty of disclosure to only those decisions which were "directly adverse." We then continued:

> We would not confine the Opinion to "controlling authorities" — *i.e.*, those decisive of the pending case — but . . . would apply it to a decision directly adverse to any proposition of law on which the lawyer expressly relies, which would reasonably be considered important by the judge sitting on the case.

> The Committee then concluded that, in the case before them, the lawyer was duty-bound to disclose a court decision that could reasonably be interpreted as directly contrary to his position: Under one interpretation of the decision, it is clearly "directly adverse to the position of the client." And it involves the "construction of a statute on which there is a dearth of authority."

The issue is potentially dispositive of the entire litigation. [A lawyer's] duty as an officer of the court to assist in the efficient and fair administration of justice compels plaintiff's lawyer to make the disclosure immediately.

In a strikingly similar case, *Seidman v. American Express Company*, 523 F.Supp. 1107 (E.D.Pa.1981), the court, applying DR 7-106(B)(1), came to the same conclusion on the duty to disclose as does the Committee in this opinion. There a trial court commended defendant's lawyer for calling attention, after oral argument, to a recent case that severely undercut the position defendant had taken at oral argument. . . .

Under the interpretation of Rule 3.3(a)(3) espoused in these ABA ethics opinions, a court decision can be "directly adverse" to a lawyer's position even though the lawyer reasonably believes that the decision is factually distinguishable from the current case or the lawyer reasonably believes that, for some other reason, the court will ultimately conclude that the decision does not control the current case.

This interpretation of a lawyer's duty to cite adverse authority was adopted by the New Jersey Supreme Court in *In re Greenberg*, 104 A.2d 46, 48–49 (1954). It was also anticipated (four years before the ABA issued Ethics Opinion 280) by the California Supreme Court in *Shaeffer v. State Bar of California*, 160 P.2d 825 (1945).

In *Shaeffer*, a lawyer relied on a decision of the California Supreme Court to argue that his opponent's complaint was flawed and should be dismissed. The lawyer failed to mention that the California Court of Appeal had issued a decision expressly rejecting the lawyer's interpretation of the supreme court case. When the court of appeal's decision was discovered, the lawyer declared that he omitted telling the trial judge about that decision because he thought that the court of appeal's discussion of the point was *dictum*, and that there was still no controlling authority contrary to his interpretation of the supreme court case. The California Supreme Court viewed the matter differently:

> In view of [the attorney's] familiarity with the [court of appeal] case, he should . . . have directed the trial court's attention to the decision and [openly] argued [his] contentions . . . that the case was not controlling.

See also *Mannheim Video, Inc. v. Cook County*, 884 F.2d 1043 (7th Cir.1989), in which the Seventh Circuit indicated that it would have upheld sanctions against a lawyer who engaged in similar conduct:

> [C]ounsel argues that [sanctions would be inappropriate because] he believes that [the] *Ciotti [v. County of Cook*, 712 F.2d 312 (7th Cir.1983)]* [decision] is not controlling. . . . *Hill [v. Norfolk & Western Railway*, 814 F.2d 1192, 1198 (7th Cir.1987),] and *Bonds [v. Coca-Cola Company*, 806 F.2d 1324, 1328 (7th Cir.1986),] made clear that an attorney should not ignore potentially dispositive authorities; the word "potentially" deliberately included those cases arguably dispositive. Counsel is certainly under obligation to cite adverse cases which are ostensibly controlling and then may argue their merits or inapplicability.

This same interpretation of a lawyer's duty has also been endorsed by legal commentators. For instance, in their work *The Law of Lawyering* (2nd ed.1998), Professors Geoffrey C. Hazard and W. William Hodes write:

> The requirement that the authority be "directly adverse" has caused some problems of interpretation. Almost any adverse precedent can be distinguished. . . . Some might argue, therefore, that precedent which can be distinguished is not "directly" adverse and need not be revealed in the first place. This interpretation trivializes the rule and does not adequately protect the court.
>
> Formal [Ethics] Opinion 280 (1949) sounded the right note on this issue when it suggested that the standard should be whether the omitted authorities "would be considered important by the judge sitting on the case," or whether the judge might consider himself "misled" if he remained unaware of them.

Similarly, in his book *Professional Responsibility* (3rd ed.1992), Professor Ronald D. Rotunda writes:

> [T]he rule does not speak of "controlling authorities.". . . ABA Formal Opinion 280 (June 18, 1949) rejects the narrow view that a lawyer must only cite decisions that are decisive of the pending case. Rather, the disclosure rule applies to . . . "a decision directly adverse to any proposition of law on which the lawyer expressly relies, which would reasonably be considered important by the judge sitting on the case. . . ."

In their work *Professional Responsibility in a Nutshell* (2nd ed.1991), Professors Robert H. Aronson and Donald T. Weckstein echo this view of Professional Conduct Rule 3.3(a)(3) in even stronger language:

> It has been settled that a lawyer has an obligation to avoid knowingly making a false statement of law.. . . Thus, to assert that a particular proposition is the law in the controlling jurisdiction, when that proposition appears to have been completely or partially undermined by a recent case, is a misrepresentation of the state of the law, tantamount to making a false statement of law, and is different only in degree, not in kind, from citing an overruled case.
>
> Of course, if the recent adverse case is distinguishable . . . or is otherwise construable as not controlling, these points can and should be raised.

Using this definition of "directly adverse," did Mr. Cyrus know that McGhee was directly adverse to the position he was advancing in Tyler's appeal?

Turning to the facts of Tyler's appeal, and using the test explained in the previous section, it is evident that the supreme court's decision in *McGhee* was "directly adverse" to the position that Mr. Cyrus was arguing in Tyler's appeal.

McGhee is the only Alaska Supreme Court decision (to our knowledge) that addresses the question raised in Tyler's appeal — the effect of a withdrawn plea and a re-conviction of DWI when a defendant faces harsher penalties if the defendant is found to be a repeat offender. The result reached in *McGhee* is the opposite of the result that Mr. Cyrus advocated in Tyler's appeal. And, although the matter was obviously debatable, one could reasonably interpret *McGhee* as being directly inconsistent with, or at least substantially undercutting, the argument that Mr. Cyrus was making in Tyler's case. Further, even if Mr. Cyrus thought that *McGhee* was distinguishable because of its procedural context, Tyler's appeal involved a novel issue on which there was a dearth of authority, and *McGhee* was the only Alaska decision that came close to addressing this issue.

Given these circumstances, *McGhee* was "directly adverse" to Mr. Cyrus's position for purposes of Professional Conduct Rule 3.3(a)(3). In the words of ABA Formal Ethics Opinion 280, *McGhee* is a decision "which would reasonably be considered important" by this court, a decision "which the court should clearly consider in deciding [Tyler's] case".

We recognize that advocacy invariably includes a process of separating wheat from chaff, of deciding which arguments and legal authorities are important to a case. Moreover, as we stated earlier, an attorney's ethical duties must not be judged in hindsight. When an attorney consciously decides not to cite a court decision or a statute, the attorney's choice should not — and does not — become a violation of Professional Conduct Rule 3.3(a)(3) simply because the court later concludes that the omitted decision or statute is directly adverse to the attorney's position. Rather, an attorney violates Rule 3.3(a)(3) only if the *attorney knew* that the omitted legal authority was directly adverse to the attorney's position.

But in Mr. Cyrus's response to our order to show cause, he does not claim ignorance of *McGhee's* potential importance to Tyler's appeal. Rather, he claims that he was not obliged to bring *McGhee* to our attention because he honestly believed that *McGhee* was factually distinguishable from Tyler's case and that, therefore, *McGhee* did not control our decision.

As explained above, this does not excuse Mr. Cyrus's failure to cite *McGhee*. When an attorney knows of a decision that is "directly adverse" under the test we have explained, and when opposing counsel fails to cite that decision, Rule 3.3(a)(3) requires the attorney to reveal the decision even though one could reasonably argue that it does not control the case at hand.

We assume that reasonable attorneys and judges might conclude that *McGhee* did not dictate our decision in Tyler's case (because of its different procedural setting). Nevertheless, *McGhee* was directly adverse to Mr. Cyrus's position within the meaning of Professional Conduct Rule 3.3(a)(3). Mr. Cyrus was the attorney who litigated *McGhee:* he knew about the case, and he understood its relevance to Tyler's appeal. Even assuming that Mr. Cyrus had a good faith and reasonable belief that *McGhee* could be distinguished, he was obliged to bring *McGhee* to our attention once he realized that the State's attorney had failed to cite the case.

We readily acknowledge that appellate litigation is a contest, not a seminar. The lawyers who appear before us do so as adversaries and advocates. Our adversary system is based on the belief that the fairest results and the best rules of law are discovered through vigorous presentation of opposing viewpoints. But attorneys are officers of the court, and they owe a duty of candor to the court:

Although a lawyer's paramount duty is to pursue the client's interests vigorously, that duty must be met in conjunction with, rather than in opposition to, [the lawyer's] other professional obligations. . . . Implicit in the lawyer's role as officer of the court is the general duty of candor.

This duty of candor includes the obligation imposed by Professional Conduct Rule 3.3(a)(3) — the obligation to disclose legal authorities that the court should, in fairness, consider when making its decision, even when these authorities are adverse to the lawyer's position. As explained in the Comment to Alaska's Professional Conduct Rule 3.3(a), A lawyer is not required to make a disinterested exposition of the law, but must recognize the existence of pertinent legal authorities. . . . The underlying concept is that legal argument is a discussion seeking to determine the legal premises properly applicable to the case. Comment to Rule 3.3, third paragraph, "Misleading Legal Argument."

In Great Britain, barristers are under "an unquestioned obligation" to cite all relevant law, both favorable and unfavorable. Professional Conduct Rule 3.3(a)(3) does not impose such a broad duty on Alaska attorneys. But although our state's duty of disclosure is narrower, enforcement of this duty remains important.

The process of deciding appeals involves the joint efforts of counsel and the court. As the Supreme Court of New Jersey has noted, "[i]t is only when each branch of the profession performs its function properly that justice can be administered to the satisfaction of both the litigants and society". Only then can an appellate court "[develop] a body of decisions . . . that will be a credit to the bar, the courts[,] and the state."

When a lawyer practicing before us fails to disclose a decision of the Alaska Supreme Court (or one of our own published decisions) that is directly adverse to the lawyer's position, the lawyer's conduct will, at the very best, merely result in an unneeded expenditure of judicial resources — the time spent by judges or law clerks in tracking down the adverse authority. At worst, we will not find the adverse authority and we will issue a decision that fails to take account of it, leading to confusion in the law and possibly unfair outcomes for the litigants involved. This potential damage is compounded by the fact that our decision, if published, will be binding in future cases.

*   *   *

Professional Conduct Rule 3.3(a)(3) is based on the notion that "[t]he function of an appellate brief is to assist, not mislead, the court." We endorse the words of the Florida Court of Appeal in *Forum v. Boca Burger, Inc.*, 788 So.2d 1055 (Fla.App.2001):

Although we have an adversary system of justice, it is one founded on the rule of law. Simply because our system is adversarial does not make it unconcerned with outcomes. . . . We do not accept the notion that outcomes should depend on who is . . . [most] able to misdirect a judge. . . .

Much is written about "professionalism" today. It is on the agenda at every [legal] symposium or continuing education conference, and our professional journals are filled with pleas for greater attention to punctilious conduct in all things. But . . . we [must now] pass from exhortation to [action].

Although we accept Mr. Cyrus's assertion that he honestly and reasonably believed that *McGhee* could be distinguished from Tyler's case, Mr. Cyrus does not contend that he was unaware of *McGhee's* potential importance to the decision of Tyler's appeal. *McGhee* was the only Alaska appellate decision that discussed, or came close to discussing, the issue that Mr. Cyrus knew would determine the validity of Tyler's *Cooksey* plea. And the result in *McGhee* was the opposite of the result advocated by Mr. Cyrus in Tyler's case.

Mr. Cyrus knew that *McGhee* could reasonably be interpreted as rejecting or casting substantial doubt on his position. *McGhee* was therefore "directly adverse" authority for purposes of Professional Conduct Rule 3.3(a)(3), and Mr. Cyrus was obligated to bring *McGhee* to our attention when he realized that the State had not cited it. Mr. Cyrus failed in that duty.

We acknowledge that Professional Conduct Rule 3.3(a)(3) has not previously been interpreted by the appellate courts of this state. Given that fact, Mr. Cyrus might plausibly have been unaware of the definition of "directly adverse", and he might honestly have thought that Rule 3.3(a)(3) only required him to cite adverse authority if that authority unquestionably controlled the litigation. But, as we have explained here, the American Bar Association and various courts and commentators have adhered to a broader definition of "directly adverse" for more than half a century. While Mr. Cyrus's misunderstanding of the rule may be a mitigating circumstance, it does not justify his conduct.

Conclusion: Mr. Cyrus is ordered to pay a $250 fine

* * *

NOTES

1. In *Tyler*, was the lawyer's position that the decision in *McGhee* was distinguishable reasonable? If so, why was he sanctioned?

2. For purposes of adverse authority, what distinction does the *Tyler* court draw between "directly adverse" and "controlling/dispositive"? What was the basis of the lawyer's defense that *McGhee* was not directly adverse?

3. The obligation to cite authority adverse to a client's claim seems at odds with the lawyer's obligation to represent her client zealously. What is the justification for the rule requiring citation to adverse authority?

4. Compare the court's response in *Tyler* with *Com. v. Frisino*, 488 N.E.2d 51 (Mass. App. 1986), in which the court explicitly commended a lawyer on citing authority adverse to the lawyer's position. The adverse authority had been decided after the briefs were filed. The court noted:

The *Weaver* case was decided after the briefs were filed in this case. The Commonwealth, commendably, directed the court's attention, by way of memorandum and again at oral argument, to *Weaver* as well as another later decided case. Both decisions supported a position adverse to the Commonwealth. Such advocacy comports with the highest level of professionalism and deserves to be praised as exemplary ethical conduct.

Id. at 54 n. 7.

vi.   Plagiarism

There are a variety of rules of professional responsibility which impose an obligation on lawyers to be truthful. This requires that lawyers refrain from acts involving dishonesty, deceit, or misrepresentation towards clients, other lawyers, third parties, and the court.

IOWA SUPREME COURT BD. OF PROFESSIONAL ETHICS AND CONDUCT v. LANE
642 N.W.2d 296
(Iowa 2002)

After the conclusion of a trial in federal court in which Daniel Sicard claimed a violation of the Americans with Disabilities Act, attorney Lane submitted a post-trial brief to the court. The legal portion of the brief was in great part plagiarized from a treatise written by Barbara Lindemann and Paul Grossman. *See* Lindemann & Grossman, *Employment Discrimination Law* (3d ed.1996). Lane later applied to the court for attorney fees. Among other charges, Lane requested compensation for eighty hours of work spent to prepare the questioned brief. Charging $200 per hour, Lane asked for $16,000 to write the brief that was largely copied from an uncredited source. In total, Lane requested $104,127 in attorney fees plus $13,363.29 in costs for his representation of Sicard.

On May 5, 1998, there was a hearing on Lane's attorney fee application. The United States magistrate judge stated it did not appear to him that Lane wrote the legal portions of the brief. Lane responded,"I borrowed liberally from other sources. Yes, your Honor." The court noted,

> [b]ecause of the consistency of style and the sequence of footnotes, the court assumes that [the brief] is from a particular source. If the source is a published treatise, it can simply be identified by name, author, and publisher.

To address this suspicion, the judge ordered Lane to explain or identify the sources cited in his brief within ten days. At the end of the ten days, Lane did nothing to comply with the court's order. On June 4, 1998, a member of the judge's staff asked Lane if he intended to respond to the order. Only days later, a fire at Lane's home destroyed many of his files and records in the Sicard matter. In July 1998, Lane closed his office, but continued to practice out of his home.

Four months passed and Lane still did not respond to the judge's order. On September 30, 1998, the judge entered an order awarding Lane $20,000 in fees in the Sicard case. The judge stated "there [were] many serious problems with plaintiff's fees and cost claim." The court was particularly concerned because Lane did not support his contention he was entitled to receive compensation at the rate of $200 per hour for his services. Lane also requested $9000 as compensation for the time he spent preparing his bill. The judge stated Lane requested $16,000 for the lifted brief but failed to comply with the court's order to"disclose the sources from which counsel 'borrowed liberally.' "Lane also requested compensation for fifty-nine hours of legal research preceding the trial. The court concluded

> it is not reasonable to bill 59 hours of legal research in the two weeks prior to trial. . . . If counsel spent this amount for time performing research, it is further evidence that he does not possess the skill and experience of those who charge $200 per hour.

The court further explained its reduction of the attorney fees awarded by citing to Lane's charges of $5.00 per telephone call, $1.00 per page of facsimile transmissions, $191 for long distance transmission, and $.50 per photocopy. Finally, the court stated Lane did not cite authority for the ability to charge for estimated pretrial travel expenses. Lane did not appeal the $20,000 award of attorney fees.

On October 30, 1998, Lane filed a compliance with the judge's order to document his sources but the judge was not made aware of the compliance until March 1999. When the judge read Lane's compliance he did not notice any reference to the primary source of the legal portion of Lane's brief. Lane's compliance constituted four pages of single-spaced lists of authorities. Among them was the Grossman treatise. However, no particular attention was drawn to this source. Consequently, the judge undertook his own investigation and discovered Lane took the legal portion of his brief verbatim from the Grossman treatise.

* * *

The Ethics Board alleges violations of DR 1-102(A)(1), (3), (4), (5), and (6). This rule provides in part, a lawyer shall not

- Violate a disciplinary rule;
- Engage in illegal conduct involving moral turpitude;
- Engage in conduct involving dishonesty, fraud, deceit or misrepresentation;
- Engage in conduct that is prejudicial to the administration of justice; and
- Engage in any other conduct that adversely reflects on the fitness to practice law.

The Ethics Board also charges Lane with a violation of DR 2-106(A) which states,"[a] lawyer shall not enter into an agreement for, charge, or collect an illegal or clearly excessive fee."The Commission found Lane violated DR 1-102(A)(1), (3), (4), (5), and (6) and DR 2-106(A) by his handling of the Sicard case.

Ethical Violations

Lane plagiarized from a treatise and submitted his plagiarized work to the court as his own. This plagiarism constituted, among other things, a misrepresentation to the court. An attorney may not engage in conduct involving dishonesty, fraud, deceit, or misrepresentation. This issue is akin to the matter of ghost-writing attorneys who "author pleadings and necessarily guide the course of the litigation with unseen hand. In this situation, an attorney authors court documents for a pro se litigant who, in turn, submits the court document as his or her own writing. This practice is widely condemned as unethical and a "deliberate evasion of the responsibilities imposed on attorneys." Just as ghost writing constitutes a misrepresentation on the court, so does plagiarism of the type we have before us.

Plagiarism itself is unethical. "Plagiarism, the adoption of the work of others as one's own, does involve an element of deceit, which reflects on an individual's honesty. Use of "appropriated material . . . cannot go undisciplined, especially because honesty is so fundamental to the functioning of the legal profession. . . ." Undoubtedly, Lane's plagiarism reflects poorly on both his professional ethics and judgment.

It was not difficult to find similarity between Lane's post-trial brief and the Grossman treatise. The legal argument of Lane's post-trial brief consisted of eighteen pages of plagiarized material, including both text and footnotes, from the treatise. In copying this material, Lane cherry-picked the relevant portions and renumbered the footnotes to reflect the altered text. Examination of Lane's brief does not reveal any independent labor or thought in the legal argument.

On the first occasion plagiarism became an issue, Lane appeared to be forthcoming with the court and admitted "[he] borrowed liberally from other sources." It also appears Lane attempted to identify the source of his writing before the court but was unable to recall the exact title of the treatise. Lane later had the chance to identify his source to the court, but when he responded to the court's order, he failed to specifically draw the court's attention to the Grossman treatise. Instead, Lane buried the title within a list of over 200 other sources. Though a technical compliance with the court's order, Lane's continued lack of candor indicates he hoped, by concealing the treatise among 200 other titles, the judge would not recognize the extent of Lane's plagiarism.

We do recognize Lane's personal circumstances shortly after the time of the court's order were not ideal. Lane's home was nearly destroyed by the fire forcing him and his family to live in a motel for two months. However, this does not excuse his failure to comply with the court's order in a timely fashion. We will not excuse the seriousness of passing off another's work as one's own. We find the record shows Lane knowingly plagiarized and intended to deceive the court.

Equally troubling is Lane's application for attorney fees. Lane copied the entire portion of his legal argument out of a book and then claimed it took him eighty hours to write the brief containing the copied material. He requested attorney fees for this work at the rate of $200 per hour. Other than Lane's assertions that perhaps he works less efficiently than other lawyers, there is little in the record to indicate Lane actually spent this amount of time writing the brief. Because he plagiarized the entire legal argument, the chances are remote that it took Lane eighty hours to write the argument. Rather, the facts show Lane stole all eighteen pages of his legal argument from a single source. Then to justify his request for attorney fees for the eighty hours it took to"write" the brief, Lane submitted a list of over 200 legal sources to the court. In doing so, Lane attempted to have the court believe he researched and relied on each of these sources in writing the brief. These circumstances only support the conclusion Lane endeavored to deceive the court.

The Ethics Board argues Lane's plagiarism was part of a larger scheme to defraud the court by means of inflated time and expense billings. When Lane requested compensation for time he did not spend working on the case, he violated the professional rule forbidding a lawyer from entering into an agreement for, charging, or collecting an illegal or clearly excessive fee. Even after the plagiarism issue arose, Lane continued to assert he was entitled to receive $200 for the eighty hours it took him to copy the material in his brief. He did not at any time admit that it did not take, nor could it have taken him that long to simply copy his legal argument out of a treatise. Charging such a clearly excessive bill brings Lane's integrity into question and the entire legal profession into disrepute.

It is important to note that Lane's request for attorney fees in this case is not similar to cases where the attorney is simply not awarded the fee requested. Lane relies on one particular case in which the district court reduced the attorney's fee application of over $171,000 to $95,000. The dispute in *Lynch* involved the attorney's expenditure of time, effort, and money in representing her client. There, the trial court properly considered several factors in reducing the award of attorney fees. These factors included: the time necessarily spent; the difficulty of handling and importance of the issues; the responsibility assumed and results obtained; the standing and experience of the attorney in the profession; and the customary charges for similar service. In *Lynch*, there was no suggestion of impropriety or intent to deceive the court on the part of the attorney who submitted the fee application. Moreover, the record contained no evidence to contradict the evidence supporting the fee application.

In many cases a fee application may not necessarily be a precise measure of the time an attorney spent on a particular case. Ethics concerns are not unavoidably raised where the court reduces the attorney fee award merely reflecting considerations that do not bring into question the attorney's honesty or integrity in submitting the fee application. On the other hand, although ethics is not a matter of degree of misstatement-any knowing misstatement to the court being unethical-the nature and depth of Lane's misrepresentation speaks of knowing deception.

The record before us amply supports the conclusion Lane's conduct rises to the level of intent to deceive. Action based in the hopes of deceiving the court are not the same as those arising from simple negligence or even recklessness. A lawyer who knowingly submits a fee application to the court and thereby attempts to misrepresent the amount of time he or she spent working on a case has committed serious ethical violations. Accordingly, we will not treat all of the cases the same. When the fee application involves culpable conduct, the seriousness of the offense will be considered in fashioning the appropriate sanction. We conclude the record supports the Commission's findings that Lane charged a clearly excessive fee in the Sicard case.

Discipline

In determining the proper sanction, we consider the particular facts and circumstances of each case. Among the factors we give weight to are the need for deterrence, protection of the public, maintenance of the reputation of the Bar as a whole, and the violator's fitness to continue to practice law. We also consider any aggravating or mitigating circumstances.

One such aggravating circumstance is a lawyer's prior disciplinary history. Lane has once before faced attorney disciplinary proceedings. In 1997, the Commission sanctioned Lane for failing to respond to an inquiry. He was publicly reprimanded for conduct prejudicial to the administration of justice contrary to DR 1-102(A)(5) and conduct adversely reflecting on his fitness to practice law contrary to DR 1-102(A)(6).

A mitigating factor to consider is Lane's recognition of some wrongdoing. Lane filed "Respondent's Statement" with this court. Although not evidence, we will treat this statement as a supplemental brief. Lane stated,

> I can accept that my behavior was the result of bad judgment, ignorance, even stupidity or carelessness, or sloppiness, or any number of things, such as laziness, negligence, arrogance, indolence, pettiness, or just plain old incompetence. . . .

Lane asserted he did not intend to deceive the court and cited his reputation for honesty. In support of this contention, several character witnesses testified on Lane's behalf at the hearing before the Commission. Despite Lane's statements to the court, he still does not appear to comprehend the wrongfulness of his actions. In requesting excessive and unreasonable attorney fees for a brief he did not write, Lane was not negligent, or even reckless. Rather, more seriously, he intended to deceive. Lane's purported acknowledgment of misconduct fails to recognize the full extent of his wrongdoing.

Mitigating factors alone do not overcome our responsibility to the public and to the legal profession. Though Lane offered evidence of difficult personal circumstances, this does not excuse his unethical conduct. Taking all of the above factors into consideration, we conclude in cases of this type, fairness and justice require discipline be imposed to deter future misconduct, protect the public, and maintain the reputation of the Bar as a Whole. Lane's excessive billing for writing a largely plagiarized brief cannot go undisciplined. Honesty is fundamental to the functioning of the legal profession, and Lane's conduct in this case has compromised that honesty. Moreover, Lane has jeopardized the integrity of the Bar and the public's trust in the legal profession. We conclude a six-month license suspension is warranted. We therefore suspend Lane's license to practice law in the State of Iowa, with no possibility of reinstatement for a period of six months from the date of the filing of this opinion. Upon application for reinstatement, Lane shall have the burden to prove he has not practiced law during the period of suspension and that he meets the requirements of Iowa Court Rule 35.13.

The costs of this action are assessed against the respondent in accordance with Iowa Court Rule 35.25.

LICENSE SUSPENDED.

NOTES

1. Lawyers routinely rely on prepared forms in pleadings and drafted documents. This enables a lawyer to practice efficiently, avoid duplication of effort, and save clients fees. Plagiarism with regard to legal argument, however, is a different matter. What was the primary source of the infraction in *Lane*?

2. In *In re Burghoff*, 374 B.R. 682 (N.D. Iowa 2007), a lawyer, Cannon, filed a 19 page brief, 17 pages of which was a verbatim excerpt from a published article by two other attorneys. Cannon failed to cite the article. *Id.* at 683. Cannon's only modifications to the article were deletion of certain sentences and citations contrary to his position. *Id.* Moreover, Cannon charged his client $5,737.50 which represented 25.5 hours of work in preparing the two briefs. *Id.* at 686. The court held that Cannon had committed plagiarism, thereby violating Iowa Rule 8.4 which prohibits lawyers from engaging in conduct involving dishonesty, fraud, deceit, or misrepresentation. *Id.* The court noted:

> In addition to exposing himself to significant sanctions, Mr. Cannon's acts of plagiarism burden the Court, undercut his client's cause, and

generate criticism of the legal profession. Moreover, parroting a scholarly article in this way is not an effective type of advocacy. More fundamentally, Mr. Cannon's disregard for the true authors' property rights in their ideas reveals a lack of integrity that reflects poorly on the legal profession.

Id. In determining the appropriate sanction, Cannon proposed an apology to the authors of the article, community service, and a disgorgement of the fees. *Id.* at 684. Unconvinced that the sanction was appropriate, the court ordered Cannon to enroll in an ethics course at an accredited law school, reasoning, "[b]ecause Mr. Cannon does not appreciate the nature of plagiarism, a continuing education class will not cure his ethical shortcomings. Mr. Cannon's deficiency calls for the more-involved method of instruction offered in a law school course on professional responsibility." *Id.* at 687.

II. FORMAT AND PRACTICE CONSIDERATIONS

An attorney has a professional obligation to prepare briefs that conform to local rules. A failure to conform to those rules subjects the attorney to reprimand, either privately or publicly, and — perhaps more importantly — diminishes the credibility of the lawyer with the court. As a practical matter, it is damaging to a lawyer's reputation (and therefore her business) to be publicly reprimanded for a failure to follow court rules, particularly when the lapses relate to merely technical matters. The following case discusses the practical implications of a lawyer's disregard for local rules pertaining to the format of an appellate brief.

REYES-GARCIA v. RODRIGUEZ & DEL VALLE, INC.
82 F.3d 11 (1st Cir. 1996)

Since appellate judges are not haruspices, they are unable to decide cases by reading goats' entrails. They instead must rely on lawyers and litigants to submit briefs that present suitably developed argumentation with appropriate citations to applicable precedents and to the record below. A party who honors the minimum standards of acceptable appellate advocacy only in the breach frustrates effective review and thereby jeopardizes its appeal. The case at bar is a paradigmatic example of a situation in which a party, by ignoring the rules, invites serious repercussions.

We sketch the underlying facts as best we can, resolving infrequent conflicts in favor of the jury verdict.

In 1987, defendant-appellant Rodriguez & Del Valle, Inc. (R & D), a general contractor, executed an agreement with a public agency, the Urban Renewal and Housing Corporation of Puerto Rico (the Corporation), to renovate several residential buildings in the Puerta de Tierra Housing Community, San Juan, Puerto Rico. Without obtaining the permission required by relevant regulations — or any other semblance of permission, for that matter — R & D levelled speed bumps on a road that provided entry into the Housing Community. Though flattening the protuberances facilitated access to the work site by R & D's vehicles and heavy machinery, the changed configuration also effectively converted the roadway into a drag strip for high-speed racing. Dismayed residents soon petitioned the municipality to reconstruct the speed bumps. The powers-that-be acquiesced and the municipality rebuilt the moguls (spacing them at their original fifty-foot intervals, rather than at the 100-foot intervals then mandated by applicable highway safety regulations). The drag-racing ceased and traffic slowed to a snail's pace.

R & D was not to be inconvenienced. It again levelled the speed bumps on its own authority. Not surprisingly, drag-racing resumed and the pace of traffic accelerated. When R & D finished the renovations limned by its contract, it departed the site without restoring the roadway to its original humpbacked condition. Residents alerted the authorities, warning that lives were at stake. After conducting an investigation, the municipality concluded that someone had best rebuild the speed bumps.

History teaches that at one point Rome burned while the Emperor fiddled. On September 18, 1990 — while various parties (including R & D and the Corporation) were fencing over who had the responsibility to restore the speed bumps — a motorist named Jose Flores, travelling at high speed on the roadway, lost control of his automobile and struck plaintiff-appellee Maria del Carmen Reyes-Garcia (Reyes) as she stood on the sidewalk. The impact caused permanently debilitating injuries, including the severance of a limb.

Invoking diversity jurisdiction the plaintiff, by then a citizen of New Jersey, sued several parties, including R & D, in the United States District Court for the District of Puerto Rico. At trial plaintiff advanced a golconda of tort theories against R & D, claiming *inter alia* that R & D had violated a highway safety regulation requiring contractors to seek permission from the municipality prior to removing speed bumps, and that R & D's conduct had transgressed the general duty of care owed under Puerto Rico law.

After a six-day trial, a jury found for the plaintiff and awarded her $700,000. It apportioned the damages 80% against the Corporation and 20% against R & D. The district court denied a variety of post-trial motions. R & D now appeals.

The appellant's submissions to this court are in utter disregard of the applicable procedural rules. It filed a nine-page opening brief that did not contain a table of contents, a list of legal authorities, a jurisdictional statement, a statement of the case, a précis of the issues presented for review, or a summary of the argument. The merits section of the brief lacked developed argumentation, eschewed any meaningful citations to pertinent legal authority, omitted particularized references to the record evidence, and did not discuss the applicable standard(s) of review. To cap matters, the appellant failed to prepare a record appendix. In short, the brief violated a whole series of requirements imposed by applicable procedural rules.

The plaintiff moved to dismiss the unleavened appeal. R & D responded in fits and starts. It filed two addenda to its opening brief (neither of which satisfactorily repaired the manifold defects in its original filings). Without consulting the plaintiff . . . R & D also prepared and filed a thirteen-page record appendix. This submission lacked vital excerpts from the trial record. It also lacked, among other things, an index, relevant docket entries, the notice of appeal, and the opinion of the district court denying the post-trial motions. The principal document in the appendix was in the Spanish language, without translation. These shortcomings violated the rules several times over.

Procedural rules are important for two overarching reasons. One reason is that rules ensure fairness and orderliness. They ensure fairness by providing litigants with a level playing field. They ensure orderliness by providing courts with a means for the efficient administration of crowded dockets. In both these respects rules facilitate the tri-cornered communications that link the opposing parties with each other and with the court.

The second overarching reason why procedural rules are important has a functional orientation: rules establish a framework that helps courts to assemble the raw material that is essential for forging enlightened decisions. In an appellate venue, for example, rules provide the mechanism by which the court, removed from the battlefield where the trial has been fought, gains the information that it requires to set the issues in context and pass upon them. When a party seeking appellate review fails to comply with the rules in one or more substantial respects, its failure thwarts this effort and deprives the appellate court of the basic tools that the judges of the court need to carry out this task . . .

In this instance the second reason is of paramount importance. The deficiencies in the appellant's submissions are pervasive. They frustrate any reasonable attempt to understand its legal theories and to corroborate its factual averments. Canvassing the appellant's arguments illustrates the point.

The appellant's principal claim is that it enjoyed a privilege to remove the speed bumps because they were placed at shorter intervals than prescribed by the governing municipal regulation. This paralogism, however, is unsupported by any citation either to legal authority or to record evidence. Therefore, we must treat the argument as forfeited. *See Ryan v. Royal Ins. Co.*, 916 F.2d 731, 734 (1st Cir.1990) ("It is settled in this circuit that issues adverted to on appeal in a perfunctory manner, unaccompanied by some developed argumentation, are deemed to have been abandoned."); *United States v. Zannino*, 895 F.2d 1, 17 (1st Cir.) (same); *see also* Fed.R.App.P. 28(a)(5) (explaining that an appellate "argument must contain the contentions of the appellant on the issues presented, and the reasons therefor, with citations to the authorities, statutes, and parts of the record relied on"). To make a bad situation worse, the argument is bereft of any indicium that it was seasonably advanced and properly preserved in the lower court.

The appellant's next asseveration is that the evidence does not support the jury verdict. Here, too, the appellant offers us no assurance that the necessary steps were taken below to preserve the point, and the fragmented record that it has produced does not afford any reliable way to tell. At any rate, the appellant furnishes no citations to the record in support of its rhetoric, but asks in effect that we take its rodomontade at face value. There is no justification for doing so.

* * *

The appellant's final argument is that it is entitled to a new trial because the district court allegedly declined to name Flores, the driver of the speeding car, on the verdict form. But the meager record that we have before us does not indicate that R & D preserved an objection on this ground at trial, and preserving the point is a prerequisite to a successful appeal. *See, e.g., Putnam Resources v. Pateman*, 958 F.2d 448, 456 (1st Cir.1992) ("Silence after instructions, including instructions on the form of the verdict to be returned by the jury, typically constitutes a waiver of any objections."). In all events, the appellant neglects to mention the singularly important fact that Flores was not a party to the lawsuit; the plaintiff had failed properly to serve him, and the appellant had not seen fit to implead him. The appellant offers no plausible theory why the district judge, under these circumstances, should have inserted Flores' name on the verdict form — and we can think of none.

The parties to an appeal must recognize that rules are not mere annoyances, to be swatted aside like so many flies, but, rather, that rules lie near the epicenter of the judicial process. This case shows why that is so; indeed, we have canvassed the appellant's asseverational array mainly to demonstrate that, even if we were inclined to do R & D's homework — and that is not our place — R & D's substantial noncompliance with the rules would hamstring any attempt to review the issues intelligently. Of course, there must be some play in the joints. No one is perfect, and occasional oversights — fribbling infringements of the rules that neither create unfairness to one's adversary nor impair the court's ability to comprehend and scrutinize a party's submissions — ordinarily will not warrant Draconian consequences. But major infractions or patterns of repeated inattention warrant severe decrees. "In the long run,. . . strict adherence to . . . procedural requirements . . . is the best guarantee of evenhanded administration of the law."

We hold that a party's persistent noncompliance with appellate rules, in and of itself, constitutes sufficient cause to dismiss its appeal. *See Kushner v. Winterthur Swiss Ins. Co.*, 620 F.2d 404, 407 (3d Cir.1980) (dismissing appeal for failure to comply with Fed. R. App. P. rules); *see also Mortell v. Mortell Co.*, 887 F.2d 1322, 1327 (7th Cir.1989) (observing that failure to comply with the rules can be "fatal" to an appeal); *Katz v. King*, 627 F.2d 568, 571 n. 3 (1st Cir.1980) (warning that failure to observe the rules may "result in the loss of valuable rights" and listing dismissal as an appropriate response to such violations); *see also* Fed.R.App.P. 3(a) (stipulating that the "[f]ailure of an appellant to take any step other than the timely filing of a notice of appeal" may be grounds "for such action as the court of appeals deems appropriate, which may include dismissal of the appeal"). We need not tarry in applying this holding to the case at hand. Appeals must be prosecuted in substantial compliance with applicable procedural rules and this appeal fails that test.3 The violations here are nothing short of egregious. Dismissal is plainly warranted. Accordingly, the appeal is dismissed with prejudice.

* * *

NOTES

1.　The *Reyes-Garcia* court explains two primary reasons why compliance with the appellate procedure rules is essential. First, compliance with the rules ensures fairness and orderliness among litigants, creating an even playing field and an efficient environment in which the court resolves disputes. Second, and related to the orderliness function, the rules provide a framework within which the court performs its essential function. The obligation imposed by the federal appellate rules of procedure therefore relates to the Model Rules' ethical obligations with regard to candor and the proper administration of justice.

2.　The reputation a lawyer forms within a jurisdiction clearly has an impact on her ability to persuade the court. It also affects her ability to attract and retain clients. Consider the impact of a public reprimand by a court for a failure to follow court rules. In *Westinghouse Elec. Corp. v. N.L.R.B.*, 809 F.2d 419 (7th Cir. 1987), lawyers for Westinghouse were criticized for failure to adhere to court rules limiting the number of pages in an appellate brief. Westinghouse had requested permission to file a longer brief, and when the request was denied by the court, submitted a brief in excess of the page limits but which attempted to disguise the error with various typographical variations. The court admonished:

> This presents a serious question about how lawyers respond to this court's orders. We expect counsel to respond to our orders by complying rather than seeking ways to evade them. In this case counsel tried to evade both the appellate rules and our order. . . . Fed.R.App.P. 32(a) requires typed briefs to be double-spaced and to observe specified margins. Briefs also must have type 11 points or larger, ruling out elite type. Westinghouse disregarded all of these rules. It filed a brief with approximately 11/2 spacing, with type smaller than 11 points, and with margins smaller than those allowed. The effect was to stuff a 70-page brief into 50 pages. One has the sense that the lawyers wrote what they wanted and told the word processing department to jigger the formatting controls until the brief had been reduced to 50 pages. Our clerk's office did not catch the maneuver. The judges did, and when we required Westinghouse to file a brief complying with the rules counsel responded by moving gobs of text into single-spaced footnotes, thereby leaving essentially the same number of words in the brief. . . . The lawyers, caught with their hands in the cookie jar, have apologized and promised not to play the same trick on us again. Perhaps they have learned their lesson. We cannot exclude the possibility that all of this was simply negligent inattention to the appellate rules.

Id. at 425. The *Westinghouse* court noted that the lawyers' behavior had multiplied the proceedings and imposed a fine of $1000.00 on the lawyers — specifically prohibiting the lawyers from passing the fine along to the client. What was the likely effect of the court's ruling on the relationship between Westinghouse and its lawyers? What was the ultimate effect on the lawyers' reputation with the court as a result of their refusal to effectively edit the document?

3.   Compare the *Reyes-Garcia* and *Westinghouse* courts' criticism of the lawyers' efforts with instances in which lawyers are praised for their professionalism. In *Pruett v. Thigpen*, 444 So.2d 819 (Miss. 1984) the court observed

> [W]e have received excellent briefs from both the attorneys representing Pruett and from the office of the Attorney General on behalf of the state . . . [I]t is appropriate that counsel be commended for the competence and professionalism . . . they have presented to the Court [in] this case which, as all know, arises out of one of the most sensationalized and emotionally charged crimes in the recent history of this state.

Id. at 828–9 (Robertson, J., concurring). Similarly, in *Quirk v. Premium Homes, Inc.*, 999 S.W.2d 306 (Mo. Ct. App. 1999), the court commented "We would be remiss if we failed to make public our appreciation for the well written briefs, superior arguments and, above all, exemplary courtesy and professionalism exhibited by counsel for both parties." *Id.* at 310 n. 5.

4.   Beyond the consequences for the lawyer, a failure to conform to court rules can result in appellate court's refusal to consider claims. In a Utah decision, the court commented on a brief's failure to conform to local rules:

> Before addressing the substance of the arguments Green raises on appeal, we pause to review the importance of complying with appellate briefing requirements "Our rules of appellate procedure clearly specify the

requirements that litigants must meet when submitting briefs to this court. The rules are easy to understand and offer a step-by-step approach to writing an appellate brief." Rule 24 of the Utah Rules of Appellate Procedure contains unambiguous requirements for a brief's organization and contents. Failure to adhere to these requirements "increases the costs of litigation for both parties and unduly burdens the judiciary's time and energy." Failure to adhere to the requirements may invite the court to impose serious consequences, such as disregarding or striking the briefs, or assessing attorney fees against the offending lawyer.

In this case, Green has failed to comply with the requirements of rule 24. Green's table of authorities lacks "references to the pages of the brief where [the authorities] are cited," and Green does not articulate the applicable standards of appellate review for each of the issues raised as required by rule 24(a)(5). Green also fails to provide either a "citation to the record showing that [each] issue was preserved in the trial court" or "a statement of grounds for seeking review of an issue not preserved in the trial court." In addition, Green's citations to the record are selective in contravention of rule 24(a)(7), which provides that "all statements of fact and references to the proceedings below shall be supported by citations to the record."

State v. Green, 99 P.3d 820, 824 (2004). Of the 39 issues raised on appeal, the court only considered three. The rest were rejected for failure to conform to the rules, including those rules that required adequate briefing of the facts and related law. *Id.*

5.   The cases included in this section consider violations for deficiencies in briefs, including missing elements, page limit violations, and inadequate references to the record. Note that scope is an important consideration in brief writing, for penalties may result from including too much information in a brief, as well as too little. *See American Surety Co. v. First. Nat. Bank*, 141 F.2d 411 (4th Cir. 1944). In *American Surety*, the court imposed costs upon a successful appellant for repro-ducing the entire record in an appendix to its brief, in violation of the rule requiring that the appendix include only those portions of the record relevant to issues. The court noted that including needless information in the appendix "adds to the expense of litigation and imposes useless labor on the Court." *Id.* at 418. The court went on to warn that aggravated violations of the rule could result in the striking of nonconforming briefs or appendices. *Id.* at 419.

6.   A court will be quick to identify and penalize formatting strategies designed to evade the rules. In *Kano v. Natl. Consumer Co-op Bank*, 22 F.3d 899 (9th Cir. 1994), a lawyer was penalized for failure to conform to a local rule requiring double-spacing and typeface size. The court noted that "lines were not double-spaced, but were spaced only one-and-one half spaces apart [and] . . . footnotes were of a typeface much smaller than that permitted by the rule." *Id.* Thus, the court "estimate[d] that the opening brief was the equivalent of at least sixty-five pages in length, far exceeding the fifty-page limit," and fined the lawyer $1,500. *Id.*

Chapter 9

DRAFTED DOCUMENTS

A badly written contract can hurt a client as deeply as a badly written brief can, and it can provoke a malpractice action or a disciplinary proceeding when it becomes clear that the lawyer's words left the client unprotected.

— Richard K. Neumann, Jr., Professor of Law, Hofstra University of Law

Drafted documents include contracts, wills, leases, waivers, releases, by-laws, statutes, and regulations. The ethical and professional considerations addressed in this chapter pertain more specifically to private documents such as contracts rather than public documents such as statutes. Public documents may raise additional ethical and professional considerations beyond the scope of this text. Private documents such as contracts and wills seek to memorialize a client's wishes with regard to a relationship or transaction. In so doing they establish, delineate, and control a legal relationship. Drafted documents may also aim to satisfy objectives of nonclients, such as an additional party to an agreement. To satisfy ethical obligations, the lawyer must be properly prepared and therefore competent to draft the document so that it indeed satisfies the client's wishes. To the extent that a drafted document seeks to satisfy future contingencies or to regulate conduct, it is essential that the lawyer explain the contents of a drafted document to a client. The lawyer may, in some instances, have a duty of disclosure and/or explanation regarding the contents of a drafted document to someone other than the lawyer's client. Finally, there are some ethical restrictions on the content of drafted documents, particularly when the document attempts to bestow a gift or other benefit on the lawyer who drafts the document.

I. CONTENT-BASED CONSIDERATIONS

A. Overview

i. Competence

Model Rule 1.1 requires that the lawyer possess the "legal knowledge, skill, thoroughness and preparation reasonably necessary for the representation." The comments acknowledge that the skill of legal drafting is required in virtually all types of legal representation. Model Rules of Prof'l Conduct R. 1.1 cmt. 2 (2008). Under both the Model Rules and the Model Code, new lawyers can satisfy the obligation of competence when faced with a novel drafting problem through "necessary study" or through "the association of a lawyer of established competence." *See, e.g.*, Model Rules of Prof'l Conduct R. 1.1 cmt. 2 (2008).

ii.   Communication

Model Rule 1.4 requires that the lawyer "explain a matter to the extent reasonably necessary to permit the client to make informed decisions regarding the representation." In drafting a document such as a contract on behalf of a client, this requires that the lawyer explain the contents of the contract and the implications for the client. In fact, the comments to the rule make clear that "in negotiations where there is time to explain a proposal, the lawyer should review all important provisions with the client before proceeding to an agreement." Model Rules of Prof'l Conduct R. 1.4 cmt. 2 (2008). With regard to clarity and client understanding, lawyers should endeavor to write drafted documents in a clear, comprehensible form. State legislatures have passed legislation requiring "simple," "clear," "understandable" language that uses "words with common everyday meanings" in consumer contracts and insurance policies. A federal Memorandum on Plain Language requires many new government documents and all proposed and final rulemakings to use plain English.

B.   Competence in Drafting

The rules on competence require that the lawyer be able to draft pleadings and documents. For a new lawyer with little experience, competence can be achieved by association with another, more experienced attorney or by adequate study by the novice attorney. Drafting an adequate and thorough document is often more complicated than the novice attorney appreciates, particularly given the availability of form agreements. To ensure that the document is adequate, attention must be paid to the details of the client's specific matter and how the client's wishes can be satisfied by the provisions in the document.

MATTER OF GREGORY
503 S.E.2d 735 (S.C. 1998)

In 1991 Luthi Mortgage Company ("Luthi") hired Respondent to conduct a title search and close a loan on a piece of residential real estate. At the time, the owner of record was Maxine Fallaw. However, a man named Lloyd Prevette had applied for the mortgage. By means of a convoluted arrangement . . . Prevette was to gain title to the property in trust and then mortgage it as trustee.

*   *   *

At the closing, the following documents, all drafted by Respondent, were executed:

(1) a deed transferring title to the property from Fallaw to Prevette as trustee with stated consideration of "One Dollar and the assumption of a mortgage to Commercial Credit Corporation with a balance of $27,300;"

(2) a promissory note to Luthi in the amount of $65,012.81, signed by Prevette, both as trustee and individually;

(3) a mortgage by Prevette to Luthi in the amount of $65,012.81, signed by Prevette, both as trustee and individually;

(4) a Land Trust Agreement creating a trust comprised of the property, designating Prevette as trustee and Fallaw as sole beneficiary; and

(5) an Assignment of Beneficial Interest in Land Trust transferring all of Fallaw's beneficial interest in the newly-created land trust to Prevette.

[After the closing, the Respondent failed to provide his client Luthi with the requested trust documents. He also failed to provide Luthi with the written authorization allowing Prevette to mortgage the property. Following a series of events, there was a foreclosure on the property. Luthi purchased the property at forclosure, but the purchase was later nullified. Judgment was rendered against Prevette and the Respondent.]

The panel found Respondent committed misconduct in two areas of this transaction. First, it found Respondent violated Rule 1.1, Rule 407, SCACR, in drafting the trust documents used at closing. Second, it found Respondent violated Rule 1.5, Rule 407, SCACR, in disbursing the loan proceeds. Respondent does not dispute these findings, candidly admitting mistakes were made in both areas.

Rule 1.1 requires an attorney to provide competent representation to a client. "Competent representation requires the legal knowledge, skill, thoroughness and preparation reasonably necessary for the representation." Rule 1.1, Rule 407, SCACR. Respondent was hired to paper a complicated real estate transaction, a primary component of which was to set up a land trust. He drafted a trust agreement whereby Prevette as trustee held legal and equitable title, and Fallaw as beneficiary retained an equitable interest. However, after creating this trust, he destroyed it with the assignment agreement. This assignment conveyed the equitable interest Fallaw had retained back to Prevette, thus merging the legal and equitable interests and as a practical matter ending the trust. We agree with the panel's finding there was no justification for this assignment agreement, which gave Prevette full title to the property to the detriment of Fallaw[6] and, ultimately, Luthi. Furthermore, Respondent did not comply with his client's request for certain important documents, and has offered no explanation for his failure to do so. As the hearing panel stated in its report:

> Although we do not find that Respondent knowingly participated in a fraud, his sloppiness in handling the closing and his lack of thoughtfulness in the documents he created for this transaction enabled Prevette to take great advantage of Fallaw, who obviously could not understand compli-cated legal documents and who came to suffer almost a catastrophic loss from the actions of Prevette. . . . At the very least, the incompetence with which Respondent handled this transaction facilitated [Prevette's] fraudu-lent attempt and embroiled Respondent's client, Luthi, in an embarrassing and expensive civil action. Furthermore, if Respondent had only complied with Luthi's request to send it the trust agreement before the closing, Luthi probably would have either objected to the trust arrangement prior to the closing, required clarification of the parties' respective responsibili-ties, or at least brought Fallaw into the later foreclosure suit. Any of these actions would have simplified things considerably.

---

[6] The extent of Respondent's duty to Fallaw is unclear given the fact he was not technically representing her. The Complainant presented expert testimony that typically an attorney in a residential real estate closing owes some attorney-client duties to borrower, lender, and seller. Regardless of any duties arising as a matter of law from this transaction, we find Respondent clearly undertook some duty toward Fallaw; his own testimony was that he drafted the trust documents for her protection.

We find Respondent's representation as the closing attorney in this matter fell below the standards set forth in Rule 1.1, Rule 407, SCACR.[7]

* * *

For the foregoing reasons, we find Respondent's representation in the above matters violated Rules 1.1 and 1.5, Rule 407, SCACR. His actions constitute professional misconduct.

We find the appropriate sanction for Respondent's conduct is a 30 day suspension. In addition, Respondent is ordered to enroll in and complete the Law Office Management Assistance Program (LOMAP). Finally, Respondent shall, within ten days from the date of this opinion, remit $ 1000 representing the undisbursed amount of closing funds in the Luthi Mortgage/Fallaw matter to the Lawyers' Fund for Client Protection of the South Carolina Bar.

NOTES

1. To whom did the lawyer owe a duty in *Gregory*? How did the lawyer violate that duty? Was there a duty owed to any non-party?

2. Note the court's criticism of the lawyer's competence in drafting the trust agreement. Specifically, in footnote 7, the court acknowledges that the client did not suffer harm from the lawyer's careless modification of the form document but that his "inattention to detail further demonstrate[d] his failure to provide competent representation."

3. In *Gregory*, the lawyer's faulty drafting was complicated by his failure to submit the documents to the client for review. What additional adverse consequences did his actions have? Can a lapse in the ethical standard of professionalism have consequences beyond the client's immediate matter?

4. Consider *Matter of Wallace*, 518 A.2d 740 (N.J. 1986), a case in which a lawyer was suspended from practice for six months. Wallace, the lawyer, represented Mrs. Zorzin, an elderly, non-ambulatory client. Mrs. Zorzin requested that Wallace prepare a promissory note to reflect a loan she had made to a third party, Leavy. Wallace prepared a note and proceeded to assist his client in the collection of money due on the note. When Mrs. Zorzin died and her granddaughter attempted to collect the money owed to the grandmother's estate, Wallace was unable to contact the borrower. The court noted that Wallace's actions were "grossly negligent and unethical. He admittedly had limited experience in the preparation of promissory notes. His draftsmanship of th[e] note was seriously deficient. The note did not include a due date, a default or acceleration clause, or even an address for the borrower." *Id.* at 742. The court further commented on Wallace's conduct following the preparation of the deficient note:

---

[7] Respondent also admitted he made mistakes in drafting the land trust agreement. He used an agreement drafted five years earlier for another transaction, merely removing the first page, copying the property's legal description, and having the parties sign blank pages at the end. As a result, the trust agreement Prevette and Fallaw executed made the law of Ohio applicable (instead of South Carolina) and had a life of twenty years (instead of one). Respondent stated he "got in a hurry" because everyone was in a rush to close. Though no harm to the parties resulted from Respondent's sloppiness, we find his inattention to detail further demonstrates his failure to provide competent representation, in violation of Rule 1.1.

More disturbing was respondent's totally unsatisfactory conduct following the loan of money to Leavy. Although he had had frequent conversations with Mrs. Zorzin, he never once inquired into Leavy's background or address so he would be able to protect her interests should a legal problem develop. * * * He kept no records of Leavy's payments except for an informal sheet which only indicated the date Leavy made the payments and not the amounts paid. At no time did he request of Leavy sufficient information so he could contact him if necessary.

Id. In sanctioning Wallace, the court reinforced the nature of his obligation to his client. "It is not enough simply to follow a client's instructions, for a client cannot foresee or be expected to foresee the great variety of legal problems that may arise." *Id.* Because a "license to practice law is a proclamation to the public that the holder thereof is one to whom a member of the public may, with confidence, entrust his professional matters, with the assurance that in the performance of legal services the lawyer will perform the basic legal tasks undertaken, competently, ethically, and in accordance with the highest standards of professional conduct," the suspension was warranted. *Id.* at 742–3. What should have alerted Wallace to the fact that the note was deficient? How might he have rectified the deficiency?

## C.	Communication with the Client in Drafting Documents

Model Rule 4.1 requires that a lawyer explain matters to a client "to the extent reasonably necessary to permit the client to make informed decisions regarding the representation." Comment 5 explains:

The client should have sufficient information to participate intelligently in decisions concerning the objectives of the representation and the means by which they are to be pursued, to the extent the client is willing and able to do so. Adequacy of communication depends in part on the kind of advice or assistance that is involved. For example, when there is time to explain a proposal made in a negotiation, the lawyer should review all important provisions with the client before proceeding to an agreement.

Model Rules of Prof'l Conduct R. 1.4 cmt. 5 (2008). In drafting documents on behalf of a client, the lawyer clearly has an obligation to explain the contents of those documents to the client so that the client understands the legal ramifications of executing the documents. In certain instances, the lawyer's ethical duty of communication and explanation may apply to non-clients as well.

The following case illustrates a lawyer's obligation to advise the client. Note that the underlying representation involved complex estate tax issues. Your focus, however, should be on the court's discussion of the lawyer's obligation to advise the client regarding the content and effect of the drafted documents.

WINSTON v. BROGAN
844 F. Supp. 753 (S.D. Fla. 1994)

* * *

The defendants were employed by Bruce and Ronald Winston in 1981 as part of a team of lawyers for the purposes of estate and tax planning for the estate of Edna Vivian Winston, widow of Harry Winston. At that time, Edna Winston's assets were valued at approximately $6,000,000, the majority of which were liquid investment assets.

[Edna was the beneficiary of a marital trust created by her husband Harry. The terms of the trust provided that Edna would receive the income from the trust during her lifetime and granted Edna the right to appoint the principal of the trust by her will. The terms of the trust further provided that, upon Edna's death, a second trust would be created for the benefit of Bruce. He would be entitled to receive the income from the trust during his lifetime, and the principal from the trust would be distributed to him in five installments payable on the 5th, 10th, 15th, 20th, and 25th anniversaries of Edna's death. In creating the trust for Edna, Harry contemplated the tax consequences of the marital trust. His will therefore provided that, if a portion of the principal was included in Edna's estate, the taxes and expenses of the marital trust were to paid from the marital trust assets.]

[Edna's] last known will was executed on July 10, 1928; it provides for outright distribution of her estate in equal shares to her two sons. Defendant Brogan recognized that Edna's move to Florida created a tax problem because, despite the provisions in Harry's will, Florida law would require that all taxes and administrative expenses attributable to the marital trust be taxed to Edna's estate. Due to the substantial value of the marital trust ($60 to $70 million), estate taxes and administrative expenses would have equalled or exceeded the liquid investment assets in Edna's estate.

The team of lawyers considered several alternative solutions to this problem. In addition to preserving the liquid assets, the solutions considered would also achieve certain income tax savings. One of the alternatives considered was to transfer Edna Winston's investment assets to the marital trust. Another was to exercise the power of appointment granted by the marital trust through a codicil to Edna's will executed by her guardians with court approval. The proposed codicil would direct that estate taxes and administrative expenses be paid from the assets of the marital trust.

On August 18, 1982, lawyers for the New York conservatorship prepared and filed a petition in the New York court for permission to make a revocable transfer of Edna's investment assets to the marital trust. Bruce was informed that the transfer would not adversely affect his rights to the investment assets as a beneficiary of Edna's will. Consequently, he verified the petition . . .

[The New York court granted the petition, noting that "[t]he Court has assured itself that . . . such transfer would not cause any individual who was a beneficiary under Mrs. Winston's will to be deprived of his or her legacy." Next, the lawyers sought to obtain authorization from the Florida court for the transfer of investment assets to the marital trust. The defendant lawyers sent Bruce a verification to sign in order to process the Florida authorization. Believing that the Florida petition would not affect his rights under his mother's will, Bruce signed the verification. The Florida court granted the petition.]

After his mother died, Bruce Winston learned for the first time that he would not receive his share of his mother's investment assets outright, as provided in his mother's will. Due to the transfer, these assets became subject to the terms of the marital trust, and would therefore be distributed to him in installments on the 5th, 10th, 15th, 20th and 25th anniversaries of his mother's death. Consequently, he filed this lawsuit against the defendants, the attorneys who advised him during the time when these actions were taken.

Discussion

In his complaint, Bruce Winston alleges that the defendants' failure to advise him of the consequences of the transfer of assets, as well as their failure to revoke the transfer after execution of the codicil, constitutes negligence which caused him to suffer damages. Specifically, he was denied the right to receive the outright distribution of his mother's investment assets as provided in his mother's will.

The defendants offer three main arguments in support of their motion for summary judgment. They assert that: (1) the plaintiff lacks the privity necessary to maintain the claims asserted against them, and that they therefore owed no duty to the plaintiff; (2) the plaintiff will be unable to prove that his damages are the result of their alleged negligence; and (3) the plaintiff is estopped from objecting to the impropriety of the defendants' actions, because he executed various petitions and pleadings which the defendants prepared.

*   *   *

Under Florida law, to maintain a legal malpractice suit the plaintiff is required to prove (1) the attorney's employment; (2) the attorney's neglect of a reasonable duty; and (3) that such negligence resulted in and was the proximate cause of loss to the plaintiff. Florida courts have uniformly limited attorneys' liability for negligence in the performance of their professional duties to clients with whom they share privity of contract. However, this rule of privity has been relaxed where it was the apparent intent of the client to benefit a third party. Although the court in *Oberon* recognized that the most obvious example of this exception is in the area of will drafting, the third party intended beneficiary exception to the rule of privity is not limited to will drafting cases.

The plaintiff argues that this case falls within the third party intended beneficiary exception to the privity requirement. At the very least, he argues, whether or not he was an intended third party beneficiary of the defendants' professional services is a disputed question of fact. The Court agrees. Although the defendants were retained by Bruce and Ronald Winston as guardians of Edna Vivian Winston, the facts as stated by the defendants as well as the plaintiff suggest that the defendants were hired to effectuate estate planning for the benefit of Edna Winston's will beneficiaries, her two sons. Thus, it would not be unreasonable to conclude that Bruce Winston personally, as one of only two beneficiaries of his mother's will, was an intended third party beneficiary of the defendants' profes-sional services.

The defendants argue that Bruce Winston could not be an intended third party beneficiary of the defendants' services, because potential conflicts of interest existed between the plaintiff as a guardian of Edna v. Winston and the plaintiff as a beneficiary of Edna v. Winston's will. They rely on *Oberon*, 512 So.2d 192, in support of this assertion. However, their reliance on *Oberon* is misplaced.

In *Oberon*, the Court stated that the plaintiff could not have been an intended third party beneficiary of the client, because there existed an obvious conflict of interest between the client and the plaintiff. In the instant case, unlike *Oberon*, there was no apparent conflict of interest between Bruce Winston as a guardian of

Edna v. Winston and Bruce Winston as a beneficiary of Edna v. Winston's will. As the evidence presented thus far suggests, the defendants recognized that their main goal when representing the guardians for the purpose of estate planning was to preserve Edna v. Winston's testamentary intent. The defendants have not suggested, nor have they offered any evidence demonstrating that Bruce Winston expressed any desire to take any action which conflicted with his mother's wishes.

The defendants argue that the instant dispute is proof that there was a conflict between the interests of the guardians acting on behalf of Edna v. Winston and the potential beneficiaries of her estate. Apparently, the defendants fail to recognize the nature of the plaintiff's claim. Bruce Winston has not alleged in his complaint that the defendants should have placed his interests ahead of those of his mother. He alleges that his mother's testamentary intent was frustrated due to the defendants' negligence, and that he suffered as a result. Thus, there is no indication of a conflict of interest which would undermine Bruce Winston's argument that he was an intended third party beneficiary of the defendants' professional services. Whether the plaintiff was actually an intended third party beneficiary, and was therefore owed a duty, is an issue of fact to be resolved by the jury.

The defendants' second argument is that the plaintiff will be unable to prove that his damages are the result of their alleged negligence. According to the defendants, the plaintiff cannot prove that the results would have been different if they had acted differently, because numerous factors might have influenced the outcome. However, the effects that these factors would have had on the plaintiff's situation, and the various outcomes which might have resulted from alternative actions by the defendants, are likewise issues of fact which remain in dispute. The plaintiff has offered sufficient evidence, including the defendants' own records, to create a question of fact as to whether his damages resulted from the defendant's alleged negligence.

Finally, the defendants argue that the plaintiff is estopped from objecting to the impropriety of their actions, because he signed the documents prepared by the defendants, which indicated that he had read and understood the documents. In addition, the defendants assert that the plaintiff had a duty as a guardian to be fully informed of all actions taken on behalf of the ward. Accordingly, they also argue that the plaintiff is estopped from objecting to the impropriety of actions which he had a non-delegable duty to be informed of and not ignore. They cite the case of *Brent v. Smathers*, 547 So.2d 683 (Fla. Dist. Ct. App. 3d Dist.1989) in support of their arguments.

However, their reliance on *Brent v. Smathers* is misplaced. In *Brent*, the Court held that a co-trustee, even though he was a lawyer, did not have a duty to explain the effects of transactions to a beneficiary/co-trustee who consented to the transactions unless an explanation was requested, or the co-trustee knew that the beneficiary/co-trustee did not have the necessary knowledge of the facts to understand the transactions. . . . Unlike the defendant in *Brent*, the defendants in this case are not co-trustees or guardians; they are counsel retained by the guardians to provide guidance with regard to the transactions at issue.

As the Court in *Dollman* pointed out, counsel is often engaged because the client lacks the knowledge and skills necessary to understand the transactions he will undertake. A client who, after receiving advice of counsel, signs a document acknowledging that he has read and understands it, should not necessarily be estopped from asserting that the advice he received from counsel was misleading. In this case, there remain questions of fact regarding the plaintiff's understanding of the transactions and the information he received from counsel. Moreover, the plaintiff is not merely alleging that the defendants' preparation and submission of certain petitions to the courts constituted negligence; he also alleges that he was damaged as a result of their failure to take other necessary actions. Questions of fact remain with regard to these allegations as well. Consequently, the Court will deny the defendants' motion for summary judgment.

Accordingly, having reviewed the motion and the record, and being otherwise duly advised, it is hereby: ORDERED and ADJUDGED that the defendants' Motion for Summary Judgment is DENIED.

NOTES

1.   To whom did the lawyers owe a duty in *Winston*? On what basis did the court conclude that the duty was owed?

2.   The lawyers raised an estoppel defense, claiming that the beneficiaries could not sue them in negligence. What was the basis for that defense? Why did the defense ultimately fail?

3.   Note that the *Winston* court focused specifically on the duty of the lawyers to properly advise the client. That duty of explanation may give rise to sanctions even where the underlying conduct of the lawyer is appropriate. In *Estate of Nevelson v. Carro, Spanbock, Kaster & Cuiffo*, 259 A.D.2d 282 (N.Y. App. Div. 1999), the court overturned a summary judgment in favor of lawyers who were charged with negligence. The court noted, "In this case, contrary to the conclusion reached by the . . . [c]ourt, the issue is not whether [the lawyers] could have come up with a better plan but whether [the lawyers] departed from the requisite standard of care in failing to adequately advise the Nevelsons and Sculptotek that their failure to substantially compensate the decedent could result in adverse tax consequences under the plan that they recommended." *Id.* at 284.

II.   FORMAT AND PRACTICE CONSIDERATIONS

A.   Overview

i.   Disclosure

In preparing private drafted documents, the lawyer often has interaction with parties other than the client. In this situation, the lawyer has an affirmative obligation of truthfulness to third parties. Model Rule 4.1 specifically prohibits a lawyer from making false statements of material fact to third parties. In addition, the lawyer is prohibited from failing to disclose a material fact to a third person when disclosure is necessary to avoid assisting the client in a criminal or fraudulent act. Model Rules of Prof'l Conduct R. 4.1(b) (2008). The obligation to disclose material facts to third parties to avoid crime or fraud by the client is tempered by the lawyer's obligation to preserve client confidences set forth in Model Rule 1.6.

ii. Conflict of Interest

Model Rule 1.8 addresses transactions that are prohibited between client and lawyer. Generally, any transaction between a client and lawyer must be fair and reasonable, must be consented to in writing by the client, and the client should be afforded a review by independent counsel. Model Rules of Prof'l Conduct R. 1.8(a) (2008). Lawyers are prohibited from preparing instruments such as wills in which the lawyer receives a substantial gift, unless the lawyer is related to the client. Model Rules of Prof'l Conduct R. 1.8(c) (2008). Finally, in relation to drafting considerations, lawyers are prohibited from preparing agreements in which the lawyer acquires literary or media rights to some aspect of the client's conduct which is the subject of the representation. Model Rules of Prof'l Conduct R. 1.8(d) (2008). In each of these prohibited transactions, there is the potential for a conflict of interest between the lawyer and the client which should be avoided as the lawyer drafts documents on behalf of the client.

B. Communication with and Disclosure to Third Parties in Drafting Documents

In *Winston*, the court discussed the duty of communication and explanation owed to a third party beneficiary of the lawyer's services in drafting documents. The court noted that the lawyer owes the client that duty of explanation and advice because the lawyer has special expertise. Indeed, the obligation is imposed under Model Rule 4.1. Lawyers who prepare drafted documents — documents that establish legal relationships applicable to non-clients — may then have an obligation of explanation to or communication with parties other than the lawyer's immediate clients. While a lawyer in this circumstance should be primarily aware of her duty to her own client, and the obligations of confidentiality associated with that relationship, she may have a duty to disclose facts to a third party where the disclosure is necessary to prevent her own client from committing a crime or a fraudulent act. Model Rules of Prof'l Conduct R. 4.1(b) (2008). The following case addresses the lawyer's duty to explain matters to a non-client in the context of a transaction.

THE FLORIDA BAR v. BELLEVILLE
591 So. 2d 170 (Fla. 1991)

We have this case on complaint of The Florida Bar for review of a referee's report recommending that Walter J. Belleville, an attorney licensed in Florida, be found not guilty of alleged ethical violations.. . .

In the summer of 1988, Belleville was retained as counsel for Bradley M. Bloch. Bloch had entered into an agreement with James F. Cowan to purchase property owned by the latter. Cowan was an elderly man, eighty-three years of age, who had a third-grade education. While the evidence showed that Cowan had substantial prior experience in selling real estate when he was younger, neither party to this cause disputes that the various written documents alleged to constitute the agreement overwhelmingly favored the buyer, Mr. Bloch. Cowan, in fact, has subsequently disputed that he ever agreed to some of the terms embodied in these documents.

Although Cowan and Bloch had negotiated only for the sale of an apartment building, the documents stated that Cowan was selling both the apartment building *and his residence*, which was located across the street from the apartments. The referee specifically found that Cowan had no intention of selling his residence and did not know that it was included in the sale. The record substantially supports this finding, which accordingly must be accepted as fact by this Court.

It is unclear whether Belleville knowingly participated in his client's activities or merely followed the client's instructions without question. Whatever the case, Belleville drafted the relevant documents to include the legal description of Cowan's house in the instruments of sale. Cowan then apparently signed the documents without realizing he was transferring title to his house. No one at the closing explained the significance of the legal description to him. Belleville only sent a paralegal to the closing and did not attend it himself. In fact, he had never met Cowan to this point in time.

In exchange for the apartment and his residence, Cowan received only a promissory note, not a mortgage. The loan thus was unsecured. This note provided for ten percent interest amortized over twenty-five years. However, the first payment was deferred for four months with no apparent provision for interest to accumulate during this time, and the note by its own terms will become unenforceable upon Cowan's death. Finally, the documents called for Cowan to pay the closing costs, which Bloch and Belleville construed as including Belleville's attorney fee of $625.

When Cowan received the promissory note and closing documents, he realized that their terms varied from the agreement he thought he had entered. Cowan contacted an attorney, who wrote a letter to Belleville explaining the points of disagreement. The next day, Bloch attempted to evict Cowan from his home.

The referee recommended no discipline based on his conclusion that Belleville owed no attorney-client obligation to Cowan. The Board of Governors of The Florida Bar voted to appeal this decision, and the Bar now seeks a thirty-day suspension.

While it is true that the factual findings of a referee may not be disturbed unless clearly and convincingly wrong we do not find that the present case turns on a dispute about the facts. The essential facts are not in question; and Belleville himself concedes with some understatement that "Mr. Cowan did not have a particularly good deal as a result of his negotiations with Mr. Bloch." Rather, the disagreement in this case is over Belleville's guilt and the appropriate discipline, if any. This is a question entirely of law that we must decide . . .

Based on the facts, we cannot accept the referee's recommendation about guilt and punishment. The referee's factual findings established that Cowan had negotiated to sell the apartment, that he did not intend to sell anything other than the apartment, and that he did not know that the documents of sale would result in the loss of his residence. It also is clear Belleville should have harbored suspicions about the documents he was preparing, because the documents established on their face a transaction so one-sided as to put Belleville on notice of the likelihood of their unconscionability.

When faced with this factual scenario, we believe an attorney is under an ethical obligation to do two things. First, the attorney must explain to the unrepresented opposing party the fact that the attorney is representing an adverse interest. Second, the attorney must explain the material terms of the documents that the attorney has drafted for the client so that the opposing party fully understands their actual effect. When the transaction is as one-sided as that in the present case, counsel preparing the documents is under an ethical duty to make sure that an unrepresented party understands the possible detrimental effect of the transaction and the fact that the attorney's loyalty lies with the client alone.

We recognize that The Florida Bar relies on *The Florida Bar v. Teitelman*, 261 So.2d 140 (Fla.1972), which is somewhat distinguishable from the present case. *Teitelman* dealt with those situations in which an attorney, while representing one party, also directly bills the other party a fee for preparing legal documents. In the present case, the parties themselves contractually agreed that one would pay the other's attorney's fee.

We do not believe *Teitelman* stands for the proposition that an agreement by one party to pay the other party's attorney fee always makes the payor a client of the attorney, provided dual representation has not occurred and provided the payor either is represented by counsel or is given the warnings required in this opinion if the payor is relying on legal statements or documents prepared by the attorney for the client. However, *Teitelman does* stand for the proposition that an attorney must avoid the appearance of simultaneously representing adverse interests, especially where the opposing party may be unfairly induced to rely on the attorney's advice or skill in preparing legal documents. Here, Belleville breached that duty.

For the foregoing reasons, we adopt the referee's findings of fact but reject the recommendations regarding guilt and discipline. The violation Belleville committed is a serious one in light of the fact that he previously has been disciplined for an ethical violation. Accordingly, we grant the request of The Florida Bar. Walter J. Belleville is hereby suspended from the practice of law for a period of thirty days, commencing on January 6, 1992. Belleville shall take all steps necessary to protect his present clients' interests and shall provide them with notice of his suspension, as required by the Rules Regulating The Florida Bar. He shall accept no new business from the date this opinion is issued. Judgment for costs in the amount of $1,220.30 is entered against Belleville in favor of The Florida Bar, for which sum let execution issue.

It is so ordered.

NOTES

1. In *Belleville*, the court noted specific ethical obligations imposed upon a lawyer who prepares a document which imposes disproportionate obligations upon an unrepresented party. What are those obligations? What is the basis for the obligations?

2. The *Belleville* court, citing *Teitelman*, noted that an agreement by one party to pay the attorney's fees on behalf of another party does not always entitle the payor to an attorney-client relationship with the lawyer. When does such a payment arrangement create an attorney-client relationship?

3. Do the obligations imposed by the *Belleville* court apply where the opposing party to the transaction is represented by counsel?

WRIGHT v. PENNAMPED
657 N.E.2d 1223 (Ind. App. 1995)

Donald H. Wright appeals the trial court's order of summary judgment in favor of the defendant-appellees, Bruce M. Pennamped and his law firm, Lowe Gray Steele & Hoffman ("the Appellees"). Wright is seeking damages arising from the Appellees' alleged deceptive and fraudulent conduct during a commercial loan transaction. Wright raises four issues for our review, which we consolidate and restate as whether the trial court erred in granting summary judgment. We affirm in part and reverse in part.

Facts

The facts most favorable to Wright, the nonmoving party, are as follows. Wright is a self-employed general contractor and real estate developer who lives in Beech Grove, Indiana. He owns and operates a sixty unit apartment complex in Beech Grove called the Diplomat Apartments. In early 1991, Wright began looking to refinance the Diplomat Apartments in the amount of $500,000.00.

On May 29, 1991, Ray Krebs, the vice president of mortgage banking at SCI Financial Corporation ("SCI"), submitted a proposal of financing to Wright. In pertinent part, the proposal provided:

[SCI] is please [*sic*] to submit the following proposal for financing for the Diplomat Apartments. This proposal is . . . offered subject to final credit approval by SCI and any funding participant(s). Final terms and conditions will be established by SCI and its legal counsel during review of the information requested herein.

*   *   *

PREPAYMENT: Not available during the first 12 months. Thereafter, at an amount consistent with the Federal Home Loan Bank of Indianapolis prepayment formula.

*   *   *

DOCUMENTATION: All documentation must be in a form and substance acceptable to SCI and its assigns.

Wright accepted the proposal on June 3, 1991. Wright did not understand the prepayment provision prior to signing the proposal and anticipated that he would have his attorney, Richard L. Brown, explain any provisions Wright did not understand when Brown received the proposed loan documents prior to closing. Brown had acted as Wright's counsel for approximately thirty years. Wright had regularly consulted with Brown with regard to real estate transactions and utilized Brown's services in connection with the loan transaction underlying the present litigation.

After signing the proposal, Wright provided Brown's name, address, and telephone number to Krebs. Krebs then relayed this information to Pennamped. Pennamped, a partner in the law firm of Lowe Gray Steele & Hoffman, became involved in the loan transaction on July 2, 1991, when he had a luncheon meeting with Krebs. SCI retained Pennamped and the firm to represent its interests and to prepare the necessary loan documents. At the direction of Krebs, Pennamped began drafting the loan documents on or about July 15th. Pennamped drafted the loan documents on July 31, 1991, and forwarded copies marked "DRAFT DATED 7-31-91" to Krebs and Brown.

A draft mortgage note was among the many draft loan documents hand delivered to Brown. The prepayment provision of the draft note read:

> Borrower may not prepay the principal balance of the Loan, or any part thereof, at any time during the first (1st) Loan Year of the Loan. Borrower shall have the right to prepay the Loan, in whole but not in part, upon ten (10) days written notice first given Lender, after the first (1st) Loan Year. The Borrower, in the event of prepayment, shall pay Lender a fee equal to one percent (1%) of the then outstanding principal balance together with accrued interest until payment is received by Lender.

On Friday, August 2, 1991, Brown reviewed the draft documents and discussed them with Wright. Brown and Wright discussed the prepayment provision as well as additional terms in the draft documents. Wright did not indicate to Brown that the prepayment provision in the draft note was any different than the one in the proposal for financing. Based on their discussion, both Wright and Brown accepted and approved the form and substance of the draft documents.

On August 1, 1991, Krebs mailed a copy of the draft documents to Don Wilson, Senior Vice President of Kentland Bank which was the funding bank. Wilson received and reviewed the documents on August 2nd. Wilson marked various provisions of the loan documents, including the prepayment penalty provision. At his deposition, Wilson testified the prepayment penalty provision was to be consistent with the Federal Home Loan Bank prepayment penalty, rather than a flat one percent. Upon completion of Wilson's initial review, Wilson and Krebs discussed a number of changes to be made to the draft loan documents, including those necessary to the prepayment penalty provision.

Late in the day on Friday, August 2, 1991, Krebs contacted Pennamped regarding Wilson's request for changes to the draft loan documents. Pennamped's timesheet for August 2, 1991, includes an entry identified as "revise documents" which indicates that he spent a quarter of an hour working on the loan transaction. Krebs pursued the Friday conversation with Pennamped on the morning of Monday, August 5th. Krebs sent a facsimile transmission of the changes, including a new prepayment penalty clause, to Pennamped with a cover transmittal sheet that stated "Don Wright Loan Document changes per our discussion."

Also on Monday, Brown and Pennamped discussed the transaction and the draft loan documents. Pennamped asked Brown if he had any problems with the proposed loan documents, and Brown responded that he did not. Brown informed Pennamped he had two cases set for the following morning and he would be unable to attend the closing set for 9:00 a.m. on August 6, 1991. Brown also spoke with Krebs on August 5th. Neither Pennamped nor Krebs informed Brown that they anticipated making any changes to the loan documents. Brown prepared his opinion letter for the closing with specific reference to the draft loan documents dated July 31, 1991.[1]

---

[1] The Appellees contest whether Krebs telephoned Pennamped on the afternoon of August 2nd regarding the changes requested by Wilson. Pennamped testified at his deposition that he may have had "some peripheral conversation" regarding the transaction with Krebs between July 31st and receiving

After Pennamped received the facsimile of the changes, he spoke with Krebs and indicated that somebody needed to speak with the borrower, Wright, to explain the changes in the prepayment penalty clause. Krebs informed him that he would take care of it. Pennamped neither attempted to reach Brown to inform him of the changes nor followed up to see if Krebs had contacted Wright with the changes. Pennamped completed the changes to the loan documents on the afternoon of August 5, 1991. Krebs did not inform Wright of the changes.

The loan closing occurred on Tuesday, August 6, 1991. Because Brown was in court, Wright attended the closing alone. Pennamped, Krebs, Wilson, and a representative of the title insurance company who acted as the closing agent were also at the closing. The closing agent handed Wright each of the loan documents and identified each document for Wright. Wright executed the documents as they were presented to him, including the revised note and mortgage that had been changed the previous afternoon. Wright did not review the documents prior to signing them because he believed them to be the same documents that his attorney, Brown, had reviewed. Wright was never informed of the revisions that had been made to the draft loan documents. After the documents were signed, Kentland disbursed the loan proceeds to Wright.

In September of 1992, Wright obtained a favorable refinancing commitment from another lender. Brown contacted Kentland Bank to obtain a payoff statement. The prepayment penalty quoted by Kentland Bank was far greater than the one percent Brown had anticipated. Brown requested and obtained a copy of the note via facsimile.[3]

The note signed by Wright contained a formula for the prepayment penalty, rather than the one percent penalty that appeared in the draft note. Brown never saw the prepayment provision contained in the final note prior to receiving the facsimile from the bank. The final note contained the following prepayment provision:

> Borrower may not prepay the principal balance of the Loan, or any part thereof, at any time during the first (1st) Loan Year of the Loan. Borrower shall have the right to prepay the Loan, in whole but not in part, upon ten (10) days written notice first given Lender, after the first (1st) Loan Year. The Borrower, in the event of prepayment, shall pay Lender a fee equal to the greater of: i) the sum of (a) the present value of the scheduled monthly payments on the Loan from the date of prepayment to the maturity date and (b) the present value of the amount of principal and interest due on the maturity date of the Loan (assuming all scheduled monthly payments due prior to maturity were made when due) minus (c) the outstanding principal Loan balance as of the date of prepayment. The present values described

---

the facsimile from Krebs on August 5th, but that he did not know that there were any conversations of substance regarding the draft documents during that time frame. Pennamped also testified that he believed that his August 5th conversation with Brown occurred prior to receiving Krebs' facsimile, because if that conversation had occurred after receiving the facsimile, he would have discussed "that issue" with him . . .

[3] Wright testified that upon learning of the higher prepayment penalty demanded by Kentland Bank, he contacted Wilson and requested copies of the final loan documents. Wright had requested copies of the loan documents at the closing. Krebs indicated that he had to provide Brown with copies, and that Wright should obtain his copies from Brown. However, Krebs did not provide Brown with copies of the documents.

in (a) and (b) are computed on a monthly basis as of the date of prepayment discounted at the rate of the U.S. Treasury Note or Bond closest in mautrity [sic] to the remaining term of this Loan (as reported in the Wall Street Journal on the fifth business day preceding the date of prepayment) plus 250 basis points; ii) one percent of the then outstanding principal balance.

On July 1, 1993, Wright paid $595,799.09 to Kentland Bank, under protest, representing payment in full of the loan, including all outstanding principal and interest, as well as the prepayment penalty of $97,504.38 calculated under the terms of the final note.

As of the July 1, 1993, payoff date, the principal balance of the note was $493,148.71. Under the terms of the draft note, a one percent prepayment penalty would have been $4,931.49. This amount is approximately $92,500.00 less than that amount required under the terms of the final, revised note. In addition, the prepayment penalty charged by Kentland Bank was approximately $60,000.00 greater than the amount charged under the Federal Home Loan Bank formula. On July 18, 1993, Wright filed a complaint for damages against Kentland Bank, Krebs, SCI, Pennamped, and Lowe Gray Steele & Hoffman. Wright sought recovery from the defendants based on fraud, constructive fraud and breach of fiduciary relationship, obtaining money and property by false pretenses, deception, criminal mischief, conversion and theft, and forgery. Wright subsequently amended his complaint to include a count based on breach of implied contract.

On September 8, 1993, the Appellees filed their motion for summary judgment. On December 1, 1993, Wright filed his opposition to the motion for summary judgment. Following a hearing on December 21, 1993, the trial court took the motion under advisement. On March 4, 1994, the trial court issued its order granting the Appellees' motion for summary judgment. The trial court found that an essential element of each of Wright's non-contractual theories is the intent to deceive and that Wright failed to come forward with any evidence supporting an inference of fraud. The court held that the Appellees had no contractual duty to Wright and therefore, Wright's breach of implied contract claim must fail. The trial held there was no just cause for delay and ordered the entry of final judgment in favor of the Appellees. Wright appeals this judgment.

Discussion

When we review a trial court's entry of summary judgment, we are bound by the same standard as the trial court. . . . We may not reverse a granting of summary judgment on the grounds that there is a genuine issue of material fact unless the material fact and relevant evidence were specifically designated to the court. "The appellant bears the burden of proving that the trial court erred in determining that there are no genuine issues of material fact and that the moving party was entitled to judgment as a matter of law." . . .

Thus, we turn to an examination of the specific theories under which Wright seeks recovery. We consolidate and restate Wright's theories as quasi-contract, actual fraud, and constructive fraud. We affirm the trial court's ruling with respect to quasi-contract. We reverse with respect to actual fraud and constructive fraud.

I. Quasi-Contract

Wright contends that a quasi-contract existed with Pennamped. Courts have used the phrases quasi-contract, contract implied-in-law, constructive contract, and quantum meruit synonymously. They are all legal fictions created by courts of law to provide remedies which prevent unjust enrichment and thereby promote justice and equity. Their purpose is to provide the injured party with the fair value of the work and services rendered and thus prevent unjust enrichment to another.

To prevail on a claim of unjust enrichment, a plaintiff must establish that a measurable benefit has been conferred on the defendant under circumstances in which the defendant's retention of the benefit without payment would be unjust. Principles of equity prohibit unjust enrichment in cases where a party accepts the unrequested benefits another provides despite having the opportunity to decline those benefits.

Wright claims he conferred a benefit to Pennamped when he paid Pennamped for his services out of the loan proceeds. We disagree. Recovery under quasi-contract requires the plaintiff to establish that the defendant impliedly or expressly requested the benefit be conferred. The loan transaction between Wright and SCI provided that Wright would be responsible for all transaction costs, including the fee of the drafting attorney. When Wright received the loan proceeds, Pennamped's fee had already been taken out of the proceeds. Therefore, Wright did not confer a benefit upon Pennamped, but rather relieved SCI of the obligation to pay transaction costs.

Since Wright did not confer a benefit on Pennamped, it is unnecessary to discuss whether Pennamped was unjustly enriched. We hold the trial court did not err in granting summary judgment on Wright's claim for implied contract.

II. Actual Fraud

The elements of actual fraud are: (1) the fraud feasor must have made at least one representation of past or existing fact; (2) which was false; (3) which the fraud feasor knew to be false or made with reckless disregard as to its truth or falsity; (4) upon which the plaintiff reasonably relied; (5) and which harmed the plaintiff. An intent to deceive, or "scienter," is an element of actual fraud, whether classified as a knowing or reckless misrepresentation or as an additional element to a knowing or reckless misrepresentation. Fraud may be proven by circumstantial evidence, provided there are facts from which the existence of all of the elements can be reasonably inferred.

Wright argues he has designated sufficient evidence to survive summary judgment on his actual fraud claim. Wright contends that we should reverse the granting of summary judgment because he has shown (1) that Pennamped made a representation of past or existing fact to Wright or Brown, (2) that Wright relied on representations by Pennamped, or (3) that Pennamped acted with actual knowledge of the falsity of any representations made or in reckless disregard of their falsity. We agree.

First, Wright claims Pennamped's failure to inform Brown of the changes in advance of the closing and Pennamped's presentation of the documents for Wright's signature, "while continuing to remain silent, constituted a representation by Pennamped that the documents so presented were in form and substance identical to the documents that had been submitted to Brown." Construing the facts in the light most favorable to Wright, we agree that Pennamped, by remaining silent and not informing Brown or Wright of the changes to the loan documents, impliedly represented that the final loan documents conformed to the draft loan documents which had been reviewed and approved by Brown. . . . *Midwest Commerce Banking v. Elkhart City Centre* (7th Cir.1993), 4 F.3d 521, 524 ("Omissions are actionable as implied representations when the circumstances are such that a failure to communicate a fact induces a belief in its opposite").

The Appellees contend, however, that Pennamped's "silence" cannot be construed as a representation in the present case because Pennamped had no duty to speak. We disagree.

The Appellees are correct that silence will not support a claim for actionable fraud absent a duty to speak or to disclose facts. In addition, the party alleging fraudulent concealment has the burden of demonstrating the existence of a duty to speak. We conclude, however, that Wright has satisfied this requirement.

By undertaking the tasks of a drafting attorney, including the distribution of draft loan documents and the solicitation of review and approval of the documents, Pennamped assumed a duty to disclose any changes in the documents prior to execution to the other parties or their respective counsel. *See Hughes v. Glaese* (1994), 637 N.E.2d 822, 825 (duty to disclose material information arises where there is a fiduciary or confidential relationship between the parties). The existence of such as duty is supported by common sense and notions of fair dealing. Thus, Pennamped, as the drafting attorney, had a duty to inform Brown or, in his absence, Wright, of any changes occurring after Brown's review and approval of the loan documents. Were the rule otherwise, pre-closing review of loan documentation would become a futile act, and counsel would be required to scrutinize every term of each document at the moment of execution.

Wright's second contention is that he had a right to rely on representations made by Pennamped. However, the Appellees contend Wright did not have a right to rely because he "was an experienced business man who had full access to all relevant facts at all times."

> A person relying upon the representations of another is bound to exercise ordinary care and diligence to guard against fraud. " '[H]owever, the requirement of reasonable prudence in business transactions is not carried to the extent that the law will ignore an intentional fraud practiced on the unwary. . . . A person has a *right to rely* upon representations *where the exercise of reasonable prudence does not dictate otherwise.*

Where the evidence is conflicting, the issue of whether a particular person has exercised reasonable prudence and whether the reliance was justified is for a jury's determination. Where the evidence is susceptible to only one interpretation, however, "it is for the court to determine as a matter of law whether plaintiff was justified in relying on the representation and whether he was negligent in doing so."

As has been noted recently by our supreme court, a demanding standard is applied with regard to the representations made by attorneys. "A lawyer's representations have long been accorded a particular expectation of honesty and trustworthiness." "The law should promote lawyers' care in making statements that are accurate and trustworthy and should foster the reliance upon such statements by others." Undoubtedly, Wright exercised ordinary care and diligence by having his attorney review the loan documents prior to closing. Similarly, Brown had a right to rely on the alleged misrepresentations made by Pennamped, as did Wright at the closing. Contrary to the Appellees' position, Wright was under no obligation to review documents at the closing once they had been reviewed and approved by his attorney, absent some indication from Pennamped that changes had been made. As a matter of law, Wright established a reasonable right of reliance on Pennamped's alleged misrepresentations.

Wright's third contention is that Pennamped acted with actual knowledge of the falsity of any representations made or in reckless disregard of their falsity. Wright claims the trial court erred because the presence of fraudulent intent is a factual issue for the jury and the evidence supports a reasonable inference of intent to deceive when viewed in the light most favorable to Wright. We agree.

The determination of whether fraudulent intent is present is a question for the fact finder.

> There is no precise formula for drawing the line as to when there are sufficient indicia to constitute a determination of fraud. The general rule is that when there is a concurrence of several "badges of fraud" — "an inference of fraudulent intent *may* be warranted." . . .

In the present case, the Appellees contend the trial court correctly determined the intent issue as a matter of law because the only reasonable inference to be drawn from the undisputed evidence is there was no fraudulent intent on the part of the Appellees.

In issuing its ruling on the motion for summary judgment, the trial court held:

> Here, it is uncontroverted that attorney Pennamped, upon learning of his client's intention to make last minute changes in the loan documents, instructed his client to notify the Plaintiff immediately of such changes and stressed the importance of such notification. In the face of such uncontroverted evidence, it is incumbent upon the Plaintiff to come forward with some evidence supporting an inference of fraud. The Plaintiff has failed to do so.

Although we would agree that the evidence supports finding an absence of fraudulent intent, we do not agree that the evidence on this issue is uncontroverted.

Viewing the evidence in the light most favorable to Wright, Pennamped first learned that changes would be made to the loan documents on Friday, August 2, 1991. Pennamped received the changes via facsimile during the morning hours of Monday, August 5, 1991, the day prior to closing. Although speaking with Brown by telephone on August 5th, and although aware that Brown would be unable to attend the closing, Pennamped did not tell Brown the documents had been or would be changed. Pennamped neither informed Wright that changes had been or would be made after Brown's review and approval nor made any attempt to confirm that Krebs had informed Wright of the changes.

Wright has designated evidence showing that Pennamped knew there were last minute changes made to the loan documents and that Pennamped failed to inform Wright and his counsel of these changes. This is evidence from which a jury might infer an intent to deceive on the part of Pennamped and the law firm. Although the designated evidence would also allow a jury to conclude that Pennamped and the law firm had no fraudulent intent, "[t]he mere improbability of recovery does not justify summary judgment and the procedure is not intended to be a summary trial."

We conclude, therefore, that the trial court erred in granting summary judgment on Wright's claim for actual fraud.

III. Constructive Fraud

The elements of constructive fraud include:

> 1. a duty owing by the party to be charged to the complaining party due to their relationship,

> 2. violation of that duty by the making of deceptive material misrepresentations of past or existing facts or remaining silent when a duty to speak exists,

> 3. reliance thereon by the complaining party,

> 4. injury to the complaining party as a proximate result thereof, and

> 5. the gaining of an advantage by the party to be charged at the expense of the complaining party.

Contrary to the trial court's ruling in the present case, intent to deceive is not an element of constructive fraud. Instead, the law infers fraud from the relationship of the parties and the surrounding circumstances. The Appellees contend that the trial court nonetheless properly entered summary judgment in their favor on Wright's claim for constructive fraud because there is an absence of the type of relationship which may form a basis of a claim for constructive fraud. Furthermore, Appellees contend this relationship did not give rise to a legal duty to disclose.

In support of their position, the Appellees cite *Hardy v. South Bend Sash & Door Co.* (1992), Ind.App., 603 N.E.2d 895, *reh'g denied, trans. denied,* and *Comfax v. North American Van Lines* (1992), Ind.App., 587 N.E.2d 118. In *Hardy*, this court affirmed the entry of summary judgment on the plaintiff's claim for constructive fraud due to the absence of a fiduciary or confidential relationship between the parties. . . . Similarly, in *Comfax*, this court affirmed the entry of summary judgment on plaintiffs' constructive fraud claim because the plaintiff failed to demonstrate the existence of the requisite special relationship. In *Comfax*, the plaintiffs argued the existence of a fiduciary relationship was established.

As we have observed previously, however,

> Defendants are mistaken in arguing that constructive fraud can *only* exist where there is a confidential or fiduciary relationship. In Indiana, the term constructive fraud encompasses several related theories. All of these theories are premised on the understanding that there are situations which might not amount to actual fraud, but which are so likely to result in injustice that the law will find a fraud despite the absence of fraudulent intent. Defendants are correct in asserting that a constructive fraud may be found where one party takes unconscionable advantage of his dominant position in a confidential or fiduciary relationship . . . This is not, however, the exclusive basis for the theory of constructive fraud.

> In Indiana constructive fraud also includes what other jurisdictions have termed 'legal fraud' or 'fraud in law.' . . . *This species of constructive fraud recognizes that certain conduct should be prohibited because it is inherently likely to create an injustice.. . .*

Thus, we find the Appellees' reliance upon *Hardy* and *Comfax* to be of no avail.

The Appellees' also cite *Hacker v. Holland* (1991), Ind.App., 570 N.E.2d 951, *reh'g denied*, and we are similarly unpersuaded. In *Hacker*, the plaintiff, Hacker, contracted to sell a tavern to Evans. The purchase price included $20,000 for the transfer of the tavern's liquor license. Evans, with Hacker's agreement, retained the defendant-attorney, Holland, as the attorney to handle the closing. Hacker did not retain independent counsel.

Holland prepared the closing contract and warranty deed pursuant to Evans' instructions. Under the contract, $20,000 for the liquor license was expected as payment upon the transfer of the license. The $20,000 balance owing was not secured, and the contract made no provision for interest payable on the balance. At the closing, Evans and Hacker individually read the contract, and then Holland read it aloud to them prior to execution. Evans and Hacker each paid $80 of Holland's $160 fee. Following the transaction and certain payments from Evans to Hacker, a balance due of $13,000 remained, for which Evans gave Hacker a note. Hacker was unsuccessful in her attempts to collect the $13,000 balance from Evans, but she never brought suit on the note.

Hacker sued Holland for legal malpractice and argued that Holland had negligently breached his duty of care to her. In support of her case, Hacker argued that an attorney-client relationship existed between Holland and her and that Holland had breached his duty of care to her by failing to secure Evans' debt or to provide for interest payments on the debt. The controlling inquiry was whether Holland acted solely as Evans' attorney or as attorney to both Evans and Hacker. This court wrote in part:

> In the context of real estate transactions, it is most difficult for the disgruntled party on one side of the transaction to demonstrate an attorney-client relationship with the attorney for the other party to the transaction. This is so because attorneys do not owe a duty of care to non-clients except in the context of third party beneficiaries . . . and because the interests involved are usually in opposition. . . .

This court held that although Hacker and Holland could have had an attorney-client relationship, Holland's preparation of the closing documents and control over the closing were insufficient standing alone, to create such a relationship or to render Holland liable for negligence. In a separate discussion, the court rejected Hacker's claim for constructive fraud, noting in pertinent part Hacker had "alleged no deceptive silence or representations by Holland as Evans's attorney which would constitute a breach of duty."

In the present case, Wright neither asserts that an attorney-client relationship existed between Pennamped and him, nor alleges a breach of a duty of care. Instead, Wright focuses on the duty to disclose which is a duty independent of the attorney-client relationship between Wright and Pennamped. Unlike the plaintiff in *Hacker*, Wright alleged deceptive silence or representations by Pennamped as lender's counsel. We find *Hacker* to be inapplicable to the present case, and the

Appellees' reliance upon this case is misplaced.

Considering the facts in the light most favorable to Wright and contrary to the Appellees' contentions on appeal, this case is amenable to the application of the doctrine of constructive fraud. The facts as alleged by Wright suggest a situation that is so likely to result in injustice that the law will find a fraud despite the absence of fraudulent intent. The material alteration of loan documents after the review and approval of those documents by opposing counsel and the presentation of the revised documents for execution with no indication that changes have been made is the sort of conduct which "should be prohibited because it is inherently likely to create an injustice. . . ." In the alternative, Appellees contend this relationship did not give rise to a legal duty. Appellees claim that Pennamped did not owe Wright a duty to disclose the changes made to the loan documents. Furthermore, Appellees argue that even if Pennamped did have a duty, Pennamped satisfied this duty by delegating the performance to Krebs. We disagree.

A party to a contract has a duty to the other party to disclose changes. The Appellees argue that although Pennamped altered the contract, he did not owe a duty to Wright because Pennamped was not a party to the contract.

Contrary to Appellees' contention, as discussed previously, we find that Pennamped had a duty to disclose. As the drafting attorney, Pennamped assumed a duty to inform Wright of any changes to the loan documents prior to their execution.

In opposing the motion for summary judgment, Wright submitted the affidavit of Richard L. Johnson, the senior partner in the law firm of Johnson Smith Densborn Wright & Heath. The significance of this affidavit was to establish the customs and practices of financing transactions. Johnson commenced the practice of law in 1972 and has concentrated his practice in the areas of banking law, real estate law, and commercial law. After setting forth his qualifications and extensive experience as lender's counsel and in drafting or preparing documents to be used in lending transactions, Johnson's affidavit states:

> Based upon my experience as lender's counsel, I believe the following to be the customs and practices in the industry in relation to real estate and/or commercial financing transactions:
>
> (a) At any time changes or revisions are made to draft or proposed loan documents by the attorney charged with the responsibility of drafting such documents — no matter how trivial or seemingly insignificant such changes or revisions may be — it is expected and understood by all other attorneys involved in the transaction that the drafting attorney will take whatever steps are necessary and/or appropriate to fully disclose and identify all such document changes and revisions to other attorneys involved in the transaction.
>
> (b) Typically, when any changes or revisions are made to proposed or draft loan documents, the drafting attorney will circulate, in writing, a 'red-lined' copy or some other written materials which will highlight and/or more particularly identify and/or describe the changes and revisions that have been or are contemplated to be made.
>
> (c) At the very least, the drafting attorney is responsible to verbally disclose to all other attorneys involved in the transaction — prior to

execution of final documents — any and all changes and revisions that the drafting attorney has made to previously-distributed draft documents.

(d) Any changes or revisions to the substance or form of documents which have been previously circulated to the participating attorneys should be fully disclosed to such other attorneys.

(e) The closing of the transaction should not occur until final revisions to the loan documents have been fully disclosed to and approved by all parties and their respective counsel.

Based on this relationship, Wright could expect that Pennamped would inform him of any changes in the loan documents. Therefore, Pennamped had a duty to disclose material information to Wright concerning the loan documents.

Furthermore, Appellees' argument is in contradiction with Rule 4.1(b) of the Rules of Professional Conduct which states, "[i]n the course of representing a client a lawyer shall not knowingly . . . (b) fail to disclose that which is required by law to be revealed." Ind. Professional Conduct Rule 4.1(b). As previously stated, the drafting attorney assumes a duty to disclose any changes in the documents prior to execution to the other parties.

Courts hold attorneys to a separate and more demanding standard than the attorneys' clients. Pennamped may have assisted his client, Krebs, in the commission of constructive fraud by failing to disclose to Wright that Pennamped changed the loan documents. Since Pennamped knew the documents were altered, he had a duty to disclose.

We conclude, therefore, that the trial court erred in granting summary judgment on Wright's claim for constructive fraud.

To sum up, while we affirm the trial court's entry of summary judgment for the defendant on the theory of quasi-contract, we reverse summary judgment on the theories of actual and constructive fraud. The case is remanded to the trial court for further proceedings consistent with this opinion.

AFFIRMED IN PART, REVERSED and REMANDED.

NOTES

1. The *Wright* court concludes that Wright did not have a claim against Pennamped, the lawyer, for quasi-contract. Why? What facts would have supported a claim for quasi-contract?

2. On the fraud claim the court concludes that Wright had a reasonable right of reliance on the representations made by Pennamped. Further, under the constructive fraud claim, the court concludes that Pennamped had an affirmative duty of disclosure to Wright. Is this because of an implied attorney-client relationship? Do these findings place additional burdens on lawyers in transactions? Do they create a conflict in the duties owed by transactional lawyers to their clients and third parties to the transaction?

3. In *In re Rothwell*, 296 S.E.2d 870 (S.C. 1982), the court considered the duty of disclosure in connection with contract negotiations. Rothwell, the lawyer, represented a client who had negotiated a deal with his former employer in which the employer agreed to buy the client's home. *Id.* at 871. The former employer sent

a deed to the home to Rothwell together with a letter asking Rothwell to have his client execute the deed. The letter also stated, "We will expect your call if there are any questions." *Id.* Before having his client execute the deed, Rothwell inserted a paragraph that discharged his client from all liability to the employer. Once his client executed the deed, Rothwell returned it to the employer with a letter stating, "We are returning herewith your package to you duly executed. Once you have filed the deed of record, please forward on a clocked copy of same for our files. Thank you." *Id.* The letter did not mention that the deed had been altered. In a disciplinary proceeding, Rothwell argued that he did not have a duty to disclose the alteration to the employer. He argued that the deed sent by the employer was an offer and that the alteration was therefore a counteroffer. The South Carolina Supreme Court disagreed and found that Rothwell had violated several disciplinary rules, including DR 7-102(A)(3), which prohibits a lawyer from concealing or knowingly failing to disclose that information which the lawyer is required by law to reveal. *Id.* at 872. As a result of his conduct, Rothwell was publicly reprimanded.

4.   In *Skarbrevik v. Cohen, England & Whitfield*, 282 Cal. Rptr. 627 (Cal. App. 1991), the court refused to extend the duty owed by corporate counsel to the stockholders of the corporation. The court noted that transactional lawyers' obligations may extend to third parties but that the

> [d]etermination of whether in a specific case an attorney will be held liable to a third person not in privity 'is a matter of policy and involves the balancing of various factors, among which are the extent to which the transaction was intended to affect the plaintiff, the foreseeability of harm to him, the degree of certainty that the plaintiff suffered injury, the closeness of the connection between the [attorney's] conduct and the injury, and the policy of preventing future harm.'

Id. at 633. The court acknowledged that a lawyer's obligation may extend where the third party is a potential beneficiary of the lawyer's services or where the "foreseeability of harm to the third party resulting from professional negligence is not outweighed by other policy considerations." *Id.* The court specifically rejected such an extension where the third party is someone who the lawyer's client is dealing with at arms length:

> To make an attorney liable for negligent confidential advice not only to the client who enters into a transaction in reliance upon the advice but also to the other parties to the transaction with whom the client deals at arm's length would inject undesirable self-protective reservations into the attorney's counseling role.

Id. Indeed, in most transactions, the lawyer's obligation to her clients may be compromised if a duty to adverse parties were imposed. The *Skarbrevik* court specifically identifies the potential effects of imposing such a duty toward non-clients, including the potential to undermine the duty of confidentiality, create a conflict of interest, and destroy the attorney-client relationship. *Id.* at 634.

5.   For additional reading on the duty of a transactional lawyer to disclose information in the context of contract negotiations, see Nathan M. Crystal, *The Lawyer's Duty to Disclose Material Facts in Contract or Settlement Negotiations*, 87 Ky. L.J. 1055 (1999).

TABLE OF CASES

[References are to pages]

[References are to pages]

[References are to pages]

INDEX

[References are to pages.]

[References are to pages.]